The Heart Beats on the Left

THE HEART BEATS ON THE LEFT

OSKAR LAFONTAINE

Translated by Ronald Taylor

Polity

First published in 2000 by Polity Press
in association with Blackwell Publishers Ltd.

Editorial office:
Polity Press
65 Bridge Street
Cambridge CB2 1UR, UK

Marketing and production:
Blackwell Publishers Ltd
108 Cowley Road
Oxford OX4 1JF, UK

Published in the USA by
Blackwell Publishers Inc.
Commerce Place
350 Main Street
Malden, MA 02148, USA

A catalogue record for this book is available from the British Library.

Library of Congress Cataloging-in-Publication Data

Lafontaine, Oskar, 1943–
    [Herz schlägt links. English]
    The heart beats on the left / Oskar Lafontaine ; translated by Ronald Taylor.
        p.   cm.
    Includes index.
    ISBN 0-7456-2581-9 — ISBN 0-7456-2582-7 (pbk.)
    1. Lafontaine, Oskar, 1943– 2. Politicians—Germany—Biography. 3.
Sozialdemokratische Partei Deutschlands. 4. Schröder, Gerhard, 1944– 5.
Germany—Politics and government—1990– I. Title.

    DD290.33.L34 A313 2000
    943'.420878'092—dc21
    [B]
                                                                      00-039956

Typeset in 10.5 on 12 pt Sabon
by Ace Filmsetting Ltd, Frome, Somerset
Printed in Great Britain by T. J. International, Padstow, Cornwall

This book is printed on acid-free paper.

Contents

Preface to the English Edition

In this book I explain my reasons for relinquishing my position as leader of the Social Democratic Party and resigning as German Finance Minister in March 1999. By describing the policies of the SPD over recent years I hope I have provided a background against which these reasons will appear both understandable and justifiable.

A considerable part of my story inevitably concerns prominent German personalities and their relationships to each other, which means that first and foremost this is a book that deals with specifically German subject-matter. So what is its relevance to the interests of an English-speaking public?

The story of my resignation is first and foremost the story of a struggle to uphold a particular political ideal. A confrontation between two individuals is a confrontation between different political concepts, so to this extent what I have to say is relevant not only to the situation in Germany. Rather, it offers a paradigm for European social democracy as a whole. The only chance that social democrats have of winning political majorities is by representing the interests of the workers, the unemployed and the pensioners. In the corporate sector their primary concern must lie with small and medium-sized businesses. Since medium-sized firms do not depend on international finance capital to the same extent as large-scale businesses, there is less pressure on them to subordinate the achievement of their economic goals to the urge to maximize their stock exchange valuation.

My book also deals with the so-called 'Third Way' proposed by Tony Blair's New Labour. This is a subject that has been keenly discussed in Germany since the Labour Party came to power in 1997.

Shortly before the European elections in 1999 Tony Blair and Gerhard Schröder published a joint declaration calling for a left-wing supply-side policy. Generally speaking the appeal fell on deaf ears. The SPD and the Labour Party both suffered considerable setbacks. In Europe the welfare state is seen as the prerequisite for a properly functioning democracy. It is not possible for the countries of Europe to take over the present British economic model as it stands.

But in Britain, as well as in the United States, people are increasingly discussing whether this British model can in the long run survive as an alternative to the European welfare state. The former Democratic presidential candidate Bill Bradley has called for a compulsory scheme of social insurance, while George W. Bush, the Republican candidate, is worried about those who have lost out in the Stock Exchange boom. Many people realize that a free market destroys the institutions of social cohesion. The answer of Lionel Jospin, the French Prime Minister, to this development is: 'Yes' to a market economy but 'No' to a market society. A deregulated labour market is at the core of a policy which leaves to the markets decisions which are and must remain the decisions of democratically elected governments and parliaments.

Indeed, the very term 'labour market' betrays the insidious way in which society has developed. People are not chattels. There can be no objection to talking about deregulated markets for goods and services, but human beings must be allowed to work under humane conditions and not figure as mere cost factors in the production chain.

The decline in humane values is also illustrated by the fact that the concept of 'shareholder value', which we owe to the British capitalist system, has in the meantime been enthusiastically adopted in continental Europe as well. The Vodaphone takeover of Mannesmann was welcomed by the apostles of the *Zeitgeist* as the demise of 'capitalism Rhineland style' and the concept of 'Germany plc'. Scarcely a word was said about the consequences for Mannesmann's workforce, some of whom had been with the company for decades. 'What's going to happen to us?' they ask. 'We're in danger of losing our jobs.' They feel angry and sad at the same time, remembering that the company had always seemed like a family business. While the managers receive golden handshakes in the form of astronomical compensation payments or appreciating share options, the workforce lose out all round, sacrificial lambs at the altar of merger madness. In any merger large numbers of jobs are always lost. The greater the number of workers laid off, the stronger the chance that the value of the firm's shares will rise. There is a need to establish in the European guidelines for takeovers the right of the workforce to participate in the decision-making process.

What policies will Tony Blair's government adopt? Will they continue to call it 'modernization' when considerations of profitability are allowed to take precedence over a commitment to human values and solidarity?

Not long ago the *Sun* newspaper crowned me 'the most dangerous man in Europe'. The reason for this honour was my demand that a stop be put to the tax-dumping measures that were spreading throughout Europe. While taxes on wealth, business profits and capital gains are being reduced, welfare contributions, income tax and excise duties continue to rise. The victims of this disastrous development are the workers. As a result of my many years in a variety of public capacities, I have come to accept the principle of an intelligent taxation policy which strengthens the economy and helps to bolster the welfare state. But a policy of tax-dumping which always leaves the workers worse off cannot seriously be reconciled with the policies of a government which calls itself social-democratic. It is therefore high time that the British government abandon its resistance to the introduction of minimum tax levels in the interests of social justice.

For some time the heads of government of the G7/G8 countries have been demanding a restructuring of the world's financial markets. Tony Blair has been one of the most vocal advocates of such a restructuring. But so far little has happened. The most vital need is to regulate short-term movements of capital and stabilize exchange rates. Proposals to this end were put forward in 1994 by a Bretton Woods commission chaired by Paul Volcker, former head of the American Federal Reserve. If we go on playing fast and loose with the world's finances, the next crisis is just around the corner, as Michel Camdessus, the retiring Director of the IMF, pointed out last February.

On Wall Street, however, huge amounts of money continue to be made through macroeconomic speculation. It is therefore questionable whether the next President of the United States will be prepared to act against the short-term interests of Wall Street and agree to reorganization of the world's financial markets. Given its traditional ties with the United States, the British government would be in a good position to play a mediating role in achieving this end.

As the United States and Great Britain are justifiably criticized in Europe for their plans for the deregulation of the labour markets and the dismantling of the welfare state, so at the same time there is a lot that Europe could learn both from America and from Britain in matters of economic management. In the early 1990s America and Britain reacted to the recession and the rise in unemployment with a policy of monetary and fiscal expansion. In Britain there was the additional factor of the weak pound, which propped up the export trade.

But at present it is not possible to pursue a similar policy in Europe because the stability pact and a strict monetary policy stand in the way of a reduction in the level of unemployment. If Britain were to join the single European currency, it should therefore insist that European fiscal and monetary policies should rather follow the American and British models. The European ideology, which maintains that the sole purpose of monetary policy is to ensure price stability, hinders attempts to get unemployment down and should give way to a policy aimed at growth and employment, as successfully adopted in America by Alan Greenspan, to international approval.

If one accepts the view of prominent economists at the Massachusetts Institute of Technology that monetary policy plays a decisive role in determining levels of employment, then the principle of the independence of the European Central Bank, which has since become dogma, presents a problem. If governments put the fight against unemployment at the centre of their policies, it is hardly possible to de-politicize and de-democratize the very institution that is chiefly responsible, according to this view, for getting unemployment down. The European central bankers naturally deny that there is a link between monetary policy and unemployment.

Compared with that of the European Central Bank, the constitution and field of responsibility of the Federal Reserve is far more modern and far better adapted to contemporary needs. Even the status and functions of the Bank of England are more clearly defined. In Great Britain the Chancellor of the Exchequer sets the rate of inflation. Of the nine members of the Bank of England committee that sets interest rates, seven are nominated by the Chancellor or the Prime Minister. Their term of office varies between three and five years. The term of office of the directors of the European Central Bank, on the other hand, is – for no good reason – eight years. The European Central Bank is right – Europe needs structural reform. Especially the Bank itself.

My book is an earnest plea for a model of a European welfare state without which there can be no stable democratic order. It is also concerned with the absence of a sound infrastructure in Britain, a subject brought to the fore by recent rail crashes.

Another reliable indicator of the health of a society is the number of children living below the poverty line. According to a study by the Institute for Fiscal Studies over 4 million children in Britain are living in poverty today – one-third of the child population. The Rowntree Foundation states that 20 per cent of children in England live in households in which nobody has a regular income. When one also considers the critical state of the National Health Service, one must realize the need, I believe, for an objective debate to prove that a fully functioning welfare state must be the cornerstone of a truly democratic social order.

On a number of occasions in my book I have had cause to refer to the work of the sociologist Anthony Giddens, with which I agree to a far larger extent than has been made out, especially in Germany, where these matters have been discussed only on a very superficial level. Maybe the gap between the capitalist model in Britain and the welfare state model in Europe is not as wide as commentators have made out. Be that as it may, I would be glad if this book helped to bridge the gap, as well as to promote a greater degree of European cooperation and encourage people to overcome their narrow national concerns. It is more important that men and women live full and healthy lives than that shareholder values rise.

Oskar Lafontaine
April 2000

Preface

At the time I resigned my office in the German government I had no intention of explaining what had led me to make this decision. It seemed to me more important to maintain my solidarity with my party and its leaders than to indulge in explanations and justifications. All too often such explanations are perverted by one's political opponents to suit their own ends. Reflecting on the European elections, together with the provincial and local elections in Germany, I had no desire to engage in a dispute that would have embarrassed the Social Democratic Party, and therefore gave just one brief interview a few days after my resignation, in which I drew attention to the lack of team spirit in the government. My meaning, I thought, was obvious enough, and I reckoned that the party and its supporters would be able to put two and two together. I was gravely mistaken.

Nor did I change my mind when various people with no love lost for me portrayed my resignation as the action of a man who had simply abandoned his responsibilities. Resignation is a political decision firmly embedded in the democratic system. A minister should resign, not only when the media urge him to do so in response to an act of personal misconduct, but above all when he no longer agrees with the policies of his party or its leader. Sections of the public seem to have completely forgotten this.

A classic case is that of Gustav Heinemann, who resigned as Minister of the Interior over the rearming of the Bundeswehr and Adenauer's authoritarian style of leadership. At that time discussions on the democratic constitution of the German Federal Republic still dominated people's thoughts to such an extent that no one would have dreamt of accusing him of dereliction of duty. It was inevitable that he should also give up his position as chairman of the party, since a running battle between Chancellor and Party Chairman could only have caused the government and the party great damage.

After my resignation the policies of the red–green coalition between the SPD and the Greens took a turn which I would never have thought possible and which filled me with alarm. That a German government, led by the Social Democrats, of all parties, should have taken part in a war that infringed international law and was incompatible with the constitution of the Federal Republic, was something that stuck in my gullet. The war in Kosovo struck at the very heart of the political principles of the SPD. By 8 June 1999 at the latest, shortly before the European elections, the day Gerhard Schröder and Tony Blair issued *The Third Way* and Hans Eichel, the Federal Finance Minister, published his programme for the year 2000, I felt I could no longer keep silent. We had won the election of 1998 on a pledge to embark on new policies and to introduce a greater measure of social justice into our society.

Four months after my resignation Gerhard Schröder disassociated himself from my finance policy. 'I am of the view that the correct course would have been to adopt Eichel's policies from the beginning,' he said. 'And if that is taken as a criticism, then so be it.'

Remarks such as these betray a lack of fairness and honesty. It is for the Chancellor to lay down the political guidelines. The cabinet, with the Chancellor's consent, approves the finance bill which is then finally passed by the Bundestag. Schröder, Eichel and Foreign Minister Joschka Fischer had urged me not to take any unpopular decisions before the elections in Hesse. When, shortly afterwards, I saw Schröder taking a tough line towards the farmers, it reminded me of how he had insisted only a few months earlier that I should not make any cuts in the tax breaks enjoyed by these very same farmers. Otherwise Karl-Heinz Funke, the Federal Agriculture Minister, would not have joined the government in Bonn. As a result there was an annual loss to the exchequer of 1.7 billion marks.

Equally false is Schröder's *post factum* declaration that he had always considered it pointless to argue with the Bundesbank – 'but I never said anything.' Shortly after his election as Chancellor he stated at a meeting of trade unions: 'I have great respect for the Bundesbank but it should not only be concerned with the stability of the currency – it should also shoulder responsibility for promoting economic growth throughout the country.' I would be prepared to ignore Schröder's lack of frankness and fairness towards me personally. But I cannot sit idly by and watch the trust of the electorate being betrayed by a political volte-face on the part of the government.

My book is therefore a protest against the radical change of direction on the part of the red-green coalition towards a policy of neoliberalism, and against the way they have reneged on their electoral promises. I was involved in producing the policies that we promised the electors we would carry out, and I still feel bound by it. The only chance that the Social Democrats have to gain political majorities for their policies is by representing the interests of the working population, the unemployed and the retired. In the field of business they must concern themselves above all with the needs of small and medium-sized firms. If they allow themselves to be led astray by the prattle of a minority which has for years been urging restraint and seeking to introduce reforms at the expense of the weaker groups in society, while enabling the prosperous and well-to-do classes to pay as little tax as possible and transfer as much of their income as possible abroad, then they will be deserting their cause.

The past few years have been governed by the political tensions generated between these two worlds. I wish to describe once again the nature of these tensions, since I was caught up in the middle of them. By so doing, I hope to prevent Germany from going any further down the wrong road – the road of neoliberalism. The SPD cannot be allowed to barter its soul.

The following pages are thus not to be taken as my memoirs. My concern is with the deep-seated conflict that lies at the heart of the SPD. In the course of my account of our discussions and decisions I shall not shrink from identifying the mistakes that I have made myself, while also criticizing the mistakes made by others, sometimes trenchantly and scornfully. But it is my own mistakes that annoy me most.

Hanging on the wall in my house, in full view of visitors, is a cartoon by Peter Gaymann. It shows a number of clean, smart young chickens squatting on the rungs of the ladder leading to their coop. But on the top rung sits a mud-stained pig. One chicken says to the other: 'I wonder how we can get to the top without collecting dirt.' By adopting a detached, sometimes ironical tone, I hope I have avoided the danger of paying too little attention to the wishes and interests of others in the pursuit of my own objectives.

Oskar Lafontaine
Autumn 1999

1

In the Wake of
Willy Brandt

A fatherly friend

I saw Willy Brandt for the first time in 1966, when I was a student and he was still Governing Mayor of Berlin. He was giving a speech at a party rally in Saarbrücken, in the course of which he emphatically rejected any thought of a grand coalition. A few days later the grand coalition was formed, with Brandt as Foreign Minister. It was my initiation into the reality that in politics the spoken word is not always to be taken literally.

As Foreign Minister, Brandt rapidly gained trust and respect throughout the world. He continued to seek a relaxation of tension through the step-by-step policy that he had successfully launched in Berlin. In this he received vital support from Egon Bahr. In the eyes of us students he quickly became a hero, especially as, in contrast to many other politicians, he had fought in the wartime resistance against the Nazis. He had emigrated to Norway as a young man in 1933 and returned to Berlin after the war. Many political fellow-travellers vilified him for leaving Nazi Germany, while Adenauer attacked him for being an illegitimate child.

His first statement of policy as German Chancellor in 1969 had as its motto 'Pluck Up Courage for More Democracy'. This was a cry that united the hopes of the younger generation. And the coalition of Social Democrats and Free Democrats did indeed succeed in introducing a series of important reforms. Brandt's slogan was no empty promise.

In 1979 I was elected to the party executive of the SPD and came into close contact with Brandt. He denied that there was a need for further nuclear rearmament, rejecting the view that it was necessary to counter the threat from Soviet SS20s by stationing Cruise missiles and Pershing II rockets in Germany and western Europe in order to preserve the balance of nuclear power. This was a policy in stark contrast to that of his successor Helmut Schmidt. I remember him saying quite spontaneously during a meal in a Bonn restaurant: 'It must be possible for a major industrial nation to escape from this never-ending spiral of arming and rearming.'

During the Christmas holidays of 1981 Willy Brandt invited me to join him on the island of Cyprus. It was then that I came to realize what international esteem and admiration he enjoyed. Spyros Kyprianou, President of Cyprus, hoped that Brandt might intercede in the Cyprus problem. The organization of Brandt's journey to Cyprus had been in the hands of a Greek journalist called Basil Mathiopoulos, a political refugee from the time of the Colonels. Brandt had managed to secure an exit permit for Mathiopoulos to return to Germany at the moment when the Colonels were on the point of ordering his arrest during a visit to Athens.

In the course of this visit to Cyprus I got to know Willy Brandt more closely as a man. He kept himself to himself, rarely revealing his feelings and emotions. He found it hard to establish intimate relationships. We swam in the sea and travelled round the island. He talked on political subjects while I sat at his feet like a disciple. As so often on such foreign trips, the programme planned for him proved to be too arduous. When, after a whole series of official engagements, a member of the Cypriot peace movement asked for an interview with him, he put on his familiar smile and said: 'Oskar, here's one for you!' So I proudly carried out my first diplomatic mission and undertook the interview on Willy Brandt's behalf.

This was the time when Jaruzelski, the Polish Prime Minister, declared a state of emergency, fearing a Russian invasion. In our hotel we learned from a ticker-tape report that Bettino Craxi, the then Deputy Chairman of the Socialist International, had condemned Jaruzelski's action. He had done this without consulting Brandt, Chairman of the Socialist International. Brandt considered Jaruzelski a patriot and had no wish to condemn his decision out of hand. As we walked together along the beach he was visibly worried and muttered, with Craxi in mind: 'That scoundrel, of all people!'

Later I read in Mitterrand's memoirs that his view of the situation coincided with Brandt's. Referring to his meeting with Jaruzelski on 9 March 1990, Mitterrand wrote:

This was no longer the man who had explained his dilemma to me at the time he had imposed martial law. What was he to do – play the hero and refuse to go along with the state of emergency, thereby delivering his country to destruction, or rescue what he could from the situation and submit to Moscow's demands? Patriotic hero or traitor? To his contemporaries, maybe a traitor. To history, without doubt a hero. He knew that he had to take ruthless steps to deal with his people, and that he would bring down their hatred and contempt on his head. But he bore this burden. It was his duty, he told me. Instead of seeing his country occupied by the Red Army for the second time and left to the whims of the Soviet government, he considered it his bounden duty to avoid such a fate and prevent at least the worst consequences.

I learned that when it came to dealing with international problems, it is better to assess the situation with caution than to pass an over-hasty judgement. Looking back, I am convinced that Brandt's assessment of Jaruzelski was more accurate than that of many politicians and journalists in the West who had immediately joined the chorus of indignant protest at the time.

After this vacation in Cyprus Brandt and I formed a closer personal relationship. In the summer of 1984 he invited me and my family to join him in his cottage in the Cévennes. I still regard it as a particular gesture of affection that he and his wife Brigitte put their own double bed at our disposal because we had our two-year-old son Frederic with us, and the spare bed would have been too small. I bought fresh baguettes, sausage and cheese every morning and prepared breakfast. Besides this we did our best to cook attractive meals for the Brandts – to Brigitte's strong disapproval, because she was worried that her husband would put on weight. She was in any case less interested than her husband in the Saarlanders' love of good eating and drinking. On one occasion, when without warning we set about cooking roast leg of lamb, we almost came to blows. This, however, had nothing to do with the coolness that later developed between Brandt and myself.

Brandt's 'grandchildren'

Brandt had made up his mind to bring the younger generation into the leadership of the Social Democratic Party. In 1987 he proposed that I should succeed him as Party Chairman, referring to me and others of my generation as his 'grandchildren' – a cunning designation which clearly implied that he wanted to bypass the intermediate generation of his 'children'. It was an appellation that came to be an embarrassment to those concerned – Herta Däubler-Gmelin, Hans Eichel, Björn

Engholm, Karl-Heinz Hiersemann, Klaus Matthiesen, Uli Maurer, Rudolf Scharping, Gerhard Schröder, Heidemarie Wieczorek-Zeul and myself, among many others. Although we had almost reached the age of grandparents, the newspapers continued to refer to us as 'Brandt's grandchildren'.

For my part, I viewed Brandt's plans with a sceptical eye. To be frank, I did not feel up to taking on the job of Party Chairman. I found it inconceivable that Egon Bahr, Horst Ehmke, Erhard Eppler, Peter von Oertzen, Johannes Rau, Hans-Jochen Vogel, Hans-Jürgen Wischnewski and the others of this generation would agree to Oskar Lafontaine as party chairman. The events of 1990 were to show how right I had been. At the time I felt instinctively that the new leader would have to be acceptable to the majority of the senior members of the party. In the mid-1980s it was unthinkable that anyone of my generation should have taken over as Chairman. Then, in 1987, came Brandt's surprising resignation when many in the party refused to confirm the appointment of Margarita Mathiapoulos, from outside the SPD, as the party's press spokesman.

On the evening before resigning, Brandt assembled his 'grandchildren' in Norderstedt, outside Hamburg, in order to discuss the succession. At this meeting Brandt canvassed more or less openly for me as his successor but for the reasons I have given I declined to stand. This must have deeply disappointed him, and from that time onwards I felt there was an ever-widening rift between us, which became even wider after 1990, the year of German reunification. The other 'grandchildren', too, were disgruntled. When, in that year, I declined the party chairmanship for the second time, a number turned their backs on me and wrote me off.

In 1987 Hans-Jochen Vogel was elected Chairman of the SPD, with Johannes Rau and myself as his deputies. I also took on the chairmanship of the party policy committee, with Christa Müller as secretary.

For all its problems this new job gave me considerable pleasure. Firstly it taught me a great deal. The new policy document that we produced, and that was approved at the party conference in Berlin in 1989, pledged the party to international cooperation, equality of opportunity for women in employment and in society, ecological modernization of the economy, and structural reform of working conditions and the social security system. My opposition to a reduction in working hours with consequent loss of pay, to more shift working and to weekend working, gained me the reputation among the public of being a 'reformer' and a 'modernizer'. Within the Social Democratic Party itself there was resistance from the trade unions. But it had always been our intention to deal with the question of weekend working and increased shift working in consultation with the employees and works councils. The 'uniform principles' so widespread today, which rest entirely on market forces, had at this time not yet become so firmly established as to undermine the right to consultation and involvement in the decision-making process.

As a result of my work as chairman of the policy committee, my name was included among those to go forward for the choice of SPD candidate to contest the election to Federal Chancellor in 1990. Wisely, Hans-Jochen Vogel stayed in the background for a long time. That was in my interests, for I had learnt at the time of the choice of Johannes Rau for the election contest of 1986 that it is a mistake to choose one's candidate too early. A public accustomed to novelty and sensation can become too familiar with a particular name, so that after a while that person comes to attract criticism rather than support.

The SPD's victory in the 1990 *Land* elections in the Saarland, with a turnout of 54.4 per cent, resulted in my adoption by the SPD executive as their candidate in the election for Federal Chancellor later that year.

After the *Land* election in 1990 I went with Christa Müller to Granada. In the *parador* in the famous Alhambra palace we discussed in detail the economic, social and financial consequences of a one-to-one currency conversion which had been proposed by a number of Social Democrats as a way of solving the economic problems in the eastern provinces of the now reunified country.

Egon Bahr faxed us a paper written by Kurt Biedenkopf which forecast a rapid economic up-turn in Eastern Germany. Christa and I had serious doubts about this prediction, suspecting rather that in the euphoria of reunification basic economic principles would be thrown overboard. From Granada I telephoned Helmut Schmidt, Karl Otto Pöhl, Jacques Delors, Franz Steinkühler and a number of others in order to help myself form a balanced judgement. Almost all of them were opposed to the plan for a conversion rate of one West Mark to one East Mark, especially our partners in Europe. Opposition from the public, on the other hand, was less clearly in evidence.

I was surprised, after Chancellor Kohl's announcement of a one-for-one conversion rate, that Karl Otto Pöhl, President of the Bundesbank, did not immediately resign. Not only had Kohl failed to consult him – he literally steamrollered him. It was instantly obvious to me that Kohl's decision would make the economy of the former East Germany uncompetitive overnight and create millions of unemployed. Equally clear was that there would have to be tax rises and increases in welfare contributions, and that for many years the West would be compelled to pay out billions of marks in order to stimulate economic recovery in the East.

After I got back from Granada I cautiously began to moot my opinions in party circles, until the attempt on my life on 25 April 1990 suddenly changed everything. During the time the course was being set for the selection procedure, I was prevented from playing my part in the formulation of vital political decisions. By the time I came out of hospital the resolution to proceed on the basis of a one-for-one currency conversion rate had been passed and was now inviolable.

In an interview with Dirk Koch and Klaus Wirtgen of the magazine *Der Spiegel* I again put forward my objections. But the SPD delegates in the Bundestag were determined to agree to the plan. Thus not only was I physically weak and psychologically shattered after the attempt on my life but I also had to accept the fact that in this vital matter of the future development of an economically and financially unified Germany, the party did not share my views. I therefore decided to withdraw my bid to become the SPD's candidate for Chancellor and prepared the following detailed statement:

To the Members of the German Social Democrat Party:
In the run-up to the selection of the party's candidate for Federal Chancellor I approached Hans-Jochen Vogel, Johannes Rau, Björn Engholm and Walter Momper and asked them whether they would be prepared to stand. They all had good reasons for declining.

In the final phase of the election campaign for the Saarland Hans-Jochen Vogel, Herta Däubler-Gmelin and Johannes Rau all publicly proposed me as the SPD candidate for Chancellor. During a brief vacation after the Saarland election I had time to decide whether to take on the job. In the face of the strains I had undergone in recent years I would have been best served by playing a less demanding role. In the end I decided against my personal interests to serve the common cause.

Having made my decision, I considered it important to attend the party conference in Leipzig, and during the final stages of elections to the DDR Volkskammer, to put forward my objections to the hasty introduction of the Deutschmark in the German Democratic Republic. I knew that this would be unpopular. But my personal credibility as a politician was on the line, and credibility lies at the heart of any long-term political success. I imagined the questions that people in Germany, East and West, would ask, and the problems – financial, economic, social – that the succeeding years would bring.

The alternative to the immediate introduction of the Deutschmark in the DDR would be to make the East mark a convertible currency and establish a fixed rate of exchange.

After the elections to the East German Volkskammer the SPD executive unanimously selected me as their candidate for Chancellor. Before my nomination I had asked for the chosen candidate and the majority of the party to be of one mind on the important political issues, because this is a precondition for a successful election campaign. At the same time I had made no bones about my opposition to the hasty adoption of the Deutschmark in the DDR. On 27 March 1990, before my nomination, I once again, at a meeting of party officials in Hanover, stated my arguments against an ill-considered rush to make the Deutschmark the currency of the East as well as the West. And I again took the occasion to point out that a successful election campaign depended on there being firm agreement on all fundamental political issues between the majority of the party and their candidate for Chancellor.

On 25 April 1990, at an election meeting in Cologne, an attempt was made on my life. Nobody could have foreseen it, but for me it had the inevitable consequence of forcing me to make up my mind once again whether I had the strength to continue as the SPD's candidate for Chancellor. I came to the conclusion that I had to ask the party to find someone else to take on this responsibility.

It was a decision made easier, though not directly precipitated, by the attitude of the parliamentary party of the SPD in the Bundestag towards the introduction of the Deutschmark in the DDR on 1 July. All my colleagues assured me that the vast majority of the parliamentary party had resolved to vote for this motion – the central issue in the treaty between the two Germanies. At the same time they demanded the right, which I respected, not to be made to vote against their convictions. It therefore followed that the members of the parliamentary party would continue to agree to the motion even if the party's leading candidate for Chancellor exercised his right not to embark on a campaign which did not carry his full conviction.

Over the coming months and years it will become clear that the government's decision to introduce the Deutschmark into the former DDR on 1 July 1990 will exacerbate social tensions and bring about an intensification of the divisions that already exist in German society, in the West as in the East.

At the party conference in Berlin I had made it clear that in my view the concept of the nation state could no longer form the foundation for progressive political policies at the end of the twentieth century. What we need are policies that link up with the tradition of social-democratic internationalism and give social and ecological questions precedence over those of the newly unified nation. That is what our manifesto states.

Many members of our party have written to me in recent weeks, offering me their support. I am deeply grateful. Many have urged me to continue, while at the same time acknowledging that after the attempt on my life I must be left to make my own decision about my future.

I did not send this letter, because Hans-Jochen Vogel was out of the country at the time and I did not want him to learn about it while he was still abroad. In the meantime my friends in Bonn had got wind of what I was thinking. Many of them came to see me to try to persuade me to change my mind. One evening almost all Brandt's 'grandchildren' gathered in my house, including Willy Brandt himself. He was angry with me, because he too had put his weight behind the proposal to introduce the Deutschmark into the East in July 1990, so that those living in the DDR could have hard currency for their summer holidays. Like the others, he had come with the object of making me change my mind. I responded by asking him to take over the candidacy himself, since he was held in high esteem in the East. This idea came, among other people, from the artist Georg Meistermann, who had written to me to suggest that in this highly unusual situation I should try and get Brandt to run. But he refused, as did Vogel and all the other 'grandchildren' whom I sounded out once again.

Vogel later wrote in his memoirs:

> Many people have since asked me why I did not simply accept the risk that Lafontaine would withdraw his candidacy. But there were times when I felt I had reached the limits of my self-respect. Nevertheless I continue to believe, for a number of reasons, that I acted correctly. In the first place, after the trauma of having almost lost his life, Oskar Lafontaine was entitled to be treated with a sympathy and consideration befitting his position. It was therefore a matter of course that I should travel to Saarbrücken and that our discussions should be held there. Sarcastic references in the press to 'pilgrimages' to Lafontaine's house left me cold.
>
> Secondly, Lafontaine's withdrawal would have caused a crisis in the party. Both inside the party and beyond he had a highly motivated band of supporters who would not have accepted such a decision without a struggle. A new candidate – which could only have meant me – would have had to fight on two fronts, with only a section of the party behind him in the campaign against Helmut Kohl.

With none of the senior figures in the Social Democratic Party willing to stand for election, I found myself in a serious predicament. I was like a general without an army. My reservations over the precipitate decision in favour of the one-for-one currency conversion were held up as demonstrating my opposition to German reunification. What I had said was that the most important thing was not that the people live together in one state but that they should live in freedom in a democracy, should have the same living conditions and should not lose their jobs, and that the collapse of the Berlin Wall should bring about a marked improvement in the quality of their lives.

I often thought in those days of Konrad Adenauer, who in a speech to the Bundestag back in 1958 put forward the idea of an 'Austrian' solution to the problem of the DDR. In 1962 he went on to claim that the West German government was prepared to discuss many questions with the 'other' Germany, provided 'our brothers and sisters in the Russian Zone' could live their lives as they wished. 'Humane considerations matter more to us than national considerations', declared Adenauer.

I envisaged a path similar to that adopted in the Saarland in 1955. On that occasion the achievement of economic and monetary union was spread over a period of four years, allowing the economy of the area time to adjust to the change. But as far as the former East Germany was concerned, the vast majority of the population took precisely the opposite view, and the conversion of the East mark into the Deutschmark at an exchange rate of one for one was Kohl's trump card in the election campaign. When it subsequently emerged that these euphoric economic expectations were all built on sand, the excuse was made that is always trotted out when things go terribly wrong: 'We had no alternative.'

The attack

After I resigned all my political functions in March 1999, Wolfgang Schmidbauer, a psychoanalyst, wrote in the magazine *Der Spiegel*:

> Oskar Lafontaine's resignation came to almost all of us like a bolt from the blue. It had a determination about it which was as incomprehensible as hara-kiri is to a non-Japanese. One way of setting about understanding it is through trauma psychology . . . In so far as his aim was to goad the SPD into action, unite its conflicting tendencies and work for a change of government in Bonn, Lafontaine had qualities that seemed incompatible with his latest move . . . The most frequent after-effect of a psychological trauma seems to be an intensified sense of vulnerability, coupled with a determination not to accept anything that is less than perfect . . .
>
> Already launched on a career that would have led to the most influential political position in the country, Lafontaine was seriously wounded in the course of a demonstration. If we were to believe that after his wound had been successfully dealt with, the affair would be over and done with, we would have learnt nothing about the nature of psychological trauma. It shows how transient are the forces of power, influence and political success . . . At the time he made a superhuman effort to suppress as completely and as quickly as possible the pain of his psychological wound – most probably in order not to disappoint his friends . . . It is reasonable to assume that the impetus that he injected into the party after his electoral defeat is linked with a compensatory urge . . . Now excluded, in his own eyes, from the race for Chancellor,

he stood aside, ignored his own emotions and made way for another candidate. After the SPD's victory he was no longer part of a movement but a martyr sacrificed by a power bloc that scorned his visions and devalued his practical aspirations.

I have often been asked how I came to terms with the attempt on my life. Today I think I can distance myself sufficiently from the event to say something about it. I was fully aware of the attack itself. I knew exactly what was happening. I was conscious for some time afterwards. I asked the security guards and the others who had stopped to help, to call a doctor. I was losing blood heavily and could have bled to death. I thought of Christa, of my son Frederic, my mother and others who were close to me. Scenes from my earlier life flashed through my mind before I finally lost consciousness.

The memory of those dramatic moments will never leave me. When I woke up in hospital and the surgeons had finished the operation, I knew that I had survived. The security guards were standing by the wall, watching me, their faces as white as a sheet. I gave them a reassuring wink with my right eye. Soon I was able to receive visitors – first Christa and Reinhard Klimmt, then many more.

I well remember Professor Müller, the friendly and highly efficient senior surgeon in the hospital, coming to me during the evening after the operation and saying: 'In order to help you sleep, either I can give you a pill or you can drink a glass of red wine.' It was not a difficult decision to make. I only tell this story in order to show that, apart from my relief at having survived, I felt the need to enjoy life more fully in future.

During the days that followed, the humdrum events of everyday life seemed to me totally unimportant. Even the day-to-day news seemed trivial. I felt like a wanderer who had reached the coast and saw nothing in front of him but the endless ocean and the unbroken blue sky. I had become aware how insignificant things like power, fame and political success were. I left hospital a week later. It did not take long for me to recover from the physical effects of the attack but I realized that it was going to take much longer to get over the psychological scars.

The attack had changed me. To put it precisely – I had learnt that life can be cut off from one moment to the next. Reflecting on my past life and summing up the situation, I came to the conclusion that from then on I would do only what I could fully reconcile with my conscience. Above all I did not want to expose myself to the charge of neglecting my wife and family. And I succeeded in avoiding this danger. Even when up to my ears in work, I always found ways and means to spend time with my family. I continually asked myself whether it was worthwhile submitting myself to an endless round of speeches, meetings, press conferences and interviews. It was entirely due to the strength of my political commitment that I was prepared to accept the many sacrifices that are demanded of a leading politician. The desire to make my contribution to the peace movement, to the preservation of the environment, to equality of opportunity and to the establishment of social justice was what drove me on.

After the attempt on my life I found myself checking – probably more often than others of my age – the date of birth of people whose obituaries appeared in the papers. Time and again I observed that a number of them were younger than me. I probably reacted differently from my contemporaries in political life to the premature death of young politicians such as Karl-Heinz Hiersemann and Klaus Matthiesen. I felt much less sure of myself in public meetings than in earlier years. When strangers approached me, I used to get a feeling of potential danger. It was obvious to me, in retrospect, that had I been more on my guard, I could have defended myself against the woman who attacked me.

The radical effects of the attack and my efforts to come to terms with it also help to explain why I felt unwilling to take over as chairman of the SPD at the time of the party conference in Mannheim in 1995. This may not seem credible to anyone who has not experienced what I have gone through. Even among fellow-politicians I always felt I was misunderstood. They alleged that the change of attitude on my part after the attack was merely a smokescreen put up to conceal my overweening ambition.

In the months immediately following the Mannheim conference I told my wife Christa time and again that, as soon as the polls gave us 40 per cent of the votes, I would hand over the baton to someone else. When later, however, a good year before the federal elections, the polls came up with 40–2 per cent, I did not carry out my intention, although the birth of our son Carl Maurice in February 1997 brought a change in my life that would in itself have justified such a move. Encouraged by the results of the opinion polls, I set out to repair the damage done to myself and to the party in the disastrous elections of 1990. I wanted to play my part in ensuring that there would at last be a change of government.

I also had a new plan in mind. I was convinced that the social democratic parties of Europe had to find an answer to the anarchy in the world's financial markets. Currency speculation, which was running out of control in the whole of the world, caused crises in the economies of entire nations and led to mass unemployment and widespread misery. The great challenge facing the Socialist International was to

fight against capitalism in this radical form, and I was at that time
prepared to accept a position in the government in order to achieve a
European agreement on employment policy. But at the same time I
had also made it clear to my friends in the party executive – and this
showed the strength of my position – that in the event of my proposals
not meeting with majority support in the party, I would hand over the
chair to someone else. I was still haunted by the thought that, if my
career were to come to a sudden end, I would not have too much with
which to reproach myself. From this point of view my resignation
from all my political offices can also be seen as a delayed consequence
of the attempt on my life.

Politics and family life

A man or woman who assumes a position of responsibility in politics
will find it very hard to reconcile the demands of that position with
those of family life. Even on Saturdays and Sundays there are important meetings that have to be attended, and that weekday evenings
are taken up with appointments of one kind or another goes without
saying. Nobody gives any thought as to how the family is to be fitted
in.

Nineteen-ninety-eight was a strenuous election year which made great
demands on me as Party Chairman. There was no chance of a holiday.
After the exhausting negotiations over the formation of the coalition
government Christa and I decided to allow ourselves at least a fort-
night's holiday in Mexico over Christmas. As usual we chose a hotel
where only a few tourists were staying, so as to be able to relax in
peace and quiet. Hotels frequented by Europeans were out of the question, since people would always be coming up to talk to me and ruin-
ing any hopes of relaxation.

After our flight had already been booked, Rudolf Edlinger, Austrian
Minister of Finance and at the time Chairman of the Conference of
European Finance Ministers, had the idea of organizing a New Year's
Ball in Vienna. His intention was to invite the ministers to Vienna in
order to celebrate the launching of the euro as the New Year dawned.
I could not help thinking that there was also the Opera Ball in Vienna,
and that there would be full coverage in the press. I therefore advised
against arranging such a celebration, and for the moment the idea was
dropped.

Shortly afterwards, however, my late friend Dominique Strauss-
Kahn, then French Finance Minister, proposed that the Finance Ministers should meet in Brussels and raise their glasses there to the birth

of the euro. Should I interrupt my holiday and fly from Mexico to Brussels and back, at taxpayers' expense, just to join my colleagues in toasting the euro? It struck me as far more sensible to ask Economics Minister Werner Müller to take my place. So I did not interrupt my holiday.

Although the launch of the euro had already been officially celebrated on more than one occasion, my absence was severely criticized. Opposition politicians called it a scandal, and even party friends muttered their criticism. Esteemed commentators who would naturally never dream of cancelling their own holidays expressed their disapproval. Scarcely anybody thought of asking what difference it would have made if the group photograph at the Brussels celebrations had included the German Finance Minister instead of the German Economics Minister. If I had flown from Mexico to Brussels, you can be sure that at least one of the familiar weekly magazines would have expressed its incomprehension that a government minister should have spent so much public money merely in order to drink a glass of champagne. Surely even senior politicians ought to have the right to spend a few days of peace and quiet with their families.

But even in Mexico I did not enjoy complete privacy. President Ernesto Zedillo had got wind of my arrival and invited me to spend a day with him in Mexico City. He was a generous host, and we discussed the crisis in the international monetary system. He was able to describe to me at first hand the effects of the crisis on the peso. I was surprised how closely our views on the international monetary system coincided. The following day he sent a book to my hotel – Paul Krugman's *The Accidental Theorist* – which gave me great pleasure.

As during this vacation in Mexico in 1998–9, my political career, stretching over a number of decades, has taught me time and again that the present political treadmill cannot allow room for a normal family life. Hermann Hesse wrote: 'Exert all your powers to discover a mode of life that is congenial to you, even if it means sacrificing all your obligations. Obligations derive a great part of their power, if not all of it, from one's lack of courage in fighting for a private life.'

Many of my colleagues have told me that they did not have enough time for their children. I wanted to do things differently. During my time as Federal Finance Minister I sometimes got into my car at eight o'clock in the evening and had my chauffeur drive me from Bonn to Saarbrücken to see my wife and my two boys. I had time during the two-hour journey to work, read and make telephone calls. Sometimes it was gone eleven by the time I arrived. This gave rise to spiteful comments in the press to the effect that 'Waigel was to be found later at his desk in the ministry than Lafontaine.'

At birthdays and other anniversaries the toasting of the person at the centre of the celebrations is usually followed by an expression of thanks to his wife, since without her support her husband's achievements would certainly never have been possible. She is usually presented with a bouquet and the guests warmly applaud. But among these guests, at many such parties, is often to be found the 'second wife' of this devoted public servant – his affectionate secretary – who ministers in one way or another to his emotional needs during his absence from home. In such cases the occasion becomes embarrassing.

Long ago I came to realize – and I did not need the attempt on my life to teach me this – that in all walks of life, including politics, one cannot do one's work satisfactorily unless one leaves enough time for one's spouse, one's children and family life in general. Such is the nature of political life today that it comes as no surprise that, when politicians talk in public about their personal and family life, their words do not carry conviction. I have frequently wondered whether politics has to be organized in the way it is. Is it not ridiculous when in an election campaign photos of all the members of the candidate's family have to be included on the posters, as in America? This is what our media-driven society wants, they say. But does it not often give the impression of an idyllic family life that is far from the truth?

It was always a wrench to leave the house when the tearful little Carl Maurice used to stretch out his arms and beg me not to go. Sometimes the scene came back to me in the course of an important meeting in Bonn, when I was beginning to get bored. I was also worried by the prospect of having to move to Berlin, which would mean that we could no longer look after my eighty-four-year-old mother, as we had done up to now. My wife cooked for her and arranged for 'meals on wheels'. To be sure, we could arrange for the social services to attend to her needs but social services are no substitute for the family.

The national election campaigns

In the course of the Bundestag election campaign of 1990 I became more and more estranged from Willy Brandt. I was particularly indignant when he joined Helmut Kohl in a television programme on 30 September in support of the Chancellor's policies. 'The economic and social problems that confront us will be solved more quickly than many believe', said Kohl. 'In three to five years we shall be facing the scenario of a single nation with a single status.' To this Brandt responded: 'I believe that in five years' time a large part of today's DDR will be the more modern Germany, because when our firms invest there, they will bring with them not old equipment but the most up-to-date technology.'

Brandt's activities during the election campaign only served to drive a deeper wedge between us. I shall never forget how we stood side by side in front of the Reichstag in Berlin on 3 October, the first anniversary of the reunification of Germany. When the sounds of the national anthem had died away, Brandt shook hands with all the others who were attending the ceremony – President Weizsäcker, Chancellor Kohl, Stoltenberg, Blüm and Heiner Geissler. But he pointedly avoided me. I did not show my feelings that evening and we went together to a private room in the Reichstag, as planned, to have a drink together. But after that we never said a word to each other. Brandt was not prepared to hold a frank discussion with me in private – maybe he was even incapable of doing so. He simply took refuge in subtle hints and gestures, relying on me to understand what he meant. But there are times when it is necessary to speak out.

After the SPD lost the election in 1990, the party executive met in Bonn. Hans-Jochen Vogel proposed me for Party Chairman, as he had told me he would at the final election meeting in Saarbrücken. But I found it hard to come to terms with the defeat, as well as with the fact that certain elements in the party had turned their backs on me. And as though that were not enough, Willy Brandt used the meeting to make particularly harsh criticisms of the campaign I had conducted. Weary and psychologically shattered, I informed the party executive that I was not prepared to stand for Chairman of the party. Instead Björn Engholm was elected to the post.

It weighed on my mind that Willy Brandt and I had fallen out in this way. When he became ill in October 1991, I wrote to him and sent him a case of red wine. A year later, shortly before he died, I sent him a note consisting of just one sentence: 'Dear Willy, You are often in my thoughts and my heart goes out to you.'

In the months that followed, my political work went well. I had a substantial majority in the Saarland parliament, and the position of Deputy Chairman of the party gave me the opportunity to take part in discussions at federal level without having to be in the front line of fire. But things were to work out differently.

In 1993, following the Barschel scandal, Engholm was forced to resign as chairman of the party. Since there was no obvious person to take his place, it was decided to hold a ballot of party members to elect his successor. The candidates were Heidemarie Wieczorek-Zeul, Rudolf Scharping and Gerhard Schröder. Schröder announced that he was standing not only for Party Chairman but also as candidate for Federal Chancellor. In the course of a meeting of the party executive I got into a bitter argument with him and told him that I found it impossible to work with him. I was incensed over the fact that he had laid claim to the leadership of the party even before Engholm announced his resignation. It also offended me that, after I had supported him for many years against opposition from others, he should now have chosen to turn his back on me.

The SPD in the Saarland gave their support to Scharping, because he seemed ready to invite me once again to be the party's candidate for Chancellor. In his book *The Years of Apathy* Peter Glotz gives an account of the events of the evening of 17 May 1993:

> Eight or nine members of the party executive were sitting round the table over a drink in Lafontaine's house. Our object was clear – to persuade Scharping to accept Lafontaine as our candidate for chancellor. A two-man team. Schröder to be left out of the picture. He is consumed by the thought that the scent of power overwhelms people. So six times a day he repeats to himself the slogan 'I want everything' – which is why we must make sure that he does not get anything.
>
> Heidi Wieczorek-Zeul, who can naturally see what is going on, seems to be rather ill-humoured. The argument sways to and fro. After a while all of us, except Scharping, are a bit tipsy. Klaus Matthiesen renews his attacks on him, looking like the helmsman of a sailing ship on the high seas. Any moment now, I thought to myself, he will burst into song with a sea shanty. But he did not sing – he bellowed. Scharping remained cool and collected. And in that moment I realized that he wanted everything too – he just did not say so.

Frau Wieczorek-Zeul drew her support in the main from left-wing constituencies and associations and from women. In the event she gained 26.5 per cent of the votes; Schröder got 33.2 per cent but Scharping was the winner with 40.3 per cent. 'I have never played in a two-man team', he commented. This remark shows why Rudolph Scharping failed as Party Chairman, as the result of his own shortcomings. He was too unwilling to discuss things and cooperate with others.

I remember once calling up Johannes Rau and saying to him: 'Johannes, can you help me? Rudolph doesn't want to talk to me. Maybe you could find out what the reason is and help us to have a proper discussion.' Rau gave his inimitable laugh. 'Don't worry,' he said, 'he doesn't talk to me either.'

Scharping made a good start as Party Chairman and the press was highly complimentary about his prospects. It was obvious that no one could bar his way to becoming the party's candidate for the chancellorship, if that was what he wanted. So at the conference in Halle on

22 June 1994 he was elected as the party's candidate with 95 per cent of the votes.

After the experience of 1990 I had made up my mind to play my part on behalf of whichever candidate was selected by the party, for the lack of support that I had suffered from certain sections of the party in 1990 had proved a cruel and lasting blow.

In his account of the events of these years Gunter Hofmann, head of the Berlin office of *Die Zeit*, wrote:

> Lafontaine kept in the background. I do not recall him uttering a single derogatory or unfair word when he disassociated himself from Engholm or from Scharping, who was Chairman at the time. Often, as in the case of the asylum bill, he helped to work out compromises, and on occasion he stood out against a reversal of policy. He refused, for example, to give up his opposition to nuclear energy, or to the deployment of German troops in the Balkans. Sometimes he gave the appearance of having lost his enjoyment of politics. He worked behind the scenes in his roles of Deputy Chairman of the party and Prime Minister of the Saarland but seemed to have no further ambitions. At this time Gerhard Schröder was first secretly, then openly working his way to the top in competition with his rival Rudolf Scharping, grooming himself to be the new hero of the SPD, a man obviously determined to become Chancellor. Sometimes one had the impression that he almost scorned his own party, turning himself into the little Franz Josef Strauss of the SPD, an appellation previously attached to Lafontaine. He seemed to have become a destructive character, spreading dissension, whereas Lafontaine had assumed the quiet, neutral role of a master of ceremonies.

I supported Scharping to the best of my abilities. According to a report in the *Bild am Sonntag* I was more active during the election campaign of 1994, both in parliament and on television, than any other politician. But unfortunately this campaign showed what the federal election had already shown, namely, that it was a mistake on the part of the SPD to name their candidate for Chancellor too early. At one press conference Scharping was asked about the SPD's taxation plans, and in particular about the income limit above which the SPD proposed to introduce a supplementary levy. We had not yet decided on this limit, and Scharping found himself floundering. He was then unjustly accused of mixing up gross and net figures, and as a result public perception of him began to change. Those who had previously taken a positive view of his qualities – his deliberate manner, his apparent trustworthiness and dependability – now began to see him as boring, uninspired and lacking vitality. Scharping himself, moreover, made a series of mistakes in the course of the campaign.

We failed to get Johannes Rau elected President in May 1994. Instead Roman Herzog was voted into office. In their biography of Rau, Rolf Kleine and Matthias Struck wrote:

> The very day after Herzog's election as president the SPD, under pressure, made a serious tactical error. Disappointed by his failure to be elected, Scharping, Chairman of his party, gave a press conference in which he hinted that Herzog's election was close to being an act of dubious political legitimacy. The majority that Herzog received, claimed Scharping, did not reflect the choice of the best man but was the result of 'political machinations on the part of Helmut Kohl', in Scharping's own words. And after a majority of the Liberals gave their support to the CDU candidate in the decisive vote, Scharping went on, one was bound to ask 'whether anyone needed the FDP any more'.
>
> The papers tore Scharping to pieces, accusing him of petulance and spite and charging the party with being bad losers, who could not grasp the fact that right from the beginning they had not had the slightest chance of success. Even in the SPD itself people shook their heads in disbelief at Scharping's outburst. 'This is not the time for recriminations,' said Hans-Ulrich Klose, leader of the parliamentary party. 'Helmut Kohl is our political enemy, not Roman Herzog.' Criticism within the party itself was even more outspoken. Scharping was accused of behaving like an ill-tempered child who was prepared to smash everything up if he did not get his own way. The SPD and their leader are completely out of order.

Scharping now became the scapegoat for everything that went wrong, and by persistently criticizing the policies of the SPD and the conduct of its leader, Gerhard Schröder mounted a rival campaign to establish himself as the shining new hope of the party. The Hamburg papers in particular were favourably disposed towards him. When we saw that the results of the opinion polls were becoming worse and worse for the SPD, I had the idea of taking Schröder into our team. After some hesitation Scharping agreed and approached Schröder. So we came to form a troika.

By bringing Schröder into the team, we were able to prevent any further deterioration of our standing in the polls. It was also to our advantage that a new face now appeared on the placards, which was what the papers wanted to see. 'A masterly move by Rudolf Scharping', said the *Hamburger Morgenpost*. Under the heading 'The Best Move Scharping Could Make in the Game' Martin E. Süskind wrote in the *Süddeutsche Zeitung*: 'All this can only mean that, now the darling of the nation has become involved, the election campaign will take on a significantly livelier character.'

Four days before election day Schröder again set the cat among the pigeons. In an interview he declared that, in the event of a grand coalition being formed, he was prepared to serve under Chancellor Kohl as Economics Minister, adding that Kohl had never been a 'non-person' as far as he was concerned – rather, 'a man whose political qualitities I have never called in question'. The following day Waigel came up to me and said: 'Kohl sends his regards – but he's not interested in having Schröder.' That hit home!

The result of the election, however, was not in itself enough to bring about the demise of Kohl's government. To be sure, after the first forecasts of the final outcome Schröder had proposed the formation of a grand coalition, saying: 'It is obvious that no one can govern the country with such a ridiculously small majority.' But the coalition of CDU/CSU and FDP was determined to stay in power.

The SPD was bitterly disappointed. There was a scent of defeatism in the air. Some expressed the view that in its present form the SPD was no longer capable of gaining a majority and had become virtually unelectable. Others considered Helmut Kohl to be a consummate politician who was almost invincible and who, especially towards the close of an electoral campaign, would always set the pace. The term 'Kohl syndrome' was invented – in the early stages of a campaign Kohl always trailed, only to gather speed as the campaign proceeded and cross the winning-post to win by a whisker. Kohl won in 1994, not because he was so good but because the SPD made so many mistakes.

After the election Schröder never tired of saying: 'I would have made it.' In the months that followed Scharping and Schröder were constantly at each other's throats, and this severely damaged the party. Time and again I urged Scharping to ignore Schröder's attacks on him, since in the end he would only emerge as the loser. But Scharping saw things differently.

The affair reached its climax when Schröder was sacked as economics spokesman of the SPD, although Johannes Rau and I had advised against it. The opinion polls were casting the party in a very poor light, besides which I felt myself compelled to contradict Scharping in public over the question of the deployment of German troops outside the NATO countries. At the party conference in Bremen in 1991 the delegates had accepted a motion worked out by Björn Engholm and myself in conjunction with experts in foreign policy and matters of security. This motion approved the participation of German troops in the activities of the UN peacekeeping forces, while explicitly rejecting any military engagement outside the NATO countries.

Scharping wanted to change this. In December 1994 he sent a letter to the members of the party executive and the parliamentary party, in which he wrote: 'The participation of German troops in the NATO force to protect the UN detachments in the event of their withdrawal is not only an obligation on our part towards the countries from which those forces come but also our clear duty under the terms of our alliance, once NATO has received a mandate to this effect from the United Nations.'

In an article published in *Der Spiegel* I took the opposite view. Sidestepping the issue of Scharping himself, I aimed my criticisms directly at the government: 'The government is offering to send Tornados to protect humanitarian flights and, if necessary, bomb Serbian positions as UN troops withdraw. How disastrous this will be for our future foreign policy is shown by the fact that the government justifies its grotesque offer by referring to our duty to maintain the solidarity of the alliance, although in fact there is no challenge to NATO's treaty obligations.'

I found support for my opinion in the views of Helmut Schmidt, who had given a warning in a speech to the Friedrich Ebert Foundation some years earlier against allowing the European Union and NATO to become a political football, kicked hither and thither by the Security Council in response to short-term resolutions. This could very quickly lead to the dismantling of NATO, said Schmidt. A few years later, holding to the same opinion, he wrote:

> As we confront the problems facing the world over the coming fifty years, the expansion of NATO into an efficient, worldwide interventionist force, as Washington would like it to become, would serve little useful purpose. It could do nothing to solve future crises in Asia, in Africa or in Latin America. In Kosovo, and in the Balkan peninsula as a whole, it may succeed in suppressing conflicts by force but it cannot provide permanent solutions to them. The western military alliance can be compared to a mutual life insurance policy – neither party wants to put it to the test. But NATO is not an instrument for solving all the problems that arise outside the territories of the member states. Up to now there has been hardly any public discussion of a general extension of the powers of NATO 'out of area'. But any democrat must feel the urgent need for a thorough public debate on the issue.

In 1995 there were heated discussions in the parliamentary party of the SPD over the destruction of Serb positions by German Tornados. Some members of the party voted with the Kohl government in favour of the action. The SPD held to its original line. The NATO bombing in Krajina had terrible consequences, which the Croats used as a pretext for expelling 200,000 Serbs from the territory.

Horst Grabert, former head of the chancellery under Willy Brandt, wrote: 'The idea of cleansing Kosovo of Albanians comes from the former President of the Federal Republic of Yugoslavia, President Cošić, and was his answer to the expulsion of the Serbs from Krajina. It was his way of finding room for these Serbs.

> It is a practical solution to a practical problem, for there are more refugees from Serbia than from any other country. Everywhere there are camps housing Serbs, including many who have been driven out of Kosovo. For five years or more Milošević refused to accept this policy of expulsion but when Vojislav Seselj, the ultra-nationalist, joined the government, he abandoned his opposition to the plan. When the NATO bombing raids began, he had to decide how long he could hold out against them. He came to the conclusion that by the time they stopped, the ethnic cleansing must be complete.

The NATO bombing in 1995 and the brutal expulsion of the Serbs from Krajina convinced me that it is wrong to intervene militarily in a civil war. That is still my opinion today.

The party conference in Mannheim

During the first half of 1995 I came increasingly to suspect that Rudolf Scharping had taken on too much by seeking all three roles – Party Chairman, leader of the parliamentary party and candidate for the chancellorship. In numerous discussions I therefore argued for a redistribution of these responsibilities, thinking that Johannes Rau might be asked again whether he would take over the chairmanship of the party. I knew there were reservations about him in a few quarters but the vast majority appreciated his calm and composed manner and his ability to bring people together, added to which he enjoyed a certain authority in the party.

I did not want to offer the position of Chairman to Gerhard Schröder. He had told me on one occasion that he was not suited to the job. For a while he toyed with the idea of applying to be appointed as one of the European Commissioners. I invited Johannes Rau and Rudolf Scharping to my house one evening to try and persuade them to change the shape of the leadership of the party but we did not see eye to eye. They both opposed any change in the status quo.

The following day I asked my wife whether I had expressed my views sufficiently clearly. She replied that I could not have made them any clearer – it was simply that Rau and Scharping had been unwilling to discuss my proposals. So the party executive decided by a large majority to confirm Scharping as their candidate for party leader. Opinion polls carried out at the time showed that if there had been a general election there and then, a mere 30 per cent of the population would have voted SPD.

My wife Christa and I travelled to Mannheim confident that nothing would change. But things worked out differently. Scharping had an off day. Whoever was responsible for the arrangements for his speech, he stood on the platform alone, as though deserted by all his colleagues, and delivered a very humdrum address. The delegates present were totally at a loss as to how to react. The following day had been set aside for discussions of economic and social questions with our invited guests – Jacques Delors, Dieter Schulte, Klaus Zwickel, Hans-Peter Stihl and others. The original idea had been for the guests to disperse after Jacques Delors's speech and embark on their discussions of the most important political issues in separate groups; after that the steering committee's report would be discussed.

When I saw that the delegates were leaving the hall one by one, and interest in the proceedings was waning by the minute, I suggested to Ulrich Maurer, who was in the chair, that we bring forward my report on the steering committee's deliberations. I hoped that by so doing, we would bring the delegates back into the hall, since as a rule my contributions to party conferences commanded considerable attention. Which was indeed what happened. My speech became one of the key moments in the conference. It concluded: 'There are political initiatives which arouse enthusiasm. If we are enthusiastic about them ourselves, we can arouse the enthusiasm of others. So good luck to us all!'

According to the minutes of the meeting 'the delegates rose to their feet and applauded loud and long.' Only in the course of my speech did I realize that I had set something in motion. The argument as to whether Scharping was the right leader of the party or not, which had hitherto been carried on in whispers and behind closed doors, had now been brought into the public domain.

A number of delegates came up to me the very same day and urged me to stand for election as party leader. But I hesitated. In our discussions at home my wife had impressed on me that, with the party losing more and more support in the polls, I could not just stand idly by. To this I replied that to take over the leadership would mean that I had less time to spend with the family: the leadership was a time-consuming job, and I would have to do more travelling. Besides this, I had not expected there to be a change of leader.

That evening I happened to find myself sitting in the hotel bar with Gerhard Schröder. He too tried to persuade me to put my name forward. But even this discussion, seen by many as the final attempt by the conspirators to overthrow the current leadership, did not convince me. People called me late into the night in attempts to get me to change my mind. I spent a restless night.

The next morning Scharping asked me to come and see him. Having discussed the matter with his friends, he had now decided to demand outright that I also put my name forward. Unwilling to evade the issue any longer, I consented. I did not concern myself much with how the election would work out. If I lost, it would be no tragedy. Later that day Scharping made a statement to the conference in which he said, according to the minutes: 'We are confronted with a situation which needs to be clarified. I therefore asked Oskar Lafontaine this morning whether he was prepared to stand for the office of party leader ... Lafontaine said that he was willing to do so.' Scharping was quite certain at this time that he would receive the majority of the votes at the conference. He also calculated, correctly, that even if this majority were slim, it would strengthen rather than weaken his position.

The result – 321 votes to 190 – was unexpectedly decisive. For the first time in the history of the SPD the incumbent Party Chairman was voted out of office and replaced by a new man. I felt a great sense of responsibility but also viewed my new position as a heavy burden. Our first task had to be to halt the decline in the party's fortunes, and the cooperation between the senior members of the party executive left a great deal to be desired. My parting words to my fellow-delegates at the conference were: 'Get ready for a long haul! We shall be back!'

Although Scharping had categorically demanded that I stand for leader, in the days that followed he managed to cast himself as a martyr. The media enjoy this sort of thing. It is much more exciting to report how an upright, honest leader has been elbowed off the stage by a posse of cunning conspirators led by Gerhard Schröder and Oskar Lafontaine, than simply to announce that Rudolf Scharping had been voted out of office because the party was facing a crisis and Scharping had misread the mood of the conference. In 1998 Scharping again managed to manoeuvre himself into the role of a martyr. But more of that later.

The public is always more interested in personalities than in policies, and to start with, the actual debate at the Mannheim conference was completely overshadowed by these changes of personnel. The legend of the successful coup was to be repeated in party circles long afterwards. When I subsequently gave my account of the events in Mannheim to the senior advisory committee, the honest, upright Schorsch Leber was astonished to learn that Scharping had insisted I stand for party leader. But I grew weary of having to explain time and again what the real situation was. Time heals all wounds.

I was, however, disappointed that after my election as Chairman of the party I was not given Bebel's gold watch. Willy Brandt wrote in his autobiography: 'Some friends in Switzerland brought me a gold watch that had belonged to August Bebel. It still kept good time. The party gave it to me for safe keeping until after my death it is passed down to my successors as leaders of the Social Democratic Party.' So I was not able to hand over Bebel's watch to my own successor.

2

A New Economic and Fiscal Policy

The election of a new party leader distracted attention from the fact that in my speech to the Mannheim conference I had proposed a change of direction in the SPD's economic and fiscal policy, which had become blurred. Neoliberalism and monetarism had come to characterize the economic thinking of Social Democrats and trade unionists alike. As President Richard Nixon once observed that today we are all Keynesians, so many in Germany or in Europe could have said we are now all neoliberals and supply-side politicians. SPD politicians and trade unionists who embraced neoliberal principles and supply-side policies were described in the press as 'modernizers'.

In preparation for the Mannheim conference I had called a meeting of senior party comrades to prepare our motion on economic policy. Among these 'modernizers' were Gerhard Schröder, Henning Voscherau, Wolfgang Clement, Dieter Spöri, Siegmar Mosdorf and others. The original draft of our motion repeated the widespread complaints about the situation in Germany. The situation in Germany was serious, we said, and the country was no longer competitive. We needed to do everything in our power to catch up with the leading industrial nations and had in particular fallen hopelessly behind the economies of the 'Tiger States' in Asia.

At this meeting I went out on a limb and completely redrafted the text of the motion with the help of Heiner Flassbeck, who later became my deputy as minister. The motion now read as follows:

Objective reports show that Germany continues to be in the top rank of world economies. In both 1995 and 1996 we shall have a trade surplus of some 100 billion marks. We shall even be in surplus with the countries of eastern Europe, with their cheap labour costs, while our trade with the 'Tiger' economies of Asia is in balance. Measured by head of population, Germany is the world's leading exporting nation. The continued rise in the value of the Deutschmark also illustrates the economic strength of the country. The example of Japan, moreover, shows that high investment abroad is not an indication of a loss of competitiveness but of the industrial and economic strength of that country.

We therefore declare that, when we reflect on the economic strength of Germany, we must conclude that the country is in a position to meet the new challenges. We must draw on those qualities that have made our economy strong and efficient – a highly qualified and highly motivated workforce, the ingenuity and skill of our technicians and engineers, the adaptability and the capacity to innovate on the part of our medium-sized businesses, the determination and initiative of our industrialists and managers, the high productivity of our factories, an efficient infrastructure, social stability and the ability of society to learn . . . We propose a double strategy – a policy of supply and demand.

I made it clear to the leaders of the party that this change of tack in our economic and fiscal policy was for me the most important item on the whole agenda of the Mannheim conference. The problems of the German economy had been played up by employers' organizations in a polemical and tendentious manner, and journalists, most of them disciples of supply-side policies, took up the cry day after day. The result was that more and more people came to believe that Germany was no longer competitive. It was therefore time to prove this thesis wrong.

A programme based on wage restraint, a curtailment of welfare benefits, a reduction in corporation tax and a removal of employees' rights, which has been held up as a model for modernization, would never, in my opinion, attract a majority of votes to the SPD in the country as a whole. Curtailing employees' rights, preaching wage restraint and cutting welfare payments was something the Liberals and the CDU/CSU always did better than the Social Democrats. Moreover, reading such respected economists as the Nobel prizewinner Paul Samuelson, James Tobin, Franco Modigliani, Bob Solow and Paul Krugman, Nobel prize nominee, all working at the Massachusetts Institute of Technology, I felt confirmed in my view that the economic debate as conducted in Germany was completely missing the point.

Of course anyone who holds to a minority position is always beset by fits of self-doubt. At the beginning I could not bring myself to believe that an economic fashion could go so far as simply to blind itself to certain facts and figures, and time and again I looked for faulty conclusions in my own arguments, because I could not understand why my views differed so radically from those of the majority. But I had learnt from the natural sciences that the correctness or incorrectness of a theory depends on figures and experiments. Admittedly economics is not an exact science. But from a precise perception of reality and the appraisement of mensurable data one can come to certain conclusions. Like scientists economists can check their interpretation of events against graphs and statistics. It is a familiar and understandable fact that employers' organizations should put their own particular spin on the available information. But it is astonishing that journalists and politicians should be jumping on to the same fashionable bandwagon. Paul Krugman made the same point:

> The history of economic doctrines shows that what I described as 'the ideology of international competitiveness' recurs time and again. However often economists point out how mistaken it is to view world trade as a form of war (which exporting countries are said to win and importing countries are said to lose); however often they claim that the economic success of a country cannot be measured by its balance of trade; however much they emphasise that only on the rarest of occasions does the prosperity of other countries reduce the prosperity of one's own country – the temptation to return to a primitive view of international trade as a kind of open competition for markets appears to be indestructible.
>
> Besides this, the media have a significant role to play in the present-day scenario. Many commentators and editors prefer to rely on the shallow views of hack journalists writing with an eye on the uncritical masses rather than engage in complex discussions with those who have some conception of broad economic issues and who recognise that trade balances have something to do with the difference between saving and investing.
>
> When I survey the mass of books and articles on the subject of competitiveness, I find myself amazed over and over again by the way highly intelligent scholars simply ride rough-shod over the elementary principles of economics and make free play with the facts. They put forward proposals which masquerade as quantifiable propositions concerning finite situations but do not consider it necessary to back up their position with empirical data. It completely escapes their attention that in reality the facts say something quite different.

A similar judgement can be passed on the economic debate in Germany. It is a striking fact that it should have been the industrial nation with the greatest volume of exports that complained loudest about being no longer competitive.

After the change of economic and fiscal course had been decided upon at the Mannheim conference, I set about making it known throughout the party. There was an interesting moment when I met the leaders of the Young Socialists, who had invited me to discuss with them the future policies of the SPD. I described the basic principles underlying my economic and fiscal policy, only to find, to my great surprise, that the Young Socialists reacted as though my ideas were old hat.

What I did not know was that, at the same time as me, a group among the Young Socialists had also come round to the view that there were two words an economist needed to know – supply and demand. Older members of the party might well have taken this as an occasion to make a critical analysis of their own positions. Indeed, I had often found that younger members of the party were more likely to respond positively to the prospect of future developments than were their senior colleagues. So I was glad to meet with this reaction, which confirmed me in my views rather than caused me to doubt them. Nevertheless it was an uphill task to persuade the entire party to accept the change of policy I proposed.

Writing in the *Frankfurter Rundschau* at the time, Richard Meng and Helmut Lölhöffel gave their own assessment of the situation:

> The present basic policy of the SPD, which is prepared to meet the confrontational strategy of the Kohl government head on, has the broad approval of the parliamentary party. The change of direction launched by Lafontaine, aimed at getting away from the competition in social dumping which is already being practised by certain states, is welcomed by those on the left of the party as the basic consequence of the transfer of the leadership from Scharping to Lafontaine. The SPD intends to distance itself from neoliberal initiatives and thus re-establish its true identity. But the hazard of being caught up in another trap laid by the government and branded as out of date, remains a hurdle still to be cleared.

The media chose to play a different tune. It was far more exciting to write fanciful articles about world trade wars, about who would be the winners and who the losers, than to examine the statistics and to reach the conclusion that many undesirable economic developments are in fact domestic in origin. It was amusing to watch those supply-side supporters who joined in the public debate accusing us of trotting out the tattered old slogans of the 1970s. Their starting-point was the proposition enunciated by the early nineteenth-century French economist Jean Baptiste Say, that every supply creates its own demand.

Since I relied on facts rather than articles of faith, I always replied to the self-styled 'modernizers' that they could consider themselves lucky if the number of unemployed were today what it had been in the 1970s. The unemployment figures tell us a great deal about current economic and finance policies. If the figures constantly rise, there is something wrong with those policies. Everything else is mere ideological chatter, which comes naturally only to those who have never known what it is to be unemployed or who have come to a cosy accommodation with the existing system, including its policy of under-employment.

People like me, who accept that demand is a basic economic force, were dismissed as Keynesians. But many who talk about Keynes have never read a word of what he wrote. At the time when the Young Socialists were at their peak, in the 1960s, we used to poke fun at those whose only knowledge of Karl Marx came from dust jackets or from secondary sources. John Maynard Keynes came in for the same treatment. His doctrine was reduced to the thesis that the state had to borrow in order to stimulate the economy. 'First we dig a hole, then we fill it up', as it was ironically put. This is the 'deficit spending' that most people think is the quintessence of Keynes.

But a mere glance at the title of his main work would show that Keynes was not writing about the theory of employment and deficit spending but about 'the general theory of employment, interest and money'. In other words Keynes gave monetary policy a central role in the fight against unemployment – an approach shared by Krugman and a number of American Nobel prizewinners. As Krugman puts it:

> About every six weeks the relevant committee meets to set the para-meters of U.S. interest rates. The decisions the committee makes have a far greater influence on unemployment levels than any trade policy. In addition they constitute a reaction to the facts of the current economic situation. The decision to raise or lower interest rates represents a bal-ance between the desire to improve the employment situation and the danger of thereby stimulating inflation. Frequently the Fed gets its cal-culations wrong, with the result that inflation rises or the numbers of unemployed do not fall as expected. But whichever way it turns out, whether they prove to be right or wrong, the Fed's decisions are among the most influential factors in raising the level of employment in the U.S.A.

The view that the decisions of the Central Bank are among the most important factors that influence the growth of unemployment is dia-metrically opposed to the prevailing ideology in Europe at the present time. That ideology is based on compartmentalized modes of thought that are hopelessly out of date. Monetary policy is concerned with preserving price stability, runs the orthodoxy, and wages policy deals with levels of employment, while the state provides a framework in which the development of the economy is not impeded.

This approach is simple and straightforward, the one to which the central bankers in general subscribe. Who has not at one time or another been irritated by the behaviour of the state and repeated the mantra that it should keep its hands off the economy as far as possible?

But surprisingly, in an age when lateral thinking and coordinated action are what is required in order to meet the challenge of the future, in economic policy compartmentalized attitudes still persist. The Bundesbank was proud of its culture of stability and that this culture found expression in the Maastricht Treaty. What was, and still is, overlooked, is that this stability is the principal cause of the high unemployment rates in Germany and in Europe as a whole. It is not yet clear whether the European central bankers are going to continue to base their decisions on this false ideology.

What is certain, however, is that they want to continue to interfere in all aspects of public policy – budgetary policy, taxation policy, social policy, wages policy and so on. But woe betide the man who dares to challenge the policies of the central bankers. This authoritarian approach to monetary policy makes it harder to arrive at a rational economic policy. To seek to question their prerogative merely produces a petulant, childish reaction on their part and on the part of their followers. But their position was already weakened by the Maastricht Treaty, which stated that monetary policy should also seek to promote growth and employment, as long as there was no danger of inflation.

Article 105 of the Maastricht Treaty states that the primary aim of the Council of European Bankers is to ensure price stability. To the extent that it is possible to achieve stability without detriment to this aim, the Council is enjoined to support the general economic policy of the European Union as its contribution towards achieving the aims laid down in Article 2 of the Treaty. This Article 2 states that it is the aim of the Union to promote a high level of employment and a substantial measure of social security, the equality of men and women, constant non-inflationary growth, a high degree of competitiveness and the convergence of economic benefits, the protection and improvement of the environment, the furtherance of economic and social cohesion and the encouragement of solidarity between member states.

But the bankers' answer remains what it always was. 'We are responsible for maintaining the stability of the currency,' they say, 'and that's the end of the matter.'

Since a reduction of the number of unemployed is one of a social-democratic government's central aims, I felt I had to make a vigorous attack on this narrow-minded ideology. I knew full well that the defenders of orthodoxy would come down on me like a ton of bricks. So immediately after taking office as Finance Minister, I repeated my demand for a lowering of interest rates in order to stimulate growth and employment in Europe. A number of European finance ministers supported me. And at a summit meeting in Pörtschach in the autumn of 1998 even the heads of government of the European countries plucked up courage and declared the abolition of unemployment to be their main aim. According to a report from Reuters they even raised the question of a reduction in interest rates – an area which, as they themselves admitted, did not lie within their field of competence.

Goran Persson, Prime Minister of Sweden, noted with approval that Europe had drifted to the left. Reuters also reported that Gerhard Schröder had delighted his colleagues in the party by announcing to journalists at a crowded meeting that he was putting his weight behind the efforts of the European Union as a whole to abolish unemployment, vehemently attacking at the same time the activities of currency speculators. He denied that such a policy would destroy the economies of entire countries. Tony Blair said that the risks of international financial crises should be limited by the adoption of a common strategy, and that the European Union had to take appropriate measures in international financial organizations. The present risk, said Blair, was not of inflation but of weak demand. It was therefore necessary to discuss the matter with the various national banks and with the European Central Bank.

Massimo d'Alema was another who made a powerful demand for a reduction in interest rates. On this occasion I could therefore assume that my appeals to the national banks and the European Central Bank to lower interest rates were supported by the majority of European heads of government.

Claus Noé, not yet a member of the government at the time, wrote a polemical article in *Die Zeit* which was published after he had become a minister of state. Noé wrote:

> Tietmeyer, President of the Bundesbank, claims that the euro is 'a depoliticized currency' because the European Central Bank will operate independently of political influences exerted by governments, parliaments and European institutions. Certainly monetary policy has to be openly discussed, vigorously by some, restrainedly by others. It does little to enhance the reputation of the currency authorities when certain of them consider it better not to reply, with the result that public demands for interest rates to be raised or lowered would be met by the central bankers with total apathy, so as to show how independent and

impervious to influence they are. It is an attitude that carries a scent of defiance – a refusal to take the proper action because others have publicly demanded it. Autonomous action means taking the decision that has been objectively demonstrated to be the right one.

National bankers cannot be dismissed. That is their privilege. But in return, I maintain, they have to be publicly accountable. Only one who is confident of his own infallibility can believe that public debate does not help to produce better-informed decisions.

This was an attack that Tietmeyer and his colleagues regarded as proof that their independence was under threat.

Then something happened that really set the cat among the pigeons. In a television chat-show my wife put in her own plea for a reduction in interest rates, pointing out that the independence of the Bundesbank on the one side was matched by an absence of democratic control and public accountability on the other.

All hell was let loose. What was the Finance Minister's wife thinking of, meddling in financial affairs like that? At the heart of many critical comments lay the prejudice, implicit if not explicit, that ministers' wives should have the sense to keep out of public affairs, even if they were well informed in the field in which their husbands carried ministerial responsibility. Before our victory in the election I had been called 'the great integrator'; during the negotiations over the formation of the coalition government I was 'the great dictator'. Now I was 'the great hen-pecked husband'.

The chorus of indignation that the Finance Minister should have intervened so ineptly in matters of monetary policy grew louder and louder. Reasoned objections there were none. Three specific items of protest – better, prejudice – stood out:

(1)   It is not the job of politicians to make statements on, or interfere in matters of, monetary policy. Forgotten were the days when Ludwig Erhard and Karl Schiller, when they were economics ministers, vetoed the Bundesbank's plan to raise the bank rate. The veto served to put off the decision.

(2)   This is the moment for the central bankers to show Lafontaine who is master in the house. They are not the people to be dictated to from outside. Those who reacted like this were treating the bankers like little children – we must at all costs resist all demands, even if they are right and proper, lest we give the impression of having surrendered our independence.

(3)   Under no circumstances can a policy of 'fiscal laxity' help to stimulate growth and employment. This is an opinion that is in sharp contrast to that which prevails in America.

In 1983 the advisory committee of the German Economics Ministry also started from the assumption 'that monetary policy can and must play an important part in employment policy', and went on to call for a consensual solution between the various social groupings. But whereas, after its negative experience with a policy of high interest rates and a strong dollar during the 1980s, the United States abandoned monetarist policies, the European central banks continued to cling to them. As a result unemployment figures fell in America but went on rising in Europe. George Soros wrote: 'Monetarism worked quite well in practice, but chiefly because the theory was ignored ... The Bundesbank, on the other hand, still cherishes the illusion that all that needs to be done is to follow the basic principles of monetarism to the letter. The Federal Reserve, by contrast, takes an agnostic line, frankly conceding that monetary policy is a matter of judgement.'

3

The Rush to Lower Taxation

The third issue at the heart of the economic debate, alongside those of national economic viability and the implications of an ideologically inflexible monetary policy, is that of taxation policy. This was to become a bone of contention between the Kohl government and the SPD, and became a factor of considerable importance in the SPD's election victory in 1998.

Politicians invariably trumpet their intention to lower taxes, because that is what the electors like to hear. But reality often stands in the way of such a policy. George Bush, John Major, Jacques Chirac and Helmut Kohl all found that the reductions in taxation that they promised before the election turned into the introduction of higher taxation after the election, thereby undermining their credibility with the electorate. The FDP gave the impression that lowering taxation was the only policy they had, while the high taxes paid by journalists guaranteed that the papers carried every day their demand for tax rates to be lowered.

Their leading example was the United States. But here too they were under an illusion. In July 1999 the *Frankfurter Allgemeine Zeitung* published a comparison between the salaries of two engineers, which showed that in the USA people in fact paid more tax. Taking all the deductions into account, the American engineer was left with less than half his gross income, while the German engineer was left with two-thirds of his earnings.

Nobody expected this. There was also a desire to simplify the taxation system – remove tax concessions and reduce tax rates, and a fairer result would follow. A committee under Professor Bareis had recommended back in 1994 that tax rates should be reduced and tax subsidies abolished. We continually urged the government coalition parties to accept the Bareis report and put its recommendations into effect. I was well aware of the difficulties involved in implementing such a policy but I took great delight in making the government feel awkward when faced with their own slogans and promises.

Theo Waigel had recognized the snags involved in the Bareis proposals and had no wish to go down that particular road. In the CDU/CSU it was in particular Wolfgang Schäuble, in conjunction with the FDP, who responded to the situation with the so-called 'Petersberg Model'. But it was impossible to take Schäuble's proposals seriously, for they involved a budgetary deficit of between 30 and 50 billion marks, as well as a rise in value-added tax. This was an embarrassment to the ruling parties just before the election. They therefore kept their real intentions in the background during the election campaign. But to their discomfort Claudia Nolte, Minister for Family Affairs, let the cat out of the bag and inadvertently made a reference to the planned increase in value-added tax. Her respect for the truth brought down the collective wrath of her colleagues on her head.

Those responsible for the 'Petersberg Model' had failed to calculate the effect of their proposals on the individual taxpayer. They therefore had not realized that a whole category of workers – skilled workers on shift work, bus drivers, nurses – would be worse off under their plan. It was also intended to do away with a whole series of popular tax concessions, such as travel allowance, employees allowance and tax exemption for shift work, night work and weekend working. Finally they planned to tax insurance payments and higher pensions.

The 'Petersberg Model' gave us a golden opportunity to demonstrate to our traditional supporters what the Kohl government was really about. The coalition parties immediately adopted a defensive stance, countering our attack with a demand that the SPD produce its own tax proposals – a demand quickly taken up by the public at large. I announced that our plans would be based on those of the 'Petersberg Model', but that at the same time we would take out the clauses which disadvantaged the workers. We also took care to see that our proposals were more realistically costed than those of our opponents.

In retrospect I must admit that it was a mistake to take our lead from the Petersberg Model. So incredibly complex and confusing had the taxation system become that any thought of evolving a system that was fair and just was out of the question. What we needed was a simplification of tax legislation so radical that everybody could understand it. However, the public debate on the subject seemed to make it advisable for us to accept the outlines of the Petersberg plan as adopted by the Kohl government and set against it our own scheme, which, though similar in basic outline, could be seen by everybody to diverge markedly from that of the coalition.

On 14 February 1997 my son Carl Maurice was born. As I had a severe cold at the time, I did not visit the hospital in case I might pass on the infection to my wife and the baby. Barely had I received the happy tidings from the hospital than the telephone rang again. It was Helmut Kohl – by chance the first person to offer me his congratulations. He invited me to join him in all-party talks on the subject of tax reform, because he knew that in the Bundesrat the governments of the *Länder* with an SPD majority would have to pass new tax legislation, whatever form it took.

But it had been an unforgivable mistake on the part of the Kohl government not to have tried to reach agreement on these matters confidentially in advance, in the time-honoured way. We were all too ready to pass a new tax bill. The so-called 'modernizers' in the SPD, in particular, were fully prepared to take over proposals put forward by business organizations. But by publishing the 'Petersberg Model' without seeking the agreement of the Bundesrat, the government had got itself into a difficult situation, which gave us the opportunity to put forward our own plans with the maximum effect.

And indeed, starting with the increase in child benefit and moving on to a reduction of the lowest tax rate and the avoidance of the many injustices suffered by employees, our proposals proved far more popular than those of the government. I had firmly resolved not to agree to a compromise solution unless the SPD's demands for a fairer tax system were met. Throughout the negotiations I constantly had to keep an eye on our representatives – Rudolf Scharping, Heinz Schleusser and Henning Voscherau – to make sure they did not concede too much ground to our opponents. To be on the safe side I secured the firm assurance of the party executive that there would be no deviation from the basic principles of our plan. If there had been a serious difference of opinion, I would have called a meeting of the party in order to prevent any substantial departure from this plan. Scharping in particular, leader of the parliamentary party, was frequently tempted to make considerable concessions to the CDU, which were greeted with approval both by the coalition parties and by the press. But I was determined to see that our principle of social justice should prevail, and I was not willing to subscribe to a plan that, in addition, showed signs of having been influenced by the FDP.

My stand was vindicated. The CDU/CSU could not escape from the shadow of the FDP. Opinion polls clearly showed that our policies enjoyed greater public support. The disagreements had a further unwelcome consequence for the government. They wanted to present themselves before the elections as a government of internal reforms. But the squabbling over the tax bill made it clear to the population as a whole that the government was in fact a lame duck.

Independent of the collapse of these discussions over taxation reform, there had over recent years been a great deal of hectic activity, part of it due to the pressure exerted by the Social Democrats, over the whole question of taxation policy. One of the reasons for this was the international race to reduce taxation. After one state made a move in this direction, all its suspected rivals felt bound to follow suit with proposals of their own. In response to pressure from the 'modernizers' I therefore agreed to the abolition of trading capital tax and business property tax, although this was a measure that did not affect small and medium-sized businesses because high allowances meant that such businesses were hardly liable to pay tax in any case. After winning the elections, we made the mistake of perpetuating the hectic air surrounding the whole question of taxation reform by setting too tight a schedule for its implementation. And after I resigned, the situation was as it had been during the darkest days of the Kohl government. Almost every day politicians of one party or another were trying to attract attention to themselves by producing this or that set of new proposals.

Alongside the broad tax reforms the party attached particular importance to the reform of ecology tax. Here it was not a question of achieving greater fairness in the tax system, as with the major reforms, but of adapting a system that had developed over decades to the present needs of the environment. In this connection we had to remember that, relative to many other prices, the cost of petrol had come down. On the other hand, as Gerhard Schröder repeatedly put it, the cost of petrol was to the man in the street like the price of bread. Tinkering with the duty on fuel was always unpopular. To get the masses to accept the changes we proposed, we needed to find a way of demonstrating the advantages of such changes.

There were two ways of doing this – on the one hand by lowering the rate of income tax at the same time, to the general benefit of employees, or on the other by reducing the unacceptably high level of welfare contributions. As we had taken a decision in 1990 to reduce the incidence of direct taxation, we now proposed to lower social security contributions at the same time as introducing an ecology tax. But this still proved unpopular, and particularly the 'modernizers' in the party never tired of querying the efficacy of such a tax when they were interviewed by journalists on television or in the press.

'Modernizer' and 'modernization' have become fashionable terms which can be made to cover every thing and everybody. When one tries to discover the essence of what is 'modern' and what makes a person a 'modernizer', one finds that it means nothing more than ecological and social adaptation to the perceived forces of globalization. The application of the term 'modern' comes to be restricted to economic categories. The UK has no legislation to protect workers against summary dismissal, so we decide to be modern and repeal our own legislation. Many countries are reducing the level of welfare benefits, so let us be modern and do the same. Business taxes are being reduced, otherwise entrepreneurs will up sticks and establish themselves in business somewhere else, so let us be modern and reduce these taxes too. In America there are virtually no restrictions on the use of gene technology, so let us show how modern we are by turning a blind eye to the risks involved and removing such restrictions ourselves.

Such examples could be multiplied *ad nauseam*. Modern has come to mean simply accommodation to economic pressures. The question of how we are to live together and what kind of society we want is now branded 'un-modern' and is no longer asked.

For the Social Democratic Party, on the other hand, 'modern' means something quite different. It has nothing to do with mere adaptation to the laws of economics. It is a word that belongs in the context of the Enlightenment and is concerned with the freedom of the individual. To us Social Democrats all structural reforms that promote the freedom of the individual, removing the dependence of one person on another and opening up fresh possibilities of self-fulfilment, are modern. If the SPD were to adopt an interpretation of 'modern' that signified conformity, and thus spell the end of political independence and influence, it would be signing its own death warrant.

4

The Election Campaign

When we sat down – Franz Müntefering, our business manager, and I, together with our colleagues and advisers – to plan our strategy for the coming election campaign, we found ourselves in a parlous situation. The opinion polls showed the party to be at its lowest ebb, considered out of date and unwilling to reform itself. In a word, we presented a sorry picture. New concepts and initiatives were required because the party had been losing its social democratic credentials at an alarming rate, and its public image needed to be revamped.

One important task I had set myself was to engage young people, in particular the Young Socialists, in the election campaign. In previous years the SPD had made the mistake of neglecting the Young Socialists. Members of the party executive had made no effort to attend their conferences and there was no real dialogue between them. That was all the more remarkable in that everybody, including the leaders of all the main political parties, had come to realize that they could get nowhere without involving the younger generation.

So immediately after taking office, I entered into discussions with the Young Socialists. It was a stroke of good fortune that their leader, a young woman called Andrea Nahles, was a person of strong political commitment, one who sent a breath of fresh air coursing through the party.

The Young Socialists' main concern, understandably, was youth unemployment. They had worked out proposals for dealing with the shortage of places on training courses, demanding that firms which offered no such places should be made to pay a levy to those firms which met their social responsibility by making such places available.

Also, in common with the parliamentary party, they proposed that directly after the elections a training programme should be launched to create 100,000 jobs for trainees and youth unemployed. In order to make the public aware that we welcomed the participation of young people in the party's debates, and that they really did play a part in its decision-making, we organized a Youth Conference in Cologne on 25 November 1996.

During our preparations for this meeting 'traditionalists' and 'modernizers' occupied rival camps. But their roles were reversed. I personally was delighted to be cast as a 'modernizer' in two respects. Müntefering had proposed that the principal speakers should be Johannes Rau, me and Müntefering himself. I opposed this suggestion on the ground that, although the three of us were still undoubtedly young at heart, the average citizen's idea of a 'young' socialist was somewhat different. My idea had been that immediately after the conference was opened, Andrea Nahles should deliver a keynote speech which would carry no less authority than that of the leader of the party. Nothing like this had been known before, and to start with the suggestion met with everything from a furrowing of the brow to outright rejection. Eventually however, my proposal was accepted.

Müntefering and I had already agreed that the external image of the conference needed to be brightened up. Müntefering had the idea of inviting students from the Faculty of Design in the University of Cologne to decorate the hall – a novel idea which in my opinion worked out admirably.

On the evening before the conference opened, I insisted on joining a group of young students dancing on the stage. This performance was a gift for the press photographers present, who, with the rest, found my performance, with my grey hair and my undisguisable paunch, to be somewhat out of place. Their mocking remarks, which deliberately overlooked the self-irony of my contorted movements and did not even have the grace to compliment me on my attempts to move to the rhythm of the music, were calculated merely to damage my self-esteem.

I was delighted that the delegates enjoyed the new decor of the hall. The occasion went off without a hitch. Andrea Nahles, in a black leather jacket, gave an aggressive speech that was received with great applause. The following day her picture was in all the papers.

There was a vigorous debate on the levy for training courses. Prominent among its opponents were Gerhard Schröder and Wolfgang Clement, the so-called 'modernizers' and employers' friends. I refused to tolerate the reluctance on the part of many firms to shoulder their social responsibility, and came out in favour of such a levy. I also considered this a key moment for deciding the direction in which the election campaign should go. It was essential to win over the younger generation, in particular those active in the trade union movement or in Church and similar organizations. This inevitably involved substantive issues – specifically, the decision as to whether the question of the training levy should be made part of the SPD's election manifesto. We also needed to make it clear that the levy would be imposed only if there was a shortage of places on training courses. In other words, employers had the opportunity to make the levy unnecessary by being prepared to offer an adequate number of such places. This proposal was carried by an overwhelming majority of the delegates at the conference.

The Young Socialists had got their way. After the motion had been passed, cries of approval rang out through the hall, first from the younger delegates, then more and more from the older members of the party. I felt a considerable personal satisfaction at this outcome. It was of vital importance that the younger generation should have a hand in forming policy.

Now that we were on the move, so to speak, we set about improving the public image of the party. The first job was to find a good public relations firm. For a number of years we had used the RSCG agency to handle the affairs of the party. But over time the images that the agency had developed were becoming hackneyed, so I agreed with Franz Müntefering that we should make a change. We invited a number of agencies to submit their proposals. One put forward a plan that was clearly built round my own position. The election campaign was dominated by social and ecological issues, a policy of which I wholeheartedly approved. But I had long made up my mind to keep my own pet hobby-horses in the background and to concentrate on winning the election.

The well-known firm KNSK BBDO in Hamburg developed a publicity campaign that was clearly based on the figure of Gerhard Schröder as candidate for the chancellorship. The candidate occupied centre stage – in their presentation the firm had used the film actor Michael Douglas as the candidate, though I am not sure whether Müntefering recognized him. At all events we were both in favour of giving the commission to this agency, as we had at the back of our minds a fairly clear idea of how the election campaign should be conducted.

By designing a series of witty placards, some of them based on well-known film posters, the agency quickly captured the attention of the public. As well as devising new slogans, they had to find ways of presenting the new image of the SPD via the television screen. We spent far more money on publicity than our rivals in the CDU/CSU.

In terms of the way in which we had planned our campaign Gerhard

Schröder was the ideal candidate. His manner matched our campaign perfectly and the public gave him their approval. Our rivals, with Helmut Kohl in the centre, made a far less favourable impression at their election meetings.

I do not claim that an election can be won by the format of its campaign. Without a readiness for change even the best campaign cannot succeed. But if that readiness is there, the manner of the campaign can strengthen the desire for a change of government. That was our goal, and in retrospect we are entitled to claim that we were successful.

Our campaign was conducted under the slogan 'The New Centre', a slogan coined by Willy Brandt in October 1972. Brandt said: 'Where there is a sense of necessity, and where preservation is guaranteed by change – that is where the new centre ground lies.' Schröder and I both adopted the same approach even before it was decided who the party's candidate for Chancellor would be. In the eyes of the public Schröder already occupied the 'new centre ground', and in the event of my being nominated, the slogan would have helped to improve my image in areas in which the public found it to be deficient. Some time earlier, in Hanover, we had adopted the motto 'The New Force'. But this was also an advertising slogan used by the firm of Siemens, so we left 'The New Force' to Siemens and kept 'The New Centre' for ourselves.

Müntefering had suggested that we should concentrate on the word 'innovation' in our publicity, and the advertising agency, having tested it out, agreed that it went down well with the public. The SPD was already identified with the phrase 'social justice', so we put the two together and emphasized from the beginning the twin concepts of innovation and a fair society in our advertising material. After the question of the chancellorship was settled, the press linked the concept of innovation with Schröder and that of a fair society with me. These two attributions – the one the modernizer, the other the traditionalist – served to consolidate the party image.

In preparation for the election Franz Müntefering and his colleagues studied Clinton's presidential campaign in America, and came to the conclusion that the correct procedure would be to follow the American example and set up a new election centre in a different building from the Erich Ollenhauer House, the party headquarters.

Opinions in the party were divided over the new election centre. The party faithful in the Erich Ollenhauer House, in particular, felt they had been passed over. But Müntefering and I were sure it was a good move and succeeded in getting our way. The centre opened in April 1998 and the campaign was launched. Everything went swimmingly, and Müntefering was in his element. As the work of the centre frequently attracted the attention of the press, we always managed to keep a length ahead of our rivals. A particularly wise move had been to employ students and other young people, who brought a breath of fresh air into the activities of the centre. Indeed, so successful was it that without further ado a similar centre was set up to handle the forthcoming European elections. That those elections did not produce the desired result was in no way to be blamed on the staff of the centre.

5

Red Socks – Red Hands

Part of an election campaign consists of observing the strategy and tactics of one's opponents. As a rule it is not advisable to wage the same kind of campaign each time an election falls due. In 1994 the CDU/CSU had caused panic in the ranks of certain SPD supporters with their 'red socks' campaign. The SPD's reaction was somewhat ill-considered. Although in East Germany, at local government level, all the parties, in particular the former east-CDU and FDP – the so-called 'Block Parties' – cooperated with the PDS, Scharping and other SPD leaders considered it necessary to announce publicly, almost day after day, that any cooperation with the PDS was out of the question. On one occasion, at a meeting of the party executive, I burst out: 'Is that the only subject you've got on your mind?'

I do not think, and did not think at the time, that the CDU's 'red socks' campaign had much effect. In the East it inclined to put people off. The only success it may be said to have had was in forcing the subject to be discussed within the ranks of the SPD itself. So I was quite pleased when in 1998 the CDU planned to revive the 'red socks' campaign as the 'red hands' campaign. The time for a vilification of the PDS was over. One was entitled to expect, from all those who proclaimed time and again that one of their paramount political aims was the unity of the fatherland, an answer to the question of how they proposed to deal with those who had voted for the PDS.

Gerhard Schröder was the first to suggest that the PDS be invited to join a coalition in a provincial government. He pointed out, correctly, that once they were installed in the government of one or other of the *Länder*, their assumption of responsibility would very quickly lead them to abandon their homespun populist policies. Their ministers would make mistakes and soon their party would be treated, in East Germany too, like any normal party. Several years were to elapse, however, before, at the end of 1998, in the *Land* of Mecklenburg-Vorpommern, the first provincial government was formed with the participation of the PDS.

The second to urge a change of attitude towards those who had voted for the PDS, and that the PDS be allowed to become involved in government, was President Richard von Weizsäcker, who wrote:

> In provincial and local elections in the East German *Länder*, including Berlin, the PDS is used as a bludgeon with which one western party beats the other western party over the head. There is no doubt that this policy brought short-term advantages to one of these two camps, especially as it unsettled the other camp and forced it on to the defensive. But the real winners were the PDS itself . . .
>
> But is it not our duty to engage our strength in winning over everybody to the cause of democracy? Why do we talk about 'post-communism' to a young voter in Brandenburg or Berlin who wants to test the ideas of socialism against the criteria of the democratic process? He may find it hard but should he not, as a democrat, at least be permitted to try? And must a young East German citizen who was still a teenager when the Wall fell in November 1989, first be required to apologise for all the shootings carried out in the DDR before he can be allowed to take part in democratic elections?
>
> What has happened in reality is that the larger of the two main democratic parties set out to attack its smaller rival over its attitude to the PDS, with the result that the smaller party became weaker while the PDS itself became stronger. This can hardly be a coincidence.

Weizsäcker saw more clearly than many of my party colleagues what the CDU was up to, and he deserves our respect for speaking out.

During my time as party leader I consistently followed a policy of opposing the crude demonization of the PDS by the CDU/CSU. As Weizsäcker rightly pointed out, this demonization of the PDS was in the CDU's interest. As the smaller parties – the FDP and the combination of the Greens and the 90 Alliance – counted for virtually nothing in the East, the only coalition partner the CDU had there was the SPD. But it was a wise policy, in my view, for the SPD to try to involve the PDS step by step in the governments of the *Länder* and thereby help it to find its place in the democratic system as a normal political party.

I had occasional discussions with Gregor Gysi, leader of the PDS, which at the beginning attracted considerable attention in the press. I repeatedly asked him about his long-term political aims. After all, I pointed out, we already had social democratic policies in place, and he had declared that he no longer subscribed to communist principles. The history of the twentieth century, I added, seemed to teach that the more the left split into different factions, the weaker it became.

I had always taken the view that it was necessary to have one big, strong, popular left-wing party in order to represent employees' interests in a democracy. Everywhere in the world, including Germany, the power of the unions had been weakened as a result of globalization and the spread of the philosophy of neoliberalism. It was no accident that investors in the USA were enticed by the promise of non-unionized labour.

Gysi did not reject this view out of hand. But he did point out that the PDS would take a few years to discover its true role. As far as the longer term was concerned, I had the impression that he shared my opinion that it would not be sensible to have two parties in East Germany which both aspired to more-or-less social democratic goals.

The foundation of the coalition that was formed in Mecklenburg-Vorpommern after the federal elections had thus already been laid, and was a logical consequence of the intention to have the PDS and its supporters in the east share in the responsibilities of government. Although Germany and France are not strictly comparable, I always remembered the way Mitterrand had dealt with the French Communist Party. He had taken them into his government, thereby not strengthening their position but considerably weakening it. In the French Partie Socialiste too there were vigorous debates on the subject, some members fearing that an alliance with the communists would work to the detriment of the party. But Mitterrand held out, and history proved him right. Today Lionel Jospin leads a government in which members of the French Communist Party, now purged of their Stalinist image, also serve.

When, after the elections in Sachsen-Anhalt in 1998, the question of PDS support for the government of Reinhard Höppner arose, we again almost found ourselves sliding down a slippery slope. Schröder and I shared the view that by forming a grand coalition, we would deprive the CDU of any opportunity to play the PDS card again in the federal election. But we very quickly realized that in Sachsen-Anhalt itself there was little desire for a grand coalition. With the benefit of hindsight I regret not having recognized this development sooner. At any rate the Social Democrats in Sachsen-Anhalt said that people in the East would not understand how they could be committed by their party leadership to entering into a government with the CDU, the palpable losers in the election.

Another lesson that emerged from the elections in Sachsen-Anhalt was that, in times when there was a general feeling of social dissatisfaction, electors in the East protested by voting for one or other of the parties of the far right, in this case the DVU. I share the opinion of a number of French commentators that in the East the influence of the PDS holds the advance of far-right parties in check.

When I witnessed the protests in the east and listened to the arguments put forward by my friends in Sachsen-Anhalt, I advised the leaders of the party that we should return to our former policy. In the East, we said, it was for the parties on the spot to decide which coalitions are formed. If the party leadership had continued to insist on a grand coalition in Sachsen-Anhalt, we should indeed have had problems in the federal elections, and the east would not have understood us. Reinhard Höppner formed a government, again with the support of the PDS, and after the federal elections the first SPD/PDS coalition government took office in Mecklenburg-Vorpommern.

I am certain that the CDU's 'red hands' campaign contributed to the success that the SPD enjoyed in the East in the federal election. Members of the east-CDU were also highly critical of the campaign. All this was grist to our mill, for we knew from our own experience that parties which argued in the course of a campaign over the effectiveness of their strategies generally turned in poor results. And so it turned out on this occasion also.

During the election campaign I had to take care that the members of the think-tank known as the Seeheim Circle were not taken in by the CDU/CSU a second time. In previous years it had been easy for the CDU/CSU to provoke vehement arguments in the SPD over the subject of the PDS. In 1998, after the formation of the coalition government in Sachsen-Anhalt, we managed to avoid such arguments to a large extent. We also frequently pointed out that neither the CDU/CSU nor the FDP had the slightest grounds for criticizing the cooperation of the SPD with the PDS. They themselves, as everybody knew, were working more and more closely together in provincial parliaments and local councils, and had absorbed the former 'block parties'. In certain bodies there were still men and women working who had already been elected as representatives of the 'block parties' in DDR times. The east CDU and east FDP had both defended the construction of the Berlin Wall and the barbed-wire barriers in the days of the DDR.

The campaign of the CDU/CSU and the FDP was thus totally hypocritical. The older ones among us also remembered that the CDU/CSU had been much less forthcoming about distancing themselves from former Nazis. Hans Globke, for instance, author of a commentary on the Nazis' anti-Semitic legislation, had been appointed to the

Chancellor's staff at Adenauer's express request. Kurt Georg Kiesinger and Karl Carstens had both been members of the Nazi Party, not to mention Hans Filbinger. In the light of facts such as these the constant disparagement of the PDS cut little ice. Apart from this, as everyone could see, the PDS now counted among its ranks not only the old guard of the communist SED but young people who were still children when the Wall came down.

It is also interesting to recall that the only chance Dagmar Schipanski, the CDU/CSU candidate for the Presidency, had to be elected was with the votes of the PDS. She was quite open about this, and it is no secret that the leadership of the CDU would have welcomed it. But in such matters there is a great deal of lying and dissembling in Germany. Sections of the press also joined in the act, choosing to accept the CDU's repeated assertions that, although they were to be found working alongside members of the PDS in local councils and elsewhere, they would never dream of forming an administration with the participation of the PDS.

Given the considerable support that it still enjoys in East Germany, I not only consider the PDS to be entitled to sit in the parliaments of the *Länder* but I would also see no difficulty about including it in the federal government, if common policies could be agreed upon. My opposition to their inclusion in 1998 therefore rested on issues of substance. They rejected the euro, whereas the acceptance of European economic union and a single currency was a firm plank in our policy. Then they had a negative attitude towards NATO, whereas for us NATO was the basis of our defence policy. And their economic and social demands were purely and simply impossible to finance, whereas our own fiscal policy was aimed at putting the nation's finances on a firm footing. There was a great deal to discuss.

Since I have always tried to see politics over the long term, I should like to mention here a plan that I was unfortunately unable to put into practice in 1990. Contrary to the wishes of Brandt and Vogel I would have considered it wiser to allow a separate east-SPD to exist side by side with the main party for a long time. Such a sister-party could have represented the interests of the East Germans far better than we are doing at the present. They would also have been given the task of discussing issues firmly but fairly with the PDS itself. An alliance between an east SPD and the PDS would have been more favourably received in the West than an alliance between SPD and PDS.

Always in my mind when I reflected on these issues was, of course, the aim that two parallel parties both subscribing to social democratic ideals should eventually merge into one. Richard von Weizsäcker was right when he said: 'Why do we talk about "post-communism" to a young voter in Brandenburg or Berlin who wants to test the ideas of socialism against the criteria of the democratic process?' The character of the membership of political parties changes over the years.

The preservation of the east-SPD would have had one positive side-effect, namely that in television discussions there would be two representatives of the SPD present, to match the two of the CDU/CSU. In this way the unfair advantage enjoyed by the coalition parties would have been offset by an east-SPD.

6

Running for Federal Office

Human nature being what it is, individuals are far more interesting than policies. The question of who would be chosen as the SPD's nominee for the office of Federal Chancellor therefore dominated the public's attention. After I had been elected as Party Chairman, people immediately asked whether that also settled the question of who the party's candidate for Chancellor would be.

During our internal discussions on the matter I urged that the issue should not be decided over-hastily. I had no intention of allowing the public to force a decision on me before the time was right. Besides that, the last thing I wanted was to give the impression that my work as Party Chairman was driven by personal ambition. As a result of the attempt on my life and the defeat of 1990 I had developed a very different attitude towards such matters.

It was a matter of observation that by constantly insisting that he was the best candidate, Rudolf Scharping, my predecessor, only made his work as Party Chairman more difficult. My years as Deputy Party Chairman had taught me that initiatives were often more effective when they came from the body of the party rather than from the leader. A premature decision would also have irritated a number of other members of the party who also made bold to see themselves as potential Chancellor.

Scharping, who had not come to terms with his defeat at the Mannheim conference, was far from being the only man in this position. There was also Gerhard Schröder, who would never have given way to Scharping and who had led me to understand that he was still interested in becoming the chosen nominee. Everybody accepted that the Chairman had the right of first refusal but in practice such agreements were of slight value.

Nor were Scharping and Schröder the only ones to consider themselves suited to the position of Federal Chancellor. A few Prime Ministers of provincial governments and our colleague in Schleswig-Holstein, Heide Simonis, were among those mentioned in the papers. I was therefore well advised to keep the matter open. The news agencies in Bonn wagered that I would fail, and the public pressure on me to reveal my decision prematurely was at times almost impossible to resist. But I held out. First the publication of our new party manifesto, I said, then the question of personalities.

In retrospect I can see that this policy was of considerable strategic importance for the SPD's victory in the election. As long as the question of personalities remained open, we retained the public's interest. As time went on, it became increasingly clear that the choice lay between Schröder and me. The opinion polls gave Schröder substantial support among the public. He also enjoyed the approval of the press, with *Der Spiegel*, *Focus*, *Stern*, *Bild am Sonntag*, *Die Woche* and, to a lesser extent, *Bild* all falling over themselves in their eagerness to endorse him as the chosen candidate. In private conversations various Editors-in-Chief tried to convince me that a vote for Schröder was the only way to guarantee that the SPD would win.

It was a source of irritation for me that, as Schröder's chances were played up, so mine were denigrated in the most offensive manner. One editor boasted that he had personally selected photos of me that showed me in a particularly unfavourable light. Even the opinion research institute Forsa joined this campaign, publishing every week high ratings among the population for Schröder and poor ratings for me. I was facing a dilemma.

There was no doubt that on television Schröder cut the better figure – a matter of no little importance in a modern election campaign. Nor was there any doubt that it would be easier to win the election with the support of the Hamburg press than without it. On the other hand I had played a dominant part in the formulation of SPD policy in recent years and had greater experience in the conduct of government business. In contrast to my colleagues I had been Prime Minister of the Saarland since 1985 and before that Governing Mayor of Saarbrücken for almost ten years. During the time I held these two positions, I enjoyed absolute majorities. The basic difficulty I faced was that, by agreeing to Schröder as our nominee for Chancellor, I would be standing everything I stood for on its head – and on two counts.

In the first place I held to the opinion that our candidate had to enjoy the active support of all the members of the party. Those who carried out the humdrum, day-to-day work of the party had to be able to identify with both the candidate and his policies. But Schröder met neither of these requirements, because he had earned the support of the media by persistently throwing mud at the party and its policies. This may have made for entertaining journalism and good television but the party could hardly be expected to approve of it. I was worried lest this one example might lead to others. In the long run the unity of the party could not but be damaged if individuals assumed their right to promote their own popularity at the party's expense.

I also found myself confronting a question that struck at the heart of the democratic process. Is it permissible, I asked, for the media to have the decisive voice in a discussion over who shall lead a party into an election campaign? If the party were to answer this question in the affirmative, would it not be shedding too much of its own responsibility? And would we not be going down the road that leads to the Americanization of the German political system? In America the parties are less important than the personalities. Candidates for high office have to be successful performers on television and to have behind them the financial backing essential for a successful campaign.

A further problem was that Joschka Fischer, leader of the Greens, our potential coalition partner, had a relationship to his party similar to that of Gerhard Schröder to the SPD. Charlotte Wiedemann wrote in *Die Woche*: 'The rise of Fischer, the darling of the media, followed a straightforward path. Contemptuous of the party that had launched his political career, he established his reputation by outspoken public criticism of his colleagues. The Greens meekly accepted his behaviour and began to enjoy their subjugation.'

Had we in fact not turned long ago from being a democracy of political parties to being a democracy of the media? It was not an easy decision for me to make. In the final analysis there were three considerations that led me to offer the nomination to Schröder. Firstly, the one thing above all that I wanted to avoid was the accusation that my personal ambitions could have stood in the way of an SPD victory. Secondly, I was sure that the decision to leave Lafontaine as Chairman of the party and endorse Schröder for the position of Chancellor guaranteed that the party would put forward a united front in the campaign. I was fully confident, in the light of the widespread praise that my work for the party had in the meantime received, that I could rally the party behind Schröder.

And thirdly, I was convinced that if a final decision were to go against Schröder, the party would not project an impression of unity. Whoever was eventually chosen needed friends who would secure the support and solidarity of the party. If I turned out to be the chosen candidate, Schröder would not have been capable of holding the party together – indeed, he would not have been prepared to do so. Nor would Rudolf Scharping. And Johannes Rau, who would have been willing to take on the task, was fearful of the quarrels that he would have to face – in private conversations he admitted as much to me – in order to retain discipline in his own ranks.

All things considered, I had virtually no choice but to offer the nomination to Gerhard Schröder. The value of the support he enjoyed in the media was not to be underestimated. I often said to my colleagues, you have lauded the man to the skies – there is no way you can tear him to pieces during the election campaign. Schröder himself thought ruefully to himself: 'Those who sing your praises today will be the first to stab you in the back tomorrow.'

In the context of the question 'party democracy or media democracy?' another point occurred to me in connection with the selection of our candidate for Chancellor: power – but for what? As I had held a succession of political positions over the years, I had always found myself wondering whether there was any point in all the effort one put into election campaigns and the like – indeed, whether there was any point in political activity at all. The accusation is often levelled at politicians that the real driving force behind their activities is vanity and the satisfaction of a craving for power. I admit that there is something in this but at the same time I maintain that over the years I have increasingly concerned myself with matters of party policy and political substance. That is why I repeated time and again that what we needed was not only a change of government but also a change of politics.

This principle caused me considerable difficulties, because it was clear for all to see that Schröder attached little importance to work on the party programme. He enjoyed carrying out the activities of government in a pragmatic spirit, with little concern for programmes and manifestos. His aim was to win over public opinion to his side, rather than to develop new programmes for improving the living conditions of the country's men and women. There are, incidentally, cases where politicians who link their policies to programmatic statements of principle are forced to take decisions which go initially against public opinion. One example is when Willy Brandt forced through his *Ostpolitik*, which was far from popular at the time. Another case involves Helmut Kohl, who succeeded in imposing European economic and currency union, and thus the introduction of the euro, at a time when such a decision met with considerable opposition on the part of the population at large, including members of the CDU/CSU itself,

I was convinced that, should Schröder be nominated, he would be prepared to cooperate with me, as Chairman of the party, and give me the chance, without encroaching on the Chancellor's own areas of competence, to have a considerable say in the decision-making processes of a coalition government. I looked for a sharing of responsibility which would allow each of us to function to the best of his ability. At the same time I was well aware that the economic and fiscal policies that I considered correct represented a radical change of direction and would meet with stubborn resistance. I often asked myself, therefore, whether Schröder, as Federal Chancellor, would be able to stand up to such pressure.

As it happened, Helmut Kohl, without knowing it, also played a part in the decision as to who would be the SPD's candidate for Chancellor. I felt that Kohl had treated me unfairly after the election of 1990. He repeatedly boasted how many of Willy Brandt's 'grandchildren' he had seen off over the years, singling out Engholm, Scharping and me in particular.

What offended me was that he did not have the decency to qualify the nature of his success over me in the 1990 election. On the one hand, as he could hardly fail to realize, the attempt on my life had taken its toll and severely curtailed my activities. On the other hand I can think of no politician who enjoyed such a measure of sheer good fortune. He was the Chancellor of German Reunification, the bearer of the coveted Deutschmark. Many times in the course of the 1990 campaign I reflected that in fact he enjoyed the best conditions he could wish for to win an outright majority.

In addition, the press had changed its attitude towards Kohl. Up to the moment of the fall of the Wall and the establishment of a reunified Germany he had been regarded as clumsy and inept, a blunderer not to be taken seriously. Now he was a national hero, admired and fêted in the whole country, seemingly invincible. After a couple of beers I used to tell my friends that it was my ambition to knock the fat man out of the ring. His pompous self-importance and his scornful references to Willy Brandt's 'grandchildren' stuck in my gullet, and I kept remembering what Henning Voscherau once said: 'Our generation must be careful not to become just a footnote in the history of the SPD.'

So I decided to be on the safe side and leave Gerhard Schröder to contest the election for Chancellor. But first we had to win the *Land* elections in Lower Saxony, and we could not afford to let it become too obvious to him that I had already withdrawn my candidacy for the chancellorship. Had he known that I had decided to support him, he would have raised more difficulties over the coordination of our work in the Bundesrat. But after the earlier quarrels over Engholm and Scharping, it was essential for the SPD to have an efficient party organization in the Bundesrat if they were to win the election. In mat-

ters such as tax policy and social policy, or in issues of internal security, like bugging regulations, we had to make intense efforts to ensure
that Schröder voted with the other SPD *Länder*.

There were several reasons why I considered it right and proper that
Schröder should first clear the hurdle of winning the election in Lower
Saxony. For one thing I needed a strong argument with which to counter
a powerful faction in the party which would have preferred to see me
as their candidate for Chancellor, and a clear victory in Lower Saxony
would have been such an argument. For another thing I wanted to be
certain that Schröder's popularity would really be converted into votes
for the SPD. That could not be taken for granted, for we had often
seen, from federal down to local level, that the popularity of a party's
leader was no guarantee of that party's success at the polls.

Schröder himself had set a very modest target. If he lost more than 2
per cent in Lower Saxony, he said, he would not put himself forward
for Chancellor. I did not consider this a wise move. On the one hand it
implied that he was concerned not so much with seeing how many
additional votes he could win as with keeping his losses to a minimum. Hardly an aim likely to fill the voters with enthusiasm. And on
the other hand if Schröder really did lose more than 2 per cent, it
would leave the SPD's candidate for Chancellor, in effect the Party
Chairman, looking like a reserve who up till then had only been sitting
on the bench.

Moreover Schröder contributed an additional difficulty to his nomination by foolishly making himself an object of suspicion in another
connection. In January news leaked out that Düsseldorf Preussag AG
wanted to sell the steel company Preussag Stahl to the Austrian firm
Voest Alpine Stahl AG. Schröder immediately put a stop to the sale by
faxing Preussag's Chairman Dr Frenzel to tell him that the *Land* of
Lower Saxony would buy out Preussag instead of Voest.

This was not exactly the action of a 'modernizer' but it was at least
a correct decision as regards the election campaign in Lower Saxony,
and one calculated to meet with the approval of the workers at Preussag
Stahl. In addition it gained Schröder the support of the iron and steel
workers' union, which up to then had been somewhat sceptical of him.

But I was outraged to learn that, in his version of the affair, Schröder
claimed that Preussag's intention to sell its steel interests had been a
put-up job instigated by Johannes Rau in order to ruin his, Schröder's,
campaign for the chancellorship. This was such a ridiculous suggestion that one can only put it down to the feelings of nervousness and
uncertainty that sometimes seem to grip the front-runner in an election campaign.

Faced with this situation, I hit on a revolutionary idea that I could put forward in the event that Schröder did not prove acceptable to the party, or that he lost the Lower Saxony election. I would nominaté a woman for Chancellor and stand with her on a joint party ticket that would make us virtually unassailable in a contest against Kohl and his CDU/CSU.

I sounded out the prospects of success for the idea in a series of confidential discussions. The subsequent nomination by the CDU/ CSU of Dagmar Schipanski, a completely unknown professor from Thüringen, showed that support for a woman candidate was very quickly forthcoming, even if she was a totally unknown quantity as far as the public was concerned. But the longer the campaign in Lower Saxony went on, the more certain I became that Schröder would emerge as the clear winner, and I did not take the idea of a woman candidate any further.

Three days before the *Land* election, after a meeting in Brunswick which we had both attended, I was sitting with Gerhard Schröder in a restaurant. I felt the time had come to let him know how things stood, since I could not put off a decision any longer. Ignoring his 2-per-cent criterion, I said: 'If we get the same number of votes as we got at the last elections in Lower Saxony, or more, then you will be our nominee for Chancellor. If not, the decision will lie in the hands of the party.' That would have meant that I would have become the nominee. But it was clear to me that evening that I had in fact passed the nomination to him. Public opinion polls conducted over the whole country in recent months had shown the SPD with between 40 and 42 per cent of the vote. Lower Saxony always turned in results above the average, and Schröder enjoyed an additional personal bonus. We sealed our pact with a handshake over a drink and pledged to make all important decisions together in future.

In the early afternoon of election day I learned that the exit polls were suggesting that Schröder would end up with almost 48 per cent of the vote. I telephoned him and said: 'Well, what now, Herr Kandidat?' He was still suspicious but the results were unequivocal. He had proven that his personal popularity could convert itself into votes for the SPD.

The same evening he caused me further irritation. Interviewed on television, he made out that my friendly greeting 'What now, Herr Kandidat?' had amounted to a request on my part that he should run for Chancellor, and that he had gladly acceded to my request. I was sitting relaxed in front of the television with a glass of red wine in my hand. For him to say that I had requested him to stand was as far from the truth as one could imagine. But I had often noticed that those most anxious to thrust themselves to the fore are those who want us to believe that they have in reality been asked. Anyway the decision had been made. All we could do now was pray.

That same evening I had the opportunity to publicize the qualities of a local Saarland product, a liqueur made from the fruit of the medlar tree, known in the vernacular as 'Hundsärsch'. As often in recent years, journalists were camped out in front of my house, waiting to transmit live the comments of the SPD Chairman on the election results. As the weather was cold, I felt sorry for them and took them out glasses of this local speciality to warm them up. As a result sales of 'Hundsärsch' rose rapidly over the whole country.

7

My Friendship with
Gerhard Schröder

Throughout the period that led up to the decision over who would be the SPD's nominee for the position of Federal Chancellor, the media were naturally keenly interested in the relationship between me and Gerhard Schröder. The wildest of rumours were in circulation and the personal friendship that existed between us was not expected to survive.

Yet the basis for political cooperation between us was strong. I no longer recall when I first laid eyes on him but we got to know each other at party conferences and at the meetings of Willy Brandt's 'grandchildren', in whose hands the fortunes of the party lay. We frequently shared a platform during the 1986 elections in Lower Saxony, and I supported his campaign to the best of my ability.

This was also the time when I met Schröder's wife Hillu, and I came to admire the loyal support she gave her husband during his campaign.

In the course of a particular election meeting in Lower Saxony I became aware of something that often came into my mind later. At the end of the meeting, at which Schröder and I both spoke, we all joined in singing a political song, in the social democrat tradition. I no longer remember what song it was but I was surprised to find that Schröder, who was standing in front of me, could not sing the proper notes. To make matters worse he was standing directly in front of the microphone, so I whispered to him: 'Move away from the microphone – your singing's terrible!' Later he confessed to me over a glass of beer that he was totally unmusical. To which I replied that if we were to work together in the future, we would have to see that there was some measure of harmony between us.

But that proved a pious hope. There was considerable discord between us, and I came increasingly to conclude that he preferred vigorous argument to a painstaking search for compromise. But compromise lies at the root of any reliable cooperation. According to stories that he himself put around, he was the son of poor parents and had always had to fight his way through life, which made him a man always ready to fight his corner. This is still true of him today. In his personal relationships, on the other hand, he can be a true comrade and exude real charm – a quality he is always willing to display.

We lost the 1986 elections in Lower Saxony, and Schröder became leader of the opposition. I was Prime Minister of the Saarland. During the federal election of 1987, in which our candidate was Johannes Rau, Schröder forfeited Rau's goodwill for some considerable time by muttering in public that maybe Lafontaine would have made the better candidate.

In 1990 we found ourselves cooperating more closely. This time I had made up my mind to put my weight behind ensuring that Schröder won Lower Saxony at the second attempt. He felt somewhat depressed when he learned that the CDU intended to enhance their chances by putting up Ernst Albrecht and Rita Süssmuth as their leading candidates. I remember this very well because I had taken Schröder with me to Paris when I visited Mitterrand on 14 March. He seemed very unsure of himself. Only in the evening, when we were having dinner in the well-known restaurant 'Lucas Carton', did he gradually begin to unwind. He must also have been worried that there were sections within the party that gave him only lukewarm support. Besides that, there were many who had no confidence in his ability to win the election. I also recall almost having a stand-up argument with Richard von Weizsäcker when he remarked in the course of conversation that Schröder had no chance of beating Ernst Albrecht.

After the stabbing incident I had a visit from Hans-Jürgen Wischnewski, who had also been in the hall at the time. This was the occasion, I believe, when I came to win Wischnewski's high esteem by sharing with him a bottle of Condrieux, a white wine from the Rhône, thereby displaying, so soon after the attack, my not inconsiderable stamina. In the course of our conversation he said that he had profound reservations about Schröder and was sure he would not win. I contradicted him, and we almost fell out over the issue.

On 13 May Gerhard Schröder won the Lower Saxony election with 44.2 per cent of the vote, which delighted me. When we spoke on the telephone in the evening he said, with his inimitable charm: 'That wound in your neck earned me 2 per cent!'

After that episode in Cologne Schröder did his best to help and support me as a fellow-member of the party. On one occasion he came to visit me in the Saarland and we spent a weekend in Saarbrücken and in neighbouring Lorraine. I recall his visit with pleasure, and I am certain it contributed to my subsequent decision to withdraw from the race for the chancellorship. In the vote on the introduction of currency union he and I were the only Social Democratic Prime Ministers to vote against the motion. I have always been grateful to him for that. He was convinced by my arguments against the precipitate adoption of the Deutschmark in East Germany. As a result he later found himself exposed to the charge, like me, of having been opposed to German reunification and of not wanting to see the East Germans come into possession of the Deutschmark.

After the defeat of the SPD in the federal election of 1990 Schröder joined those who brought considerable pressure to bear on me to take over the chairmanship of the party. But at the crucial meeting of the party executive he left early, which greatly annoyed me, because at that very moment, when Willy Brandt, among others, had been roundly criticizing my election campaign, I could have done with Schröder's support. And after I had declined for a second time to accept the chairmanship, Schröder also expressed his disappointment.

I could feel that cracks were beginning to develop in our friendship. The magazine *Der Spiegel* had managed to find an expert on employment law who maintained that my salary as Prime Minister, and the way the payments had been calculated which referred to my period as mayor of Saarbrücken, were not in order. In spite of the fact that other lawyers came to quite different conclusions, I found the question of my pension under the spotlight. According to the papers Schröder remarked drily: 'Am I my brother's keeper?' And when *Der Spiegel* discovered a few years later that in the 1970s I could often be seen doing the rounds of the Saarbrücken night-clubs, the story was blown up into 'Lafontaine's Red Light Escapades' and led to the most absurd suspicions and speculations in the German press. Among Brandt's 'grandchildren', including Schröder, the realization must have dawned that it was now other people's turn.

My relationship with Schröder continued to suffer under our disagreements over the matter of who should succeed Engholm. Then the party's decline during the Scharping era brought us closer together again. With the opinion polls showing support for the SPD dwindling from day to day, he would often consult me about what to do, saying that we could not go on watching this collapse. When our support dropped to 30 per cent, he said, it was time to pack up and go home.

As newly elected Party Chairman I naturally looked to cooperate with him. Lower Saxony was a powerful force in the Bundesrat, and we could only win the federal election if Schröder played his part. Our cooperation then began to improve. One evening in March 1996 he called to tell me that he and Hillu were going to be divorced. I took this call as a mark of his trust in me. The next day the papers were full of the news. His divorce, and his new friendship with Doris Köpf, were just what the journalists loved.

I had known Doris Köpf from the time when she was a newspaper correspondent in Bonn. The couple visited us in the Saarland in August 1997, when the familiar photos by the river were taken. We promised each other to keep the question of the nomination for the chancellorship open until the elections in Lower Saxony. During a walk in the countryside Doris Köpf showed herself to be a charming and highly intelligent woman who now, as many times in the future, played a positive role in her husband's affairs and coolly ignored the occasional disparaging remarks about her in the press. For my money she had more political common sense than many of her former colleagues. When the going became hard, she always managed to find the proper words for the situation. She and my wife Christa quickly developed a rapport. The best of friendships between men suffer if their wives do not get on well with each other.

The agreement to embark on the federal election campaign under a single banner thus met with the mutual encouragement of the personalities involved. At the same time it was clear to me that, given the nature of his personality, I would have to give way to Schröder over the nomination for Chancellor if we were to make a go of things.

Everything ran smoothly throughout the election campaign. I still recall how I broke out in a cold sweat before Schröder's final speech in the budget debate in the Bundestag. The previous day I had been in good form and won the debate for our side. All now rested on Schröder's shoulders. We sat on the Bundesrat bench, presenting a solid front. Kohl delivered his broadside and Schröder countered brilliantly. Together we had won the day.

Events such as these forge friendships, and I hoped that our accord would live on after our victory at the polls.

8

Hammering out the Government's Programme

It is customary before elections for the parties involved to put forward a programme of measures they would carry out over the coming four years if they came to power. These programmes, or manifestos, are naturally hedged round with a number of ifs and buts. One is well advised, for example, to make certain reservations on the financial front, because the best of intentions cannot be put into effect if they cannot be financed. One must also gain the reputation of being open and reliable. We in the SPD wanted to make reasonably sure that we could keep our promises after the election.

Over and above this there was a particular requirement incumbent on the SPD at this time. This was, that the programme should seek to lessen, or prevent, the incidence of disagreement within the party. In other words, we aimed to make relatively clear the form that the government's activities would take over the next four years. Gerhard Schröder and I, together with our colleagues and advisers, therefore set about collecting and sifting through the material on which we would base our draft policy document.

I myself attached great importance to giving this party document a clear social democratic slant. I was firmly convinced that the reason we had won over the electorate was that the time for vague, generalized declarations of policy was over. Since the party conference in Mannheim we had been working to sharpen our image, above all in respect of welfare policy and taxation policy. As regards taxation policy we stood for a greater measure of fairness combined with tax relief for lower- and middle-income employees and for smaller and medium-sized businesses. Our social policies were based on the preservation of the welfare state. Since Norbert Blüm, CDU Minister of Labour, proudly announced that he had made annual savings of 98 billion marks in payments to pensioners and the unemployed, any further reductions in pensions and unemployment benefits were unthinkable.

Our manifesto read as follows:

> A government led by the SPD will ensure that the so-called 'generation contract' between the older and younger generations remains in force. The cuts in retirement pension made by the CDU/CSU and FDP have reduced many pensioners, both men and women, to the status of people on welfare. This is no way to treat people who have worked hard all their lives. An SPD government will therefore immediately repeal this legislation and take steps to introduce a system of guaranteed pensions that will ensure an appropriate standard of living for those living in retirement. We shall also introduce measures to raise the level of the basic state pension through private sources, occupational pensions and an increase in employers' contributions. We do not want to see old people forced on to welfare. We shall therefore introduce a basic social security scheme which will guarantee a retirement pension at a level that will prevent retired people from falling into poverty and being forced to claim welfare payments.

Interestingly enough the CDU/CSU had decided before the Bavarian *Land* elections in September 1998 that the reductions in pensions should not apply to the long-term insured. This was a decision forced upon them by the large number of people who had paid insurance contributions for over forty-five years and were not prepared meekly to accept a reduction in their pensions. It was a move that reflected a recognition of these pensioners' lifelong contributions to their pension fund but also showed to what extent the CDU/CSU had lost their sense of social justice.

For what the CDU/CSU proposed amounted to the retraction of the cuts as far as those on higher pensions were concerned but their retention for those on lower pensions. This made me furious. The whole affair was swallowed up in the hectic activity surrounding the election, and the CDU/CSU escaped the criticism of the conservative press almost unscathed. But at the same time even the most dyed-in-the-wool conservatives were forced to realize that cuts in pension payments could not be inflicted only on the poorer sections of the population.

This change of policy on the part of the CDU/CSU made it necessary for us to make clear to the electors exactly what we were promising. A vague formulation such as 'we shall amend pensions legislation', which left a number of options open, was replaced by 'we shall repeal the legislation to reduce pensions.' We could not go before the Bavarian electors and say that pensioners who had worked their whole lives and paid pension contributions for many years would be worse off under our plan than under that of the CDU/CSU.

In the area of pensions, incidentally, we tried on a number of occasions, at the instigation of our taxation expert Rudolf Dressler, to reach a consensus with the other main parties. But this became increasingly difficult, because the CDU/CSU, held in the thrall of the FDP, refused to make any agreement with us. In the end, however, it turned out that they could not do anything without our cooperation because the insurance fund was billions of marks in the red. It was the SPD, via the Bundesrat, that made it possible to put the pension fund back in the black by agreeing to a one-point rise in value-added tax and to the proposal that 100 per cent of this additional income should go into the pension fund's coffers. This also enabled us to deny the charge frequently levelled against us of blocking the passage of legislation in the Bundesrat.

I have often wondered whether, if the boot had been on the other foot, the CDU/CSU and the FDP would have voted for an increase in value-added tax immediately before the elections in order to restore the pension fund to solvency. For the SPD, at all events, it was a matter of course that in such a situation we should let electoral considerations take second place to the need to put the pension fund on a secure financial footing.

After the federal elections it emerged that the Allensbach Institute, the leading pollsters, had given the most accurate forecast of how the election would go. They also found out that the decisive issue had been that of social justice. In the Institute's view the Kohl administration was voted out of office because in the eyes of the public it gave the impression that Germany was no longer a just society. The task facing the SPD was therefore to put forward a programme which we considered the vast majority of the electorate would look to us to put into effect – a fair taxation policy, a lowering of the initial rate of income tax, an increase in child allowance and a cut in welfare contributions. These proposals became firm commitments after they had been discussed and passed by majority vote in the relevant party committees.

We also pledged to reverse the most blatant blunders of the Kohl administration. One of these was the decision to discontinue entitlement to sick pay. It was also a grave error on the part of the Kohl government, in my view, not to have made a success of the so-called 'Alliance for Jobs'. Any conservative government would have profited from joining with unions and employers in creating an 'alliance for jobs' which would have facilitated the creation of jobs by putting various structural measures in place.

But at some point the Kohl administration abandoned its role of mediator between the employers' organizations and the unions and agreed with the employers that sick pay should be scrapped. Not surprisingly the unions promptly withdrew from the Alliance. We took advantage of this situation and adopted the reinstatement of sick pay as one of the central planks of our programme. The so-called 'modernizers' in the party were less than wholly enthusiastic about this decision but the majority of the party executive had no doubt that it had to be set at the heart of our campaign.

The same applied to our proposal to restore the right to job security in small businesses. Although throughout Europe, and in Germany itself, the development of flexible labour markets had given rise to the rapid spread of part-time jobs, the Kohl administration felt it had to accede to the request of employers' organizations to restrict the right of workers in small businesses to severance pay in cases of summary dismissal. The situation in America, with its policy of 'hire and fire', was repeatedly quoted. But job security lies at the heart of the social contract as it has been developed in Europe over many years. Europe is not comparable with America in this respect. In the USA, a country in which the culture of society has been formed by settlers and immigrants, different conditions of employment are possible, whereas Europe has evolved an organic social tradition over centuries. The right of protection against wilful summary dismissal from one's place of work is a cornerstone of European social culture.

Let us be honest. No manager who spoke out in favour of doing away with this protection would be prepared to work under such conditions himself. As a rule those in management enjoy five-year contracts, with generous compensation in cases where the agreement is prematurely terminated. The biblical adage 'Do unto others as you would have them do unto you' cuts no ice in discussions over economic reforms. It was a saying I used time and again in my election speeches, and it always went down well with the audience. Indeed, it was a sentiment to which the whole population responded.

This lack of sensitivity over this particular measure, a cold-bloodedness for which the FDP bore its own degree of responsibility, was not shared by other European conservative parties. The Christian Socialist Prime Minister of Luxemburg, Jean-Claude Juncker, for instance, warned against embarking on a free-for-all to see who could produce the worst labour protection laws in Europe. This was a refreshing remark which stood in stark contrast to the crude commonplaces being mouthed by conservative circles in Germany, where the received wisdom was that the realities of the market-place compelled us to get rid of superfluous social regulations in order to compete in the economic struggle with other countries. It was comparatively late in the day that the Kohl government came to realize that, by drawing attention to the common social standards that prevailed in Europe, the SPD had caught the mood of the people far more accurately than the protagonists of neoliberal politics.

Above all, these neoliberals had no answer to the question of where this rush to dismantle welfare measures would lead and when it would stop. To restore protection against summary dismissal in small businesses thus became the second most important demand in our programme.

Our third point was the restoration of bad-weather payments. This was a measure introduced specifically for workers in the construction industry, in particular those affected by the new freedom of movement across national borders.

The extent of the black economy in Germany beggars belief. Reports in the newspapers talked of Ukrainian workers sleeping in tents and earning less than one mark an hour. If ever Marx's principle of the exploitation of the workers needed an illustration, it is to be found in the working practices of the construction industry.

This situation represented a direct challenge to the Social Democratic Party. We saw the building workers as our comrades, and did not wish to sacrifice their bad-weather payments, a concession they had struggled for years to win. We therefore took up the building workers' demand and made the restoration of these payments a specific item in our programme. With this in mind we succeeded in persuading Klaus Wiesehügel, President of the Building and Agricultural Workers Union, to stand for the Bundestag, because we needed an experienced trade unionist in the new parliamentary party.

Our policy statement read as follows:

> Social dumping, wage dumping, illegal labour practices and widespread systematic moonlighting distort welfare programmes, undermine wage agreements and threaten the existence of legally operating businesses. We need to introduce new modes of employment in the labour market but we are not prepared to tolerate unfair competition or illegal practices, nor will we allow a mass exodus from the welfare system. We shall restore justice and discipline in the labour market, and introduce an action programme to stamp out unofficial employment and illicit working practices. National and European regulations must be introduced to prevent social dumping and establish the principle of 'a fixed wage for fixed work in a fixed place'.

My answer to those who opposed these principles, especially those in the FDP, was to say that a human being is not a commodity. Where it is a question of importing bananas or industrial products, it is legitimate to talk in terms of competitive prices. But the wages and working conditions of men and women are not to be seen primarily in terms of commercial competition. To do so would fly in the face of everything that the Social Democratic Party stands for.

I was also angry with those politicians in Germany who, in spite of the poor wage rates and lamentable working conditions that existed on many construction sites, were opposed to the so-called parity bill. This bill was intended to guarantee that on building sites in Germany no wage rates should be tolerated that were far below subsistence level. To those opposed to the measure – chiefly members of the CDU and the FDP but also 'modernizers' in the ranks of my own party – I retorted that they would find themselves singing a different tune if they woke up one day to find their places in the Bundestag taken by Polish or Portuguese delegates prepared to do the work of government for 10 per cent of the money. It was a spectre that regularly produced laughter when I told the story at election meetings. Again it became apparent that the 'modernizers' were ready to propose reforms for the man in the street which they would not have dreamt of accepting for themselves.

As well as addressing ourselves to employees and pensioners, both men and women, we had a special word for young people. One of the items in our programme was an emergency measure to deal with the problem of youth unemployment. The proposal stated:

> As an urgent measure to reduce the numbers of youth unemployed, we shall put into effect as soon as possible a plan to provide training and jobs for 100,000 young people. We want to provide a job or a place on a training course for every young person who has been unemployed for more than six months. The cost of this measure will be covered by the funds that would otherwise have to be paid out in the form of unemployment benefit. Our motto is 'Training and jobs, not youth unemployment'.

One important aspect of this programme was that it gave youth organizations the chance to canvass among their members for a change of government. To complement this, the training levy was also made part of the SPD's manifesto, a move to which I attached considerable importance: 'Industry and the public sector must both shoulder responsibility for providing an adequate number of apprenticeships. Otherwise it will be necessary to pass a law to establish over the country as a whole an equitable financial balance between firms that offer training places and those that do not.'

This was an issue on which a government led by the Social Democratic Party had to nail its colours to the mast. A society that had amassed a private fortune of 14.5 billion marks must surely be in a position to offer an apprenticeship to any young person who wants one. It is not a matter of economics but a social question. How do we want to live and work together? Is it acceptable to deny young people access to a career? Our reply was clear and unequivocal. And we did not want just to content ourselves with vague, non-committal formulae but give cast-iron, verifiable assurances.

Changes were also necessary in the structure of the health system. When we wish someone 'good luck and good health', we know that it is no mere empty phrase. Everything fades into insignificance if a member of the family or a friend is suddenly struck down by some disease. It is at moments like these that one comes to appreciate the importance of an efficient health care system. There is no way in which the Social Democratic Party can stand idly by and witness a development that is leading to a situation where certain medical services are only available to those who can afford to pay for them. We therefore stated in our programme that it was our intention to withdraw the increase in prescription charges that had been recently imposed. We also announced that young people would again be entitled to free dentures. These two pledges also played an important part in the election campaign.

It was a great relief to me that we had succeeded in putting together an unmistakably Social-Democratic programme and that this programme bore the signatures of both the party's candidate for Chancellor and the Party Chairman. There were to be no arguments after the election over what our policies were. It was interesting to observe during the election campaign that it was precisely these points that proved to be of crucial importance and to be seen by the party's supporters as defining the unique character of the SPD.

There was, of course, no shortage of commentators who claimed that these pledges had been foisted on Schröder the 'modernizer' by Lafontaine the 'traditionalist'. But it was a pleasure for me to see that the protagonists of the Social-Democratic cause, including Schröder, all made reference to these points in their speeches, for they knew that they would find an echo among their audiences. No politician can make any impression with vague mantras such as 'welfare benefits are too high', or 'wages are too high', or 'working conditions must be made more flexible', or 'the rights of the workers must be further curtailed'. It may be possible to score a few points with such catchwords in meetings of entrepreneurs and managers, who are frequently irritated by the regulations governing job security or the increasing demands made by the workforce. All this is understandable. Such slogans also meet with the approval of the press. But a Social-Democratic election campaign can only be waged with Social-Democratic policies. If proof be needed, it is to be found in the federal election of 1998.

It was also essential, from my point of view, for our programme to contain clear statements on the ecological modernization of the industrial society. The mistaken view had been taken in Germany that modernization and ecological renewal were irreconcilable. Since the concept of modernization was linked to the removal of workers' rights and an erroneous interpretation of flexibility in patterns of work, the whole ecological argument was held to contradict the concept of modernization.

It is interesting to observe that those in Germany who take their lead from Tony Blair and his modernization programme overlook the fact that Blair's guru, Anthony Giddens, makes the ecological renewal of industrial society a central element in his project. In his book *Beyond Left and Right*, Giddens calls the ecology movement the most significant development of recent years. In his book *The Third Way* he writes:

> The issue of modernisation is a basic one for the new politics. Ecological modernisation is one version but there are others too. Tony Blair's speeches, for example, are peppered with talk of modernisation. What should modernisation be taken to mean? One thing it means, obviously, is the modernising of social democracy itself – the breaking away from classical social democratic positions. As an agenda of a wider kind, however, a modernising strategy can work only if social democrats have a sophisticated knowledge of the concept.
>
> Modernisation that is ecologically sensitive is not about 'more and more modernity' but is conscious of the problems and limitations of modernising processes. It is alive to the need to re-establish continuity and development social cohesion in a world of erratic transformation, where the intrinsically unpredictable energies of scientific and technological innovation play such an important role.

Giddens would not dream of palming off environmental demands as un-modern or as undermining the economy. Still less would it occur to him to make the curtailment of workers' rights a central part of the process of modernization, for this would be at the expense of 'social cohesion'.

The SPD programme thus included unambiguous demands for ecological modernization. We also promised an ecological recasting of the taxation and benefits systems. The cost of labour in Germany had become too high. Environmental consumption was relatively cheap.

As the taxation and benefits system constitutes the basic framework prescribed by the state for the functioning of a social market economy, so the ecological modernization of this system is a vital aspect of the whole process of modernization.

We demanded a reversal of energy policy and the rejection of nuclear power. We did not, however, lay down a fixed timetable. There were many practical arguments against doing so. Our programme simply stated that we intended to put an end to the exploitation of nuclear power as soon as possible:

> We look to build a bridge that will lead to the solar age. That is our vision for the 21st century. Our energy policy will be based on the use of renewable sources of energy, and the proportion of regenerative energies in our overall energy supply progressively increased. Included in this package are equitable arrangements for feeding in electricity supplies derived from renewable sources of energy, both in Germany and in Europe as a whole. Industrial mass production for modern solar technologies must be expanded, combined with which we plan to initiate a programme for solar roof panels in 100,000 houses. We shall also promote the export of solar technology to developing countries.

The two words 'innovation' and 'fairness' were no mere shibboleths. We had made them the core principles of our programme and presented them in such a way that the ordinary members of the party could communicate them to others. There is no point in drafting long-winded programmes that are intelligible only to their authors. In one's dealings with the electorate it is essential to lay out one's policies lucidly and precisely in a programme that meets with the approval of the majority and is at the same time financially viable.

9

Choosing a Team

Choosing a government team is always a tricky business. Those on whom one calls are gratified: those one passes over are disappointed. No prospective Chancellor sets about the task with any great relish. Gerhard Schröder and I had therefore agreed to announce the principal members of our team first and leave ourselves free, if called upon to form a government, to fill the remaining posts later. This meant that we did not have to decide for certain in advance who would be appointed to government office and who would not. It was a procedure that ultimately met with the party's approval.

The party's nominee for Chancellor and the Party Chairman were both members of the team as a matter of course. I declared my willingness to assume responsibility for financial matters and for Europe, but without this being finally settled. It had already been mooted that I might also take over the post of leader of the parliamentary party, so as to be able to support the prospective Chancellor in dealing with the day-to-day business of the Bundestag.

This suggestion met with broad approval, in particular from such former ministers as Horst Ehmke and Herbert Ehrenberg. We were fully aware that the work of the government could be satisfactorily carried out only if Chancellor and parliamentary leader worked closely together. There was a certain justification for the view, expressed in various quarters, that by taking on the duties of parliamentary leader in addition to those of Party Chairman, I would be shifting the balance of power to an unacceptable degree. But this did nothing to change my conviction that the work of the government could only be carried out on the basis of cooperation that was both fair and friendly.

Rudolf Scharping took over the fields of foreign policy and defence policy. Even this was not finally settled, because he also had his eye on becoming parliamentary leader. He often felt offended by remarks made by Schröder and others in public that there was nothing to stop the Party Chairman from also becoming parliamentary leader, if that was what he wanted.

In the course of one of the many discussions we held, Schröder even offered me the post of Foreign Minister in the event of the SPD coming to power. This was the position in which Willy Brandt had once acquired an international reputation. But I was not the only one to be attracted by this prospect – Scharping also had his eye on the job, while for Joschka Fischer it was that or nothing.

To be appointed Finance Minister, on the other hand, is to receive the kiss of death – it is a post in which there are only losers. I had not failed to observe that Theo Waigel, Finance Minister in the Kohl administration, was the least popular of the government ministers. But I had undertaken to make my own contribution towards reducing unemployment. It had been clear for many years to anybody who had studied the situation that the Finance Minister was in a far better position than the Economics Minister to do something about unemployment. Helmut Schmidt had even wanted to abolish the Economics Ministry altogether, saying drily that all the minister did was to open trade fairs and grant subsidies.

This is perhaps the place to mention that as the SPD's coordinator of financial affairs in the Bundesrat, I had for a long time played a prominent role in shaping the party's financial policies. And over and above this it was only right and proper that the man who had brought about a radical change of direction in the party's economic and fiscal policies should be there to stand up for his principles when government business was discussed.

Our manifesto stated:

> Our reply to economic globalization is the introduction of a policy of internal reforms and international cooperation. A move to reduce costs in order to compete with low-wage economies in various other parts of the world would be to embark on a war that Germany cannot win. If we want to compete in world markets, we must produce more and better goods than our competitors. The future of the German economy lies in the production of high-quality goods at competitive prices. We also need to embark on a search to evolve the best education system in the world, the most productive research institutes and the most modern infrastructure. The globalized markets stand in need of a new and fairer world economic order based on the principles of a social and ecological market economy. Through a balanced, pragmatic combination of sup-

ply and demand policies we aim to achieve higher growth and create new jobs.

This, briefly, is the counter-argument to supply-side politics, which rests on lowering business taxes, wage restraint, reductions in welfare payments and the abrogation of workers' rights. Supply-side policies are based on a conception of competition that equates national economies with businesses, and makes a reduction in welfare benefits a precondition for new investment and the creation of new jobs. The SPD's programme turned its back on the fashionable market-driven supply-side policies that had led to the calamitous unemployment situation. It was therefore only natural that I should take over this portfolio in the new government.

Later I appointed Heiner Flassbeck and Claus Noé, two men known to support the new economic and fiscal policies, to be my deputies. It was inevitable that they would put people's backs up from time to time. It is usually easier to garner public approval by repeating the terms of the received wisdom. It was unfair for Hans Eichel to attack them later by saying that one of them had succeeded in turning the ministry against him, while the other had embarked on a collision course with the whole world. Let it not be forgotten that Eichel was the man who managed in record time to set workers, unemployed and pensioners all against him.

Most of Flassbeck's initiatives had the support of the French and the Japanese. Because Britain, together with Bundesbank President Tietmeyer, did not see eye to eye with him was not necessarily an argument against him. Noé, too, was a firm protagonist of an economics policy that favoured supply and demand in equal measure. And he, too, met with opposition. Responsibility for continuity in the Finance Ministry rested in the hands of the long-serving Manfred Overhaus, and with Barbara Hendricks and Karl Diller as parliamentary deputies we had put together a good team.

The criticism that our ministry did not function perfectly in the first few months is not entirely unfounded. But it rebounded on the critics. People who claimed that they could have brought a large ministry under control in a fraction of the time were only displaying their ignorance. But there are also ministers who quickly find themselves in the control of their ministry. Generally without noticing it, they take over the policies of their predecessors, who were themselves in the grip of their ministries.

For the position of Minister of Justice Gerhard Schröder proposed Herta Däubler-Gmelin, the only member of the executive to have more or less openly supported him in his campaign for Chancellor. For

Research, Education and Environment we settled on Edelgard Bulmahn. Originally I had agreed with Manfred Stolpe to take Matthias Platzeck into the team, a man who had made a name for himself in Brandenburg and far beyond at the time of the flooding caused by the River Oder. He would have had responsibility for the environment but his wish to become Governing Mayor of Potsdam forced us to abandon this plan.

To represent the East we chose the attractive Christine Bergmann from Berlin, who had demonstrated her abilities as a member of the Berlin Senate and was appointed to deal with youth and family matters. Responsibility for reconstruction in the East was given to Rolf Schwanitz, a lawyer who had gained a reputation among East Germans. During the party conference in Leipzig Schröder and I agreed to invite Walter Riester to join the team, a reform-minded trade unionist who would be well suited for the post of Minister of Labour. It was Willy Brandt who had introduced the custom of appointing leading trade unionists to government posts, and I remain firmly convinced that social-democratic policies can only be successfully carried out as long as social democrats and trade unionists march together side by side.

The position of Minister of the Interior, we agreed, should go to Otto Schily, a man who had gained my particular admiration by the way he handled the complicated negotiations over the great bugging affair. He was subjected to considerable criticism from the ranks of his own party, the Greens, but he turned out to be a man of clear ideas, with the ability to put them into practice step by step. In particular he had a keen sense of which compromises could be reached between rival factions. Another to join the potential government was Franz Müntefering, the party whip, whom we intended to appoint head of the Chancellor's Office.

An especially difficult decision was whom to make Economics Minister. In one of his interviews to the press Schröder said he proposed to appoint an independent expert to the position, but I was sceptical about this. The public always approves of the idea to bring in experts from outside but it gives the false impression that there is a lack of such experts in the parties themselves. My experience had taught me that neither academic nor practical qualifications were sufficient to assume responsibility for economic or financial affairs in political life. It needs specialized knowledge to occupy a university chair, and particular skills to run a business. But the qualities demanded of an aspiring minister are quite different. Over the years politicians of all parties who specialize in economic and financial affairs acquire not only the expert knowledge they need but also the necessary political skills to be able to run a ministry in a parliamentary democracy. Besides this, in recent years – the custom goes back to Willy Brandt – we have not always had the happiest of experiences with these independent experts.

But Schröder had stated his intention, and as the matter dragged on, more and more people asked him when they could expect to see the promised independent expert or successful businessman. In fact it would not be in the professional interests of any such manager to accept a post in government. For one thing it would usually involve a drastic drop in salary. For another, a person accepting such an offer would run the danger that the party might lose the election, causing him to lose face with his colleagues and making him a laughing-stock among the voters at large.

However, in June Schröder finally called me and said he had found the right man for the job, a successful young entrepreneur from the world of computers. We arranged a meeting, and the three of us met Jost Stollmann in Bonn.

Stollmann made a good impression and gave us details of his professional career. He had studied at the Harvard Business School, had made himself a multi-millionaire with his firm CompuNet, in Kerpen, and been voted Euro-Manager of the Year in 1990. At its peak, his firm, which he had sold to General Electric, had a turnover of 1.9 billion marks and employed 1,800 workers. It was rated low in hierarchies, swift, adaptable and dynamic. The father of five children, Stollmann seemed, to judge from the course of his career up to that time, the ideal candidate for Schröder's politics of the 'New Centre', which was calculated to appeal precisely to the ambitious yuppie class.

Nevertheless I felt uneasy about his appointment, especially as I quickly became aware that Stollmann had little knowledge of the political process. I therefore asked Schröder not to announce any decision prematurely, as I first wanted to have the executive committee's approval for the plan. During my time as Party Chairman I had made it a principle to let the executive decide in difficult cases.

But I was too late. The next day the name of Jost Stollmann was in all the papers. In the weeks that followed, the general sense of delight grew and grew. Stollmann gave a series of interviews in which he praised Helmut Kohl for his fantastic achievements and declared himself highly suspicious of worker participation in the decision-making process and of the welfare state. Kohl's office put out a mocking headline: 'Stollmann is our man in the SPD's corridors of power.' We were all relieved when Stollmann withdrew from the scene.

As his answer to Jost Stollmann Kohl appointed his old adversary Lothar Späth to be chairman of an advisory committee for innovation and future development. This seemed to suggest that Kohl was clutching at straws. A Chancellor who forms an advisory committee on innovation just before an election is casting himself in the worst possible light. Our victory was coming closer.

We were also considering at this time how we could improve Schröder's reputation in France. The French had got the impression that his sympathies lay more with the Anglo-Saxon world. He had also offended Prime Minister Jospin and his government with a tactless remark that the introduction of the thirty-five-hour week in France had done Germany a favour.

We travelled together to France on a fence-mending expedition. I have close and friendly relations with the Parti Socialiste and had for a time considered proposing Jack Lang for the post of government spokesman for cultural and media matters in a Schröder administration – a position that later went to Michael Naumann. I am certain that, if he had been asked insistently enough, Lang would have accepted the post. It would have been a unique experiment in Europe which would undoubtedly have given Franco-German relations a welcome boost.

One day Schröder surprised me with the suggestion that we appoint Brigitte Sauzay, whom I had met when she was Mitterrand's interpreter, to be a kind of spokeswoman on French affairs in the Chancellor's Office. To this day I have no idea what Schröder expected to get out of such an appointment. It also caused a certain irritation in the French Foreign Ministry, which had not been informed of the proposal, and I was quickly called in to smooth things over. Brigitte Sauzay had arranged a meeting for Schröder with leaders of the conservative opposition in Paris. But it had not occurred to her to arrange a similar meeting with our friends in the Parti Socialiste, in order to avoid any possible misunderstanding.

When I got wind of the affair, I begged Schröder as a matter of urgency to go and see Lionel Jospin. At my request Jospin cancelled a number of engagements at short notice, and we avoided a major row. Schröder's well-intentioned suggestion that Great Britain should share in any future Franco-German initiatives did not meet with the most enthusiastic of responses. There were other ways and means I could have envisaged for strengthening the links between France and Germany.

10

The Formation of a Coalition Government

Observers of the political scene in Bonn will know that well before the actual election of 1998 violent arguments had broken out over what positions in a new government would be given to whom, although we had agreed that things should be handled quite differently. In human terms that is entirely understandable. An election victory is the product of the efforts of many different people who have supported the party's campaign in their various ways. Before the election I used to accept this with a good grace and send everybody to Peter Struck. 'Peter will receive applications and allocate the available jobs,' I told them. But immediately after the election was won, the agreements that had been entered into before the election began to pose problems.

I had announced that, as a matter of principle, we should first agree on the nature of the coalition, then discuss the allocation of the individual posts and functions. But the parliamentary party did not keep to this agreement. Wolfgang Thierse had for some while made it clear that he had his eye on the position of President (Speaker) of the Bundestag. Nobody could object to this – Thierse was eminently qualified for the job in personal terms, and has subsequently proven, in my opinion, to be a Bundestag President respected by all sides. But as Party Chairman I had to keep the whole picture in mind and remember that we had intended to put forward Johannes Rau for Federal President.

Johannes Rau is one of the most popular and experienced politicians in Germany today. In addition to his representative functions, the constitution gives the President considerable powers to resolve problems that may arise within the parliamentary system. Schröder had agreed that we should propose Rau for this post. I therefore suggested that we should nominate a woman for President of the Bundestag.

A number of names came to mind, among them that of Anke Fuchs. Formerly Minister for Labour and Social Affairs in Helmut Schmidt's cabinet, Frau Fuchs had been Government Whip at the time of Hans-Jochen Vogel and for many years Deputy Chair of the parliamentary party. There was no dispute, therefore, over her qualifications to become President of the Bundestag, the second woman to hold this post after Annemarie Renger. But Anke Fuchs had decided, doubtless for good reasons, that she wanted to become Vice-President of the Bundestag. Another suitable candidate was Christel Hanewinckel, from Halle, who gave a very effective election address to the parliamentary party. But we had to abide by our earlier decisions.

Another factor in the equation was that even before the election Rudolf Scharping, contrary to our agreement, began to spread the news, both among the deputies in the Bundestag and to the newspapers, that he would like to retain the post of Chairman of the parliamentary party. In the closing phase of the election campaign he wrote a letter to the members of the SPD parliamentary party and the SPD candidates for the Bundestag:

> With the agreement of the relevant committees, together with the other members of the parliamentary party, and on the basis of our electoral manifesto and of the work already done by the parliamentary party, and also having regard to the intentions of the other parties involved, I have instructed our planning committee to prepare the ground for substantive negotiations on the establishment of a coalition government, so that we can embark on our task immediately after the election. On the conclusion of these negotiations and the formation of a government we can proceed to make the necessary decisions within the parliamentary party itself.
>
> Over the few remaining days of campaigning I wish you a successful continuation of your commitment and your practical efforts, so that we may win a majority for our policies for a just and prosperous Germany. I look forward to the fruition of our joint endeavours.

Readers of Scharping's letter knew exactly what he was getting at. It was his early bid for the chairmanship of the parliamentary party. The only course left to me was simply to take no notice of such an act of disloyalty.

It would have been equally possible for a woman to take over as Chair of the parliamentary party. Herta Däubler-Gmelin had already expressed interest in doing so, while Ingrid Matthäus-Maier or Anke

Fuchs would also have been suitable. Ingrid Matthäus-Maier, whose work I had come increasingly to admire, was outstanding in financial affairs and one of our best speakers but she did not get on with Gerhard Schröder. She therefore saw no point in seeking to become Finance Minister or in putting her name forward for Chair of the parliamentary party, since in either capacity she would have had to work closely together with the Chancellor. She looked for a job elsewhere and is today a member of the board of the Bank for Reconstruction.

In the course of the negotiations over the formation of a coalition, which occupied much of our time, Scharping had managed to advance his candidature for Chair of the parliamentary party by holding meetings with deputies and journalists. In the event of the parliamentary party accepting a woman as Bundestag President, it had crossed my mind to propose Franz Müntefering for the post of leader of the parliamentary party. He had had experience of parliament, had been a party whip and had gained a considerable reputation in the Bundestag and in the party as a party manager. When we put forward his name to the new parliamentary party for the first time, the proposal was greeted with warm applause. He was also a man with no particular personal links to either Schröder or to me. He used to say, somewhat provocatively, that he was not the Chairman's manager but the party's.

But Scharping's stubbornness put an end to these plans. He persisted in maintaining, without reference either to Schröder or to me, that he would insist on remaining Chairman of the parliamentary party. This was a direct challenge to the authority of the party leader. I asked him to come and discuss the matter, and told him that I could only interpret his behaviour as a breach of our understanding. Apart from that, I went on, I did not consider that, in the given situation, he was the right man for the job. I reminded him of the hurtful and offensive arguments he had had with Schröder in 1995. I also reminded him of how, contrary to the advice of Rau and myself, he had dismissed Schröder as the party's economics spokesman. I knew that these feelings of Schröder's went deep, and that in situations of particular difficulty the Chairman of the parliamentary party needed to show an unswerving loyalty both to the Chancellor and to the party leader. And because he had never got over his de-selection at the Mannheim conference – which he himself had provoked – Scharping's relationship to me had always been touchy. No amount of affected politeness at party gatherings could conceal this fact.

In what was tantamount to a confirmation of my attitude the *Süddeutsche Zeitung* wrote shortly after my resignation: 'Well before his argument with Lafontaine over the chairmanship of the parliamentary party Scharping had delivered his judgement on the man who had cut him down in Mannheim. He put as much as possible of the blame on the shoulders of his successor as SPD leader and showed an intense personal antipathy towards him, thereby allowing himself enough scope to join Schröder in an SPD government without Lafontaine.' So wide did this scope become that in the summer of 1999 Minister Scharping was to be heard telling everyone that he considered himself competent to take on the role of Federal Chancellor.

My arguments made little impression on Scharping. He insisted on remaining a candidate for leader of the parliamentary party. I was therefore compelled to use the weapon of last resort and announce that in that case I would also throw my hat into the ring. At the same time I called a meeting of the party executive to hear what they recommended. Scharping withdrew, and we produced a face-saving statement to the effect that Gerhard Schröder had invited Oskar Lafontaine, Party Chairman, and Rudolf Scharping, Chairman of the parliamentary party, to join the cabinet. Scharping, who had broken the agreements in the first place, chose to interpret this procedure as a second humiliation at the hands of the Party Chairman, and a number of deputies who had not been informed of the true situation accepted his version of events.

The *Berliner Zeitung*, on the other hand, carried an accurate report on Scharping's behaviour for those who wanted to know the truth. 'Scharping has prepared his position,' wrote the paper.

> From the very evening of the election he adopted a strategy calculated to ensure that he retained at all costs the position of parliamentary leader, which he considers more influential than a place in the cabinet. With the help of an aggressive, albeit discreet press campaign he allowed it to be known in Bonn that he had no intention of giving way. At the same time he called to his aid all the available troops in the parliamentary party. His wire-pullers and spin-doctors worked flat out on his behalf, until the papers began to report that he had the majority of SPD deputies on his side.
>
> Scharping and Lafontaine – two men who since the party conference in Mannheim have been unable to conceal their antipathy towards each other. Each suspects sinister motives behind whatever the other says or does, and often justifiably so. Thus when Lafontaine declares that Scharping would be of more use to the party as Defence Minister, Scharping will have nothing of it. The very fact that Lafontaine made such a suggestion was sufficient for Scharping to see it as an attempt to banish him to the sidelines.
>
> This time, however, in contrast to Mannheim, Scharping considered himself well prepared to defend his position. First he made his peace with Schröder, the future Chancellor. After a series of election meetings

in Lower Saxony he paid a visit to his former rival at his house in Hanover. Schröder apologized for any offence he might have caused Scharping, and it was generally assumed that they had cleared the air. Scharping gave the same impression during the Bundestag elections. To secure his position in the parliamentary party, Scharping attended no fewer than 111 meetings with his deputies in the course of the last five weeks of the campaign. He hoped that this would help to guarantee his position as parliamentary leader. There are also said to have been discussions over appointments to particular posts in the event of Scharping retaining his position. . . .

For these reasons Scharping was unmoved when, as in Mannheim in 1995, Lafontaine threatened to run against him. Unlike Mannheim, however, he was convinced that, when the votes came to be counted, he would have a clear majority. He therefore openly stepped up the pressure.

But as in Mannheim, Scharping had again misjudged the situation. After our victory at the polls I discovered what the real position had been. I had been mistaken over the extent of my ability to set the whole procedure on a proper course. In addition, while rejecting Thierse as President of the Bundestag, Schröder had played no part in the election to that post, nor had he intervened in the question of parliamentary leader.

In the words of the *Berliner Zeitung*: 'The future chancellor is taking great pains not to be drawn into the dog-fight between Lafontaine and Scharping. On the one hand he appears to support Lafontaine's proposal that Scharping be offered the defence ministry but his support comes late in the day and lacks enthusiasm. Let the chairman of the parliamentary party deal with these individual issues, is Schröder's casual response.' This was not exactly the kind of cordial cooperation I had reckoned with after we won the election.

Moreover when I realized that many of those on the left of the parliamentary party had been taken in by Scharping's version of events, I was forced to admit that the degree of confidence that I enjoyed as Party Chairman was evidently a good deal less than my three years of work in the interests of party organization and integration had led me to expect.

The decision over the chairmanship of the parliamentary party was also linked to the question of who should take over the running of the Chancellor's Office. During the election campaign Schröder had told me that he was thinking of appointing Gerd Andres, spokesman for the Seeheim Circle, to head the Chancellor's staff. But I succeeded in talking him out of this idea. Andres had been active in internal party wrangles and intrigues but had nothing substantial to commend him.

During the election campaign I had secured Schröder's consent to the appointment of Franz Müntefering as head of the Chancellor's Office. But in the course of a meeting between us to discuss which posters we should use for the final stage of the campaign, Schröder and Müntefering got into a fierce argument, and the following day Müntefering said to me angrily: 'I'm not going to work with that man!'

I therefore suggested to Schröder that we should approach Peter Struck, a man who had already expressed an interest in the job. Struck was well versed in parliamentary affairs. He had also kept things going at the time when the parliamentary party had been very dissatisfied with its Chairman Rudolf Scharping. At first Schröder complained that Struck 'nattered too much', and the two did not get on with each other particularly well; Schröder was also in the habit of poking fun at 'mediocre members of the party' who had not yet managed to win a constituency for themselves. But in the end he agreed, and I passed on our decision to Struck.

But then, despite this agreement, Schröder surprised me one day by announcing that the job of head of the chancellery staff was to go to Bodo Hombach. I was annoyed that I now had to go to Struck and tell him that the offer I had conveyed to him, on Schröder's behalf, now had to be withdrawn. Schröder was also breaking the agreement we had made on that evening in Brunswick, when we said we would make all important appointments jointly in future.

If the new government were to be successful, the head of the chancellery staff had to enjoy the confidence of both the Chancellor and the leader of the parliamentary party. I could not see what particular abilities Bodo Hombach had that qualified him to take over the position. He had undoubtedly proven himself a capable election manager. But he had only just become Economics Minister in Düsseldorf, and had taken no part in federal politics in recent years. Nor had he been involved in the technical discussions on the reform of the taxation and welfare systems or in matters of internal security. The head of the Chancellor's staff, charged with coordinating the government's programme, needs a broad overview of the political situation, together with an awareness of the technical issues facing the individual ministries. Bodo Hombach possessed none of these qualities.

As ill-luck would have it, Frank Steinmeier, head of the *Land* chancellery in Hanover, also had his eye on the job. Steinmeier was an outstanding administrator, and we rated his work highly, especially the quiet, relaxed way in which he got to grips with difficult problems. I was gratified when he was called to take over the administrative side of the work in the future Chancellor's Office. He is extremely thorough in his work, a man who keeps a keen eye on all the contracts and agreements that have been drawn up.

With the two men working in the same office – Hombach the superficial salesman, Steinmeier the solid civil servant – the Chancellor's Office could hardly be expected to function smoothly. Hombach saw himself as a German Peter Mandelson – a man of ideas and a spin-doctor. He assembled a team of people around him to act as his assistants. I remember once reading that James Baker, the former American Secretary of State, described the State Department in Reagan's day as a veritable witches' kitchen of intrigue, jockeying for position, ego-trips and self-promotion. I was often reminded of this description as I observed the hustle and bustle in the Chancellor's Office under Hombach and his associates. The function of this cabal, cast in the mould of the British spin-doctor, lay in the publication of indiscretions and items of disinformation. Nobody dared, of course, to accuse the Party Chairman outright but it was always obvious to me where the snide remarks in the press came from.

During a conversation with Hombach I offered him a fair opportunity to cooperate, an offer he accepted. But after only two months I had to tell Schröder that I found Hombach's activities intolerable, and asked him to put a stop to them. Hombach, of course, protested that he had behaved perfectly correctly and had nothing to do with such intrigues. I pointed out to Schröder on a number of occasions that Hombach was not carrying out properly his job of coordinating the government's programme but Schröder took no action. It would be overstating Hombach's importance if, as a number of social democrats later speculated, he were to be regarded as the principal reason for my resignation. If the Chancellor's Office does not function properly, then ultimate responsibility lies, not with the head of that office but with the Chancellor himself. If he sees that that official is not carrying out his duties as he should, the Chancellor must replace him.

In June 1999 Hombach was despatched by Schröder to the Balkans as coordinator of the stability pact. Schröder had come to realize far too late that, in the face of the opposition to Hombach that had been building up, it was an inevitable decision. Naturally it was presented as a case of Hombach undertaking a mission of the utmost political significance, a mission for which the Chancellor had designated his most important man. Schröder had discussed who should fill the post with President Clinton at the G-8 summit meeting in Cologne. 'It sent a thrill running down my spine', said Hombach excitedly to the tabloid *Bild*.

The most cold-blooded obituary on Bodo Hombach's political career appeared in *Die Woche*, a journal close to Schröder:

The 'Hombach Method' was dead and buried after a mere six months. It died from his thirst for publicity, his passion for intrigue and his inability to embark on prudent forward planning. At the end of his reign his relations with the SPD parliamentary party, the Greens and important members of the cabinet were in tatters, compensation for Nazi slave labourers shunted into a siding, and the Alliance for Jobs rendered powerless by his personality cult. The only part of his machine that worked smoothly was his media department. But his personal links with influential journalists in even more influential journals became so close that everyone could see the wires hanging down in the political puppet theatre. In the end young Bodo found his throat cut by his own wires.

When I look back, I can only admire the way Hombach succeeded in wrapping journalists, including editors-in-chief, round his little finger.

When Hombach left, Hans-Olaf Henkel declared that with his departure the cabinet had lost 'a valuable supporter and the most highly qualified minister in economic affairs, a man who made a decisive contribution to the government's change of direction in its fiscal and social policies'. When I read this, I could not stop laughing.

The problems Schröder had in finding people to guarantee that the cooperation between the Party Chairman and the Chancellor would work smoothly is well illustrated by the following example.

Insiders in Bonn knew that in the Bundesrat I could always rely on the Saarland's representative in the federal government, Pitt Weber. He was one of those who shun the attentions of the public but achieve a great deal behind the scenes. By means of skilful negotiations he always managed to ensure that the Social-Democrat *Länder* in the Bundesrat voted in unison. As Anton Pfeifer had done for Helmut Kohl, so Weber offered to Schröder to coordinate the voting in the Bundesrat. Although Schröder initially felt inclined to accept this suggestion, press reports about the negotiations over a coalition government and about the dominant role that I was alleged to have played in these negotiations led him to change his mind. To have had a Lafontaine man in the Chancellor's office, the press being what it was, would in his opinion only have led to further misunderstandings.

Jost Stollmann posed a particular problem, as we had anticipated. He took part in the coalition negotiations although, since he belonged neither to the parliamentary party nor to the executive, he was not a member of our delegation. In order to ensure the coordination of our work, at this stage as at all others, we invited the candidates for office, as the occasion arose, to join in the discussions. Stollmann could not be blamed for not being fully conversant with the party's programme or with the details of its taxation and welfare policies. Given time, he could familiarize himself with these. The problem lay in the division of responsibility between the Finance Ministry and the Economics Ministry.

Partly as a consequence of the role Stollmann had played in the election campaign, I felt compelled to demand from Schröder that the Finance Ministry, assuming that I were to take it over, should be expanded into a kind of treasury, like the Exchequer in Great Britain. As models I pointed not only to the British Exchequer under Gordon Brown but also to the Finance Ministries of Bob Rubin in the USA and Dominique Strauss-Kahn in France. There was no way I could imagine myself sitting at a table with Jost Stollmann, as Waigel and Rexrodt had done. Nor was I enamoured of the idea that, while I introduced a change of direction in economic and fiscal policy in the finance ministry, Stollmann would be delivering an annual report full of the old familiar neoliberal claptrap about supply-side policies and the rest.

I therefore insisted that all the relevant departments and committees should be integrated into the Finance Ministry. But Schröder put off making a decision for the present.

Stollmann called frequent press conferences, and the papers reported that he had succeeded in getting his way in his argument with Lafontaine. Tongue in cheek, I told him he should not believe everything he read in the papers. I later found out that he had not picked up the irony of my remark. Faced with the choice between losing Stollmann or forming a cabinet of which the party chairman was not a member, Schröder finally acceded to my demand. Stollmann threw in the towel, the party breathed a sigh of relief, and after a short telephone conversation with Schröder, Werner Müller, an independent expert who, as a former manager of the VEBA concern, had been an adviser to Schröder during the consensus discussions on energy policy, took over the Economics Ministry.

The final and decisive clash between Gerhard Schröder and myself, after all these wrangles over who should be appointed to government posts, occurred when it came to deciding who should become leader of the parliamentary party. Peter Struck had indicated his interest at an early stage. But so too had Ottmar Schreiner, an expert in social affairs from the Saarland, who was held in high esteem by the parliamentary party and had always come out near the top in the elections to the parliamentary executive.

One morning, when we were holding one of our regular preliminary meetings in our North Rhine-Westphalian offices to discuss the

coalition negotiations, the news of Schreiner's nomination appeared
in the papers. Schröder appeared later with a sinister, venomous look
in his eyes, and sat down without saying a word. After I had invited him to address us, I whispered to him: 'What's wrong?' He replied: 'It seems you want to foist Schreiner onto me as parliamentary
leader.'

I told him that was all nonsense and that we must discuss the matter
immediately. He had no wish to talk to me, he snapped, and marched
out of the room in the way he always does when he is angry or when
he wants to demonstrate the isolation of a great statesman.

Only in the afternoon did I manage to confront him. I told him
outright that I would not stand for another outburst of that kind, and
that we could only function as a team on the basis of mutual comrade-
ship and trust. I had no idea, I went on, who had planted in his head
the notion that I wanted to palm Schreiner off on him but I could only
conclude that he was not prepared to show me the trust and confidence
without which any successful cooperation in the government or in the
party was impossible.

Later the same day I came to the conclusion that I would not join
the government. Schröder had confirmed the suspicions of those who
had repeatedly told me that, in the event of his winning the election,
he would prove to be utterly incapable of working in harmony with
others. I was deeply disappointed. After all, I had allowed him to be
the front-runner in the race for the chancellorship, at the expense of
my own interests, and united the party behind him in the election campaign.

I returned to Saarbrücken and told my wife what I had decided.

Late that evening the phone rang. It was Schröder's wife. She asked
me what was wrong – her husband had got home and gone to bed in a
bad temper. I told her about our argument and my decision not to join
the government. Then I handed the telephone to my wife. The two
women talked with each other for a long time. Schröder was made to
get out of bed, came to the phone and mumbled an apology. Finally I
abandoned my intention to summon a press conference at which I
would have announced that I would not be joining Schröder's cabinet.

I justified my decision by telling myself that in a double function of
Party Chairman and Finance Minister I could ensure that the promises
made in the government's programme would be kept. Maybe I had a
feeling already at that time that, if I were no longer present, Schröder
would quickly renege on these promises. I wanted to use the position
of German Finance Minister to work towards a reorganization of the
world's financial markets in such a way as to put an end to currency
speculation. As former Prime Minister of the Saarland, I felt myself

obligated to devote my energies to the realization of a number of initiatives that were of key importance to the region, such as the establishment of a Franco-German university in Saarbrücken, the linking of the Saarland to the national high-speed rail network, a reduction of the province's debt by 5 billion marks and compliance with the compromise over the coal industry. So I gritted my teeth and hung on.

During these turbulent days something happened that I was surprised had not happened years earlier. Over a number of nights I dreamt of the attack on my life – eight years after the event. The only people I told about it were my wife and Gerhard Schröder – the latter, in order to make it clear to him that I too felt the strains of the election campaign and the meetings to appoint the members of the government team.

The negotiations over the formation of a coalition government went smoothly. Both Social Democrats and Greens were anxious to reach speedy decisions. We had an argument over the reform of the tax system. The Greens wanted to reduce the top rate of tax, a measure to be paid for by the workers, but that was something we could not accept.

The terms of our withdrawal from the nuclear energy programme were worked out by Schröder, Jürgen Trittin and their advisers. Schröder had concerned himself with energy policy for many years and consulted with a number of experts on various aspects of the subject. In particular I supported his efforts to avoid raising any false expectations as to when we might finally abandon our use of nuclear energy.

In an agreed statement we said:

> Comprehensive and irrevocable legislation will be put forward in the course of the coming parliamentary term concerning the use of nuclear energy . . . In the hope of reaching a consensus, the new federal government will invite the utility companies to join in discussions on a new energy policy, on steps to put an end to the use of nuclear energy and on questions regarding the disposal of nuclear waste. The government proposes a deadline of one year after taking office for the conclusion of these discussions. When this time has elapsed, the coalition will introduce a bill which will prescribe the terms under which the use of nuclear energy will be abandoned without compensation. A set time will similarly be laid down for the compliance of the individual companies. Similar rules will apply to the disposal of nuclear waste.

A further bone of contention was the new citizenship law. Otto Schily managed to persuade the Greens to agree to a compromise which we also found acceptable. But as with the tax reforms, here too we had not allowed ourselves enough time. We ought to have discussed whether it was sensible to force through such a compromise only with a majority of the red-green coalition in Bundestag and Bundesrat.

There were also lively exchanges over the section in the coalition treaty that dealt with foreign policy. The SPD had to ward off the exaggerated demands of the pacifist wing of the Greens, which vigorously defended its position. A few weeks later it turned out that these arguments had been superfluous.

A considerable problem was posed by the way our negotiations were reported in the press. They all took the same line, namely, that Lafontaine dominated the proceedings and had got his own way. *Der Spiegel* carried a headline 'The Chancellor and His Shadow'. Under the heading 'Victor and Prompter' it claimed that I had 'blurred the outlines of Schröder's comprehensive tax reforms'. *Der Spiegel* ought to have known that the draft tax reforms had been drawn up with the help of experts from all over the country and had been passed by the party executive as a whole, including Schröder and myself.

'Almost everybody agrees,' wrote *Der Spiegel*,

> that responsibility for the half-hearted, wishy-washy coalition document lies with the man standing behind – or at the side of, or perhaps in front of – the Chancellor himself, namely Oskar Lafontaine, SPD chairman and Schröder's red shadow. Even within the new coalition itself there are those who blame Schröder's secret rival for the government's false start. According to Oswald Metzger, economics expert of the Greens, Lafontaine, protagonist of redistributive policies, is steering the country into the abyss with his 'half-baked Keynesian ideas', while Metzger's colleague Fritz Kuhn complained that the Greens had found themselves negotiating with a 'structurally conservative' SPD: 'those in the SPD in favour of reform were simply too weak.'

'All this has left the Chancellor depressed,' continued *Der Spiegel*,

> for his disappointment over the tax reforms, the squabbling over the expansion of Lafontaine's finance ministry into a treasury, the public altercation with Rudolf Scharping, ex-leader of the parliamentary party, and the replacement of Jost Stollmann, the original Finance Minister, by Werner Müller – all this has spoilt the pleasure the new Chancellor ought to have felt on assuming office. 'We could have made a better start', he muttered grimly. First bathed in the glowing warmth of victory, he now finds himself facing an alarming prospect: he occupies centre stage as Chancellor but sitting in the prompter's box is the figure of Lafontaine. With the government statement expected in two weeks' time, the seventh Chancellor of the Federal Republic of Germany will therefore set out to portray himself as his own man, a man who will address himself directly to the wizards of the technological revolution

who have hitherto cast scarcely a glance in the direction of a social democratic politician, a man determined to send a blast of fresh air through the sleepy, ossified structures of the old Germany.

There is no doubt that Gerhard Schröder suffered at the hands of the press. We have a problem of presentation, he used to say. But the election manifesto that both he and I had signed formed the foundation for the coalition negotiations. At two points I had met him half way. The first was when, at his request, I had not insisted on including the reintroduction of a private wealth tax among the items for discussion in the coalition negotiations. The second was when I agreed to leave the training levy out of the coalition agreement.

It would have been very possible to write simply that Lafontaine had given way to Schröder over these two issues. But since it is the Chancellor who lays down policy guidelines, the media found it more attractive to peddle the story that it was Lafontaine who got his own way.

This pantomime of who had got his own way, Schröder or Lafontaine, continued even after my resignation. With a number of decisions taken by the government after 11 March there was speculation as to whether I had voted for or against. In particular, in connection with the so-called Programme 2000, the press often claimed that such a programme would have been impossible with me. True, this was meant by many business correspondents as a genuine criticism but I nevertheless felt flattered that they were taking me seriously. Indeed, that programme would certainly have been impossible with me.

The election of the parliamentary leader passed off comparatively smoothly. Struck and Schreiner had discussed the matter amicably beforehand. The executive proposed Struck, who was elected by a large majority. It was a decision that proved, during my four years in government office, to be a wise one. Struck was always willing to compromise and anxious to iron out difficulties, and resisted the temptation to set up confrontations between the parliamentary party and the Chancellor or individual members of the government. Müntefering proposed Schreiner as business manager, a proposal I gladly accepted.

The remaining appointments followed the lines we had announced when we named the government team. Heidemarie Wieczorek-Zeul took over the ministry for economic cooperation, and Franz Müntefering that for transport, construction and housing. For the Greens Joschka Fischer became Foreign Minister and Jürgen Trittin Minister for the Environment.

There was a lengthy debate over who should take over at the ministry of health. Rudolf Dressler, who had been in overall charge of social policy for the SPD for many years, would have liked the job but the Greens put forward Andrea Fischer. Schröder had no particular attachment to Dressler. But personal likes or dislikes ought not to be the sole basis for such appointments. As Chairman of the working party on the problems of employees, Dressler represented an important section of the SPD, and his many years dealing with matters of social policy had given him a profound understanding of social problems. He sometimes gave me the impression, since his tragic car accident, of being prone to fits of depression, and I would have liked to see him given the Ministry of Health. It would have given him a fillip. But since I was forced to read day after day that I was dominating the government's policies and personalities, I finally gave way, and Andrea Fischer became Minister of Health. The episode still leaves a nasty taste in my mouth today.

There remained the election of the new Chancellor. In spite of everything Schröder had cold feet. He was aware that over the years he had made many enemies in the parliamentary party. As a pro-motor car man, he could not be certain that he had the support of all the Greens. Personally I felt pretty relaxed, not only because our majority ought to be sufficient to clinch the issue but also because we could count on a few votes from the FDP and the PDS.

And in fact Schröder did gain the votes of at least seven members of the opposition. Out of a total of 666 deputies 351 voted for him, which gave the coalition parties 344 seats in the Bundestag. I went up to him and embraced him. It was a totally spontaneous gesture, absolutely genuine. Then I pushed across to him a box of Cohiba cigars, decorated with a red rose.

In moments like this one forgets all internal dissensions. Every Social Democrat is a member of a large family and every family has things to celebrate, in this case the election of the third Social-Democratic Chancellor of the German Federal Republic. We had worked long and hard for this day, a day which proved that Willy Brandt's 'grandchildren' were not doomed to become just a footnote in history, as Henning Voscherau had feared many years earlier.

The victory itself was also overwhelming. Not only was the SPD the largest party in the Bundestag for the second time but the 'grandchildren' had succeeded in emphatically consigning the CDU to second place. The SPD had gained 40.9 per cent of the votes, the CDU/CSU had been reduced to 35.1 per cent, i.e. 5.8 per cent less.

Our venerated predecessors would never have believed it possible, and we felt entitled to compare our victory with that of Willy Brandt in 1972. Among those who came to congratulate the new Chancellor were the losers – Helmut Kohl, Wolfgang Schäuble, Theo Waigel, Klaus

Kinkel and others from the opposition parties. After congratulating Schröder, Heiner Geissler turned and congratulated me as well. 'This was your victory,' he said, then turned on his heel and left.

Other members of the present opposition have made similarly complimentary remarks to me but Geissler's particularly impressed me. He recognized at an early date that the CDU had abandoned the cause of social justice, which is fatal for any popular party. At this moment I could have no idea that after my resignation the new coalition government would repeat all the mistakes that had led to the downfall of the CDU/CSU and FDP.

Our remaining task was to elect a new Social-Democratic President – the second in the history of the German Federal Republic, after Gustav Heinemann. As Party Chairman of the SPD, I attached great importance to this. I was of the opinion that in previous elections to this most eminent of positions in the country the views of the SPD had not been sufficiently taken into account. I was also of the opinion that, as head of state, it was a position that should be kept free of party politics. I therefore lost no time in seeking the agreement of the CDU/CSU and FDP that the name of Johannes Rau should go forward. I also discussed the matter with Gregor Gysi of the PDS. It is deeply to be regretted that, in line of succession from Heuss, Lübke, Heinemann, Scheel, Carstens, von Weizsäcker and Herzog, the CDU/CSU and sections of the FDP were not prepared to support a Social Democrat for President.

The idea floated by the CDU/CSU that Dagmar Schipanski, an East German, would be a suitable nominee, had its attractions. All the previous Presidents had been men, and it was high time a woman was appointed to the position. But in the SPD our direction was already set. Rau, after all, had already contested the presidency with Roman Herzog. By the time a number of women in the SPD began to press for a woman candidate, it was already too late. Decisions of this kind require thorough discussion. The proposal to elect Jutta Limbach would in any case not have been the answer because it was desirable to retain a woman at the head of the Federal Constitutional Court.

Parts of the press embarked on a vicious campaign against Rau, for many years Prime Minister of the *Land* of North Rhine-Westphalia, belittling his qualities and using dishonest tricks to undermine his candidature. But I was not going to budge, and the relevant committees voted by a large majority to nominate Rau for President.

On 23 May 1999 Johannes Rau was elected eighth President of the German Federal Republic. I followed the election on television and was sorry not to be able to be there in person. Since the attempt on my life my relationship with Rau has become more intimate than is usual among politicians. We were standing side by side at that fateful moment, and the original intention of the would-be assassin, a woman, had been to kill Rau, not me. I can still see the expression on his face as I lay on the ground and the security forces moved him away from the platform.

Johannes Rau regards the position of President of the Federal Republic as the summit of his political career. Born in Wuppertal, son of a pastor, who rose to become first Governing Mayor of his home town, then leader of the SPD parliamentary party in North-Rhine-Westphalia, and finally Prime Minister of the largest *Land* in the Federal Republic, Rau is the ideal man for the office of head of state. His political slogan is 'Reconciliation not Rancour' – a motto that has led friends and opponents alike to dub him 'Brother John'.

He was the first man to speak of the SPD as a shield to protect the 'little people'. In his inaugural address as President he said:

> The most important social task confronting us today – of this I am convinced – is to create new jobs. In the first place this is the responsibility of employers. Politicians are charged with providing a proper framework for supply and demand, and with stimulating the economy correspondingly . . .
>
> It is vital for our future development that we organize and expand our patterns of work in such a way as to achieve a balance between the needs of men and women and the demands of a market economy. Work is what gives us our livelihood. That immediately gives it a value. But within it – and this gives it a further value – human capabilities unfurl. Hans Küng was right when he said: 'Without meaningful work part of a person's dignity is lost.' . . . It is no mere academic observation to draw attention to the value of work for the preservation of human self-esteem and for the cohesion of state and society. Those who see in work nothing but a cost factor which has to be kept as low as possible – however important the question of wages in the whole economic process may be – are playing with fire and threatening the very foundations of western civilization, whether they realize it or not.

I was grateful to Johannes Rau for saying this. For it is neoliberalism, which reduces workers to mere numbers, that is 'playing with fire and threatening the very foundations of western civilization'.

'Teneo quia tenor', runs the Latin tag – 'I hold fast because I am held fast.' Rau frequently quotes this saying. And I too could not help remembering it when I said after my resignation: 'Teamwork means having regard for others and supporting others, both in private and in public. Team spirit is what characterizes the work of government.'

Weeks before my actual resignation I had made up my mind to depart from the scene immediately after the presidential election. I had long put up with more than I could reconcile with my self-esteem. Agreements were broken, the government's business was not coordinated and the team spirit essential for the successful conduct of government was just not there. I had no desire to argue the matter – merely to inform the party that my role as parliamentary leader was over. We had a Social-Democratic President and a Social-Democratic Chancellor.

But as we now know, things did not work out like that.

11

The Red-Green Coalition

The coalition between the Social Democrats and the Greens – popularly known as the red-green coalition – is the product of lengthy deliberations within the SPD. Initially the majority of Social Democrats reckoned that the Greens, as a party, would not last long in the political life of the country. A coalition with this party was naturally considered out of the question. Indeed, the Greens themselves had violent arguments over whether they should remain an extra-parliamentary pressure group or become a parliamentary opposition party with the declared intention of refusing to share in government.

In my book *The Other Step Forward*, published in 1985, I took issue with this attitude and wrote under the heading 'Responsibility not Refusal' that the Greens' refusal to accept responsibility represented an apolitical attitude, and that anyone who engaged in political debate ought not to shelter behind such a negative stance but be prepared, if the need arose, to take on the responsibility of government.

In 1985 the Greens in the Saarland declared that they were not willing, in the event of a red-green majority, to accept any responsibility in government. In fact the SPD won an absolute majority in the Saarland elections, leaving the Greens, who had won seats in other states, with no representatives in the provincial parliament.

In December that same year Joschka Fischer was appointed Minister for Energy and the Environment in the *Land* of Hesse. Leading members of the Greens had formerly belonged to the SPD but disagreements over rearmament and nuclear energy led to a split and thence to the formation of the Green Party.

Erhard Eppler was prominent among those who formulated policies for the SPD that were also in the manifesto of the Greens. We too wanted to see an energy policy which excluded the risks involved in producing electricity from nuclear energy. We too wanted to see an end to rearmament, especially in the field of nuclear weapons. We too wanted a realignment of our industrial society to take account of the needs of the environment. As far back as the early 1970s conservation had been the key item on the agenda of the IG Metall union, while even earlier, in the 1960s, Willy Brandt had demanded policies which would create blue skies again over the Ruhr. But a considerable section of the party persisted for a long while in seeing conservation measures as a threat to jobs, which is why in ecological matters the SPD moved far too slowly to modernize its programme.

The Green Party emerged as a counter to this. They had four principles – their policies should be ecological, peaceful, social and democratically formulated by the grass roots of the party. I established links with them very soon after their foundation. At various mass peace demonstrations I met Petra Kelly and Gerd Bastian, and thought very highly of both of them. Their tragic death affected me deeply. I also met Joschka Fischer at an early stage and admired his political skills and his rhetorical gifts. He approached me at the time when the red-green coalition in Hesse was threatening to fall apart, and subsequently became my closest professional colleague. Otto Schily, on the other hand, had left the Greens in 1989 to join the SPD.

A friendship that has lasted over many years is that with Antje Vollmer, Vice-President of the Bundestag, whom I met, together with her son Johann, at a peace demonstration in Bonn. She visited me in Saarbrücken after the attempt on my life in 1990, and was one of the few who made the effort to come to grips with the physical and psychological effects that the attack had had on me. She showed me sympathy and support during the difficult election campaign in 1990, especially in Bundestag debates, and it was a source of great regret to me that the SPD parliamentary party behaved so ineptly when she was elected to the vice-presidency of the Bundestag. She has remained a faithful friend since I retired from politics.

Under Fischer's influence the pragmatic wing of the Greens – the so-called 'Realos' – announced that they were prepared to share responsibility in a coalition government. During the federal election of 1987, following Rau's suggestion, the SPD had rejected a coalition with the Green Party. Rau had thought that, after his spectacular victory in North Rhine-Westphalia, when he won an absolute majority, his success could be repeated at the federal level. But his strategy did not work out, and after losing the federal election, the SPD had no interest in reviving the prospect of a coalition with the Greens at provincial level, although, in response to particular local situations, various forms of ad hoc collaboration did come about.

There is no doubt that the Green party influenced the policies of the other parties. Whenever a new party comes into being – unless it belongs to the extreme left or the extreme right – and captures votes at the expense of the popular parties, those parties first react by asking themselves where they have gone wrong. Then they incorporate in their own programmes some of the points in the new party's programme. Such is the competition for votes that they are compelled to cast their nets far and wide in order to capture the support of as extensive a range of electors as possible. New ideas spring up which appeal to the voters. Ecological concerns, for instance, attracted increasing support in all parties.

The Greens succeeded in forcing the FDP into third place in the *Land* elections, while red-green coalitions became ever commoner at *Land* level. Nowhere were developments since 1987 more strikingly demonstrated than in North Rhine-Westphalia, where a red-green coalition was formed in 1995 with Johannes Rau at its head. It almost seemed a matter of course, therefore, that if we won the general election, the government itself would be a red-green coalition. Since the CDU and the FDP declared almost every day that they intended to remain partners after the election and had no intention of collaborating with the SPD, a red-green coalition in Bonn must have seemed a credible option.

Warning signs began to show themselves when the coalition in North Rhine-Westphalia threatened to fall apart. There were vehement arguments over the question of open-cast mining at the Garzweiler II plant. The late Klaus Matthiesen, leader of the SPD contingent in the North Rhine-Westphalia parliament, had not been able to find an accommodation with the Greens, blaming them for the fact that he had not been elected Prime Minister of Schleswig-Holstein in April 1979. He fell 1,287 votes short, because the Greens had put up their own candidate and won 2.4 per cent of the vote. In addition to this, wrangling had broken out in the ranks of the SPD over who should succeed Rau as Prime Minister of North Rhine-Westphalia.

So began the familiar game of indiscretions and intrigues. But the red-green coalition could not be allowed to disintegrate before the federal election, for that would have seriously damaged our chances. I therefore talked time and again with those involved in order to prevent this from happening. I spent the Christmas of 1997–8 on the island of Madeira but here too the problems of the coalition continued to dog me. I was in constant contact with Joschka Fischer, who was spending Christmas in Paris, and discussed with him how we should proceed. In the end we managed to hold the coalition together.

One Saturday afternoon in March 1998 Rau came to visit me in Saarbrücken. Schröder had meanwhile won the *Land* elections in Lower Saxony. Rau told me that he intended to resign his position as Prime Minister. In the course of our discussion I told Rau that, quite apart from any decision he might make over North Rhine-Westphalia, I still held fast to my intention to put his name forward for the office of Federal President. I passed this information to Schröder, who was in agreement.

After the differences between the parties in North Rhine-Westphalia had been ironed out, the prospect of a red-green coalition for Bonn became ever rosier. Fischer had asked me on a number of occasions to nominate Schröder as SPD candidate for Chancellor. He said he realized that I was the leader of the pack in the SPD but, the power of the media being what it was, we would have a greater chance of success if we were to put Schröder forward, the darling of the press, as our man for Chancellor. A little earlier I had learned via the familiar indiscretions of the media that Fischer had been spreading the tale behind my back that I had the evil eye and was therefore quite incapable of winning a federal election.

Fischer annoyed me particularly one day when, via his usual revelations to the press, he declared that Brandt's 'grandchildren' were not up to the job. He telephoned one day to suggest that we ought to take a leaf out of the Italians' book and nominate a 'German Prodi' for Chancellor. He urged me in all seriousness to approach Helmut Werner, who until recently had been managing director of Mercedes Benz. I began to have doubts about Fischer's powers of judgement. Apart from that, I said to Fischer, we already have one man in the motor car lobby.

This was the time when, in relative terms, the Greens were doing better at the polls than the SPD. Fischer was not the only one to make derogatory remarks about us – other leading Green politicians also chimed in. I refrained from reminding him of this later when the boot was on the other foot.

I had firmly decided that, provided we gained an adequate majority, I would set out to reconcile the rival elements in the red-green coalition after the general election. In taxation policy, even more in social policy – I am thinking of improvements in the law on summary dismissal and of entitlement to sick pay – as well as in health policy and pensions regulations, the Greens are closer to us than are the CDU or the FDP.

But some were always raising obstacles. At their conference in Magdeburg in March 1998 the Greens had proposed that the price of petrol be raised to 5 marks per litre over the course of the next ten years. A woman delegate even demanded that holiday flights to Majorca should be restricted.

The Social Democrats came down on such proposals like a ton of bricks. Schröder declared that the Greens were incapable of governing. In a number of conversations I had with him, I urged Schröder to choose his words rather more carefully, because I was convinced that after the general election the government would consist of a red-green coalition.

By March 1998 business leaders too were coming round to the view that a red-green coalition was increasingly likely. Hans-Peter Stihl, president of the DIHT, gave interviews under the heading 'Back to the Stone Age with Red-Green'. At a meeting in Munich Stihl, Henkel, Hundt and Philipp, captains of German industry, ranged themselves alongside Kohl, promising 500,000 new jobs and suddenly praising the policies of the federal government in Bonn. There could hardly have been a cruder way of doing things.

I wanted to have the Greens as our partners because I saw in them a guarantee that I would be able to carry through a socio-ecological reform programme in energy policy and transport policy, and above all promote the cause of world peace. In the ranks of my own party there were still some who remained attached to neoliberal ideas, talked in superficial terms about modernization and rejected all thoughts of an ecological tax reform. These same circles also approved of the use of nuclear energy and supported the use of military force within the territory of NATO. My expectation that the Greens would join me in my effort to keep the coalition on a socio-ecological reform course turned out to be a miscalculation.

Scarcely had they found themselves in government than the Greens began to show themselves willing to abandon vital principles in order to keep their hands on the instruments of power. For all practical purposes I had guaranteed to Fischer that a red-green coalition would come about provided a large enough majority was in favour of it. I was the only leading Social Democrat present at his fiftieth birthday celebrations in Frankfurt in April 1998. The last words in the short speech of congratulation I gave were: 'Joschka, if the majority are with us, let's do it!'

An incidental reason for my resignation from the government was that I very quickly came to recognize that the Greens had forgotten how to keep to their principles. That there should be a clash of views between us on how to amend the nationality laws, in the face of the new coalition government between the CDU and FDP formed after the elections in Hesse, was understandable. And that the Greens should have intervened and agreed a compromise with the FDP, was logical.

But under no circumstances could I accept the way they allowed themselves to be treated over the question of nuclear energy, or the way Fischer, who had barely taken over the Foreign Ministry, sucked up to Madeleine Albright, hanging on her every word. I listened with astonishment as he spoke out in favour of military involvement and made German loyalty to NATO the cornerstone of his foreign policy. In spite of his loyalty to the Western Alliance, I would have expected him to subject the measures proposed by the Alliance to some kind of critical examination, especially the attitude of the Americans.

If, in the wake of the speeches by Fischer and Scharping, Helmut Schmidt had addressed the cabinet, he would have created an uncomfortable atmosphere and been branded a trouble-maker. 'I have difficulty,' wrote Schmidt,

> in concealing my doubts about the powers of judgement of the present architects of foreign policy in Washington . . . The ruthlessness, generally motivated by internal political interests, with which Washington asserts its power and forces its will on its allies, will become a source of increasing irritation to many Europeans. The illusory vision of America, the world's one superpower, as a global policeman, creating and maintaining peace in the whole world with the help of NATO, should not be allowed to obscure the memory of Korea or Vietnam, or of 'Desert Storm' and any other 'peace initiatives' backed up with threats of military action.

Gerhard Schröder had made the abandonment of the nuclear energy programme his main priority. I played no part in the negotiations. This too went against what we had agreed. Schröder had close links with the utility companies and must have set out with the intention to find a compromise. But frictions quickly developed. In cabinet meetings one side blamed the other for its intolerance, with Trittin, Minister for the Environment, making the Chancellor's Office responsible for breakdowns in negotiations, and the Chancellor's Office laying the blame at the door of Trittin and his ministry.

Werner Müller, the Economics Minister, repeatedly complained to me, as Party Chairman, that he was never sufficiently involved in these discussions, and that he could neither follow the direction the discussions were taking nor who was supposed to be coordinating them. He told me he had considered resigning as a protest against this way of conducting government business. I advised him to approach the Chancellor personally and insist on the adoption of procedures that were rational and effective.

It never ceased to amaze me how patiently the Greens allowed Jürgen Trittin to be held up in public as a bogeyman. The spin-doctors of the

Chancellor's Office joined in the fun and Schröder himself also attacked him publicly. I told the Chancellor that, as head of the government, he must always lead his troops from the front, even if one minister or other aroused his disapproval or held views which he found unacceptable. That, at any rate, is how I see the role of a head of government. And under no circumstances would I regard it as acceptable behaviour for a member of the cabinet who is under attack from the media to be made the object of public criticism from his leader.

I was always worried that Trittin might decide he had had enough of all this and resign. I was therefore at pains to maintain friendly relations with him. But I still could not understand why Joschka Fischer and other members of the Green Party did not make greater efforts to support their embattled colleague. In my own statement of resignation I wrote: ' One cannot achieve success without having a team to work with. Teamwork means having consideration for others and sticking together – also in the eyes of the public. The work of a government rests on team spirit.' When Fischer read this, he claimed that he had never noticed anything about bad teamwork. Apparently Fischer becomes aware of humiliations only when they affect him personally. When others are humiliated, he fails to notice.

When in June 1999, at the instance of the Chancellor himself, Trittin went against his own convictions and repealed the EU regulation on toxic emissions from older motor vehicles, I could no longer understand what he was doing. Some of his friends in the party asked him whether he still recognized the man he saw in the mirror. Others went so far as to demand that he resign.

An even greater disappointment was the attitude of Fischer and his party to the war in Kosovo. The Green party, which had once upon a time taken its stand on the need to find more democratic means of reaching conclusions, and had therefore introduced the rotation principle among its members in the Bundestag, took virtually no part in the debate and left everything to Fischer himself.

Fischer, however, had decided early on to base his Yugoslavia policy on the principle of solidarity with the NATO Alliance, which implied a readiness to become involved in military action. He defended the war in Kosovo on moral grounds. A man who acts in the spirit of realpolitik knows that ethical norms cannot of themselves determine the course of political action. But a man who bases his political decisions solely on moral principles very quickly loses his essential sense of objectivity and finds himself on a slippery slope.

I have often wondered, and have continued to do so since my resignation, what differences there would have been in German foreign policy if Helmut Kohl and Klaus Kinkel had still been in charge. I am afraid my answer was and is – precious little. I had hoped to find in the Greens a partner who would help me restrain a minority in my own party which consistently favoured military intervention, even in territories outside the areas covered by the NATO mandate. True, even this minority in the SPD insisted on the approval of the Security Council of the United Nations. But that we should reach the point where, when it came to approving such military action even without a mandate from the Security Council, Joschka Fischer would outdo Rudolf Scharping, was something I had not anticipated.

Sooner or later we are going to have to answer the question – what position will the Greens come to occupy, as a party, in the party political landscape as a whole? Jochen Buchsteiner wrote in *Die Zeit*: 'The Greens of old no longer exist. But then, what sort of an organization is it that takes part in political life under the label "The Greens"? The Green Party of today is rootless, reactionary, split and paralysed. Power is perhaps their final aim.'

The central problem in this century will be that of the environment, though it does not at present arouse great interest on the part of the electors. And as to the Greens' pacifism, they finally turned their backs on that philosophy at their extraordinary party conference in Bielefeld in May 1998, if not before. For the first time in the history of the party Fischer and the Realo wing won a narrow majority. Jürgen Trittin, Ludger Volmer and Angelika Beer had followed their lead. Writing in *Die Woche*, Charlotte Wiedemann said: 'By force of circumstance the Greens have become a war party. If the general election had gone the other way, even by a few hairs' breadths, we would have now had, in this eighth week of the Kosovo war, eloquent critics of NATO in the seats of government, men and women with names like Angelika Beer, Ludger Vollmer, Kerstin Müller and probably also Joschka Fischer. And, of course, Trittin.'

In the field of economic and fiscal policy suggestions were coming forward which also gained support from the FDP. Many among the Greens, for example, were in favour of lowering the top rate of income tax and made this an issue in the discussions on the formation of the coalition. Since they were proposing to finance this measure at the expense of the workers, we had to block it. The Greens were blissfully unaware that in the 1990s even the USA had taken to taxing the better-off because consumption could not otherwise be curbed.

Then there were Greens from Swabia who wanted to reduce fiscal policy to one word – 'economizing'. One could hardly fail to notice that the new initiatives in economic and fiscal policy that I had launched, which took account of the economic cycle and similar matters and which had gained the support of the majority of my own party, were barely discussed at all by the Greens. Even after the government had taken office, it was impossible to find anyone among them who showed much interest in such questions. Naturally the press found words of praise for those who proclaimed in public the need for economy measures. But that was only because anybody who urges economies in government spending can be sure of his share of praise. The effect of such economies on the willingness of enterprises to invest or on overall demand were issues the Greens preferred not to discuss.

The Greens' change of direction became even more evident after the *Land* elections in Hesse. I had a long conversation in the Finance Ministry with Joschka Fischer. In view of the dramatic inroads the Greens had made in these elections, I asked him what line his party intended to take in order to give it a distinguishable character in the party political spectrum. To my surprise he replied that they proposed to concentrate on issues arising from the workings of a free market economy.

I was taken aback. Was this party, born in the ecology movement and constantly drawing the world's attention to the fact that there were limits to economic growth, now going to seek its future in the doctrines of neoliberalism? It had become evident in many debates, both before and after the federal election, that there was a keen rivalry between the Greens and the FDP. They apparently both found it necessary to appeal to the same sections of the electorate.

This flirting of the Greens with liberalism became still more blatant after I had resigned. Some expressed the view that the coalition now had the opportunity to make a fresh start. In June a number of young Greens decided that the entire party programme had to be modernized and old baggage jettisoned. 'Our present programme,' they wrote,

> is like an attic, a place where everything ends up that one once used to cherish but has long had no further use for, but which – one never knows – might come in useful again some time . . . The day of truces and compromises is over – the party needs clear decisions about the proper path for it to take in the future. We shall adopt clear, responsible and pragmatic positions. At the same time we demand changes in the party hierarchy . . . What confronts us is the need to redefine the meaning of a social market economy in the age of globalization. A new relationship must be forged between individual freedom and social security. Market forces and the needs of society must be brought into accord with each other, and the economic and ecological rights of future generations respected. We aim to revive the dormant legacy of a responsible liberalism and fuse it with a concern for the environment and for justice between generations present and future.

This statement drew from another group of young Green politicians a four-page riposte headed 'No New Middle Way!' 'The way forwards for the Greens', they wrote, ' is that of a pragmatic left-wing party.' In the nine months they had been in government, they went on, the party had utterly failed to satisfy the needs of society. Conservation issues must again be made a principal concern, while greater attention must be paid to social justice and to the aspirations of young people. The document produced by the young Realos was scornfully dismissed as the longest application to join the FDP that the world had ever seen.

Antje Radcke, a spokeswoman for the Greens, said: ' We have lost our identity. No one knows any longer what the Greens stand for. They express contradictory opinions on all issues of substance. This is an appalling situation that cannot be allowed to continue.' It is extraordinary to see discussions going on about the legacy of liberalism at a time when the Liberal Party cannot even reach the 5 per cent hurdle in *Land* elections. One got the impression that the SPD and the Greens had set out to drive away as many of their voters as they could.

This really was a new beginning.

We must wait and see where the Green party goes from here. If Fischer succeeds in his plan for them to 'modernize' themselves by adopting market-oriented positions, their importance will decline. The preservation of the environment, hitherto the hallmark of their identity, has all but faded from the day-to-day business of government, while their foreign policy is governed by their loyalty to the Western Alliance.

For me one justification for the red-green coalition was that in the election campaign the Greens had made similar promises on questions of social policy as had the SPD. Once this link between the two is broken, it is difficult to explain why the Greens should be a better partner for the SPD than the CDU/CSU or the FDP. Moreover the former leaders of the FDP had always impressed me with their resolute attitude to the question of bugging. Men like Genscher and Lambsdorff had made it clear that they would not vote for the extension of bugging operations to cover journalists, doctors, drug advisers and other sensitive groups. In order to hold them to their word, we sent the bugging bill back from the Bundesrat to the Bundestag. Genscher and Lambsdorff stuck to their guns, and immediately after the elections in Lower Saxony we inflicted a heavy parliamentary defeat on the Kohl government. The coalition had lost its majority in the Bundestag.

Journalists hailed it as a great victory for the freedom of the press. It was a personal source of satisfaction for me as well, because since the amendment to the press regulations in the Saarland, designed to improve the law on the right of reply, I had been held up as an opponent of the freedom of the press. It had cost me a great deal of effort to persuade Schröder to get journalists exempted from the bugging regulations. Coming on top of the brilliant victory in Lower Saxony, this parliamentary defeat weighed heavily on the government parties. A mood of despondency settled over them, and they began to wonder whether with Kohl as their leader they were still capable of winning the election. Indeed, to nobody's surprise, the FDP began to distance itself from the Chancellor. This was precisely what I had been working for. The aura of invincibility that had settled round Kohl had to be shattered. It was an aura that many Social Democrats regarded as impenetrable, and the press corps in Bonn still accepted the validity of the so-called 'Kohl curve' – at the opening of an election campaign Kohl's support lags behind but at the winning-post he has his neck in front.

When Johannes Rau announced that he was handing over to Wolfgang Clement, the pressure on Kohl grew even stronger. The argument over whether Kohl was the right man to lead the CDU/CSU continued to rage right up to the last minute. Nine days before polling day Wolfgang Schäuble wrote in *Playboy* that it had been politically inept to pronounce him after the Leipzig conference to be Kohl's successor. Our success in the election was in fact due in large measure to our ability to sow the seeds of doubt in the minds of CDU/CSU voters over the continued suitability of Helmut Kohl as Chancellor.

Willy Brandt and Oskar Lafontaine at the SPD Party Conference in
Münster, September 1988
(© Ullstein – Karl-Bernd Karwasz)

Celebrations to mark the first anniversary of German reunification. On
the balcony of the Reichstag building in Berlin. From left to right:
Oskar Lafontaine, Willy Brandt, Hans-Dietrich Genscher, Hannelore
Kohl, Chancellor Helmut Kohl and Richard von Weizsäcker
(© Ullstein – Werek)

Gerhard Schröder, Lafontaine and Rudolf Scharping after the defeat
of the SPD in the general election of October 1994
(© Ullstein – Vario-Press)

Lafontaine beats Scharping in the contest for leader of the SPD in
November 1995
(© Ullstein – Bonn Sequenz)

Andrea Nahles, Chair of the Young Socialists, in conversation with
Lafontaine in October 1997 in Dortmund
(© Süddeutscher Bilderdienst – imwo/Ute Grabowsky)

At the summit of the G-7 Finance Ministers in Bonn, February 1999:
Robert E. Rubin (USA), Lafontaine, Dominique Strauss-Kahn (France)
(Associated Press/Fritz Reiss)

The SPD campaign team for the federal election of June 1998. From left to right: Franz Müntefering, Oskar Lafontaine, Edelgard Bulmahn, Rudolf Scharping, Herta Däubler-Gmelin, Gerhard Schröder, Otto Schily, Christine Bergmann, Rolf Schwanitz, Walter Riester
(Associated Press/Jan Bauer)

Gerhard Schröder, Joschka Fischer and Lafontaine celebrating the conclusion of the coalition agreement in Bonn on 20 October 1998
(Associated Press/Roberto Pfeil)

Lafontaine embraces Schröder on his election as Chancellor,
27 October 1998
(© dpa – Bildfunk)

Lafontaine with Johannes Rau, who had been present when
Lafontaine was stabbed
(© dpa)

Press ball in Bonn, 13 November 1998: Lafontaine with his wife
Christa Müller and Schröder with his wife Doris Schröder-Köpf
(Associated Press/Roberto Pfeil)

Lafontaine with his mother, Käthe, in February 1992
(© Süddeutscher Bilderdienst – F. Hartung)

Lafontaine the family man at his home in Saarbrücken, with his son
Carl Maurice, 13 March 1999
(© dpa)

12

Getting off on the Wrong Foot

As we took up the task of government, it became increasingly clear that we were confronted by a structural problem. Whereas formerly there had been one decision-making centre, and only one, namely the executive committee of the party, we now had four centres – the Party Executive, the Chancellor's Office, the Parliamentary Party and the Bundesrat. From the very beginning, therefore, there was a need for close cooperation between these four centres, which would only have been possible if there had been consistent collaboration between Gerhard Schröder and myself. And of that there was no hope.

It all started with the government's statement of intent. The statement had been drafted by Schröder's close advisers, led, presumably, by Bodo Hombach. There was no discussion with the chairman of the party. Nevertheless I managed to get hold of the text on the evening beforehand and run a cursory eye over it. The first thing with which I found fault was that it did not begin with a sketch of Schröder's new policies. The proper way of launching a new government would have been to say, right at the beginning, these are the things we intend to achieve for our country over the coming years. Instead, as early as page two, the statement complained about the huge debts that we had inherited from the Kohl administration. I communicated my objections to Schröder's advisers but to no avail.

When Schröder reached the following passage in his text, my hair stood on end:

We do not intend simply to abolish the category of casual so-called

630-mark jobs* but plan to absorb them gradually into the compulsory welfare insurance scheme. The new threshold will be set at 300 marks. Since we propose at the same time to abolish the flat-rate tax, these measures will not lead to an unreasonable rise in costs. It can therefore be seen that the government firmly recognizes the need and desirability of such modes of employment, not only for employers but also for the employees concerned, as well as for consumers. With the cooperation of employers' organizations and trade unions we shall, however, rigorously seek to stamp out abuses of the system.

To this day I have not been able to find out who wrote this passage of the Chancellor's speech. It represented a clear breach of promises that Schröder and I had given during the election campaign. With the particular interests of women in mind who, their children now having left home, supplemented their income with part-time work, we had consistently emphasized that we aimed to make casual earnings below 630 marks per month subject to welfare contributions but in such a way that those dependent on these earnings should not suffer financial hardship. At the same time we were fully aware that those who were better off would enjoy incomparably greater advantages. Not for nothing had these part-time jobs come to be called 'the poor man's tax haven'.

At a meeting of the parliamentary party I emphasized the promise we had made and said that in no way could I support the plan drawn up between members of the parliamentary party, the Ministry of Labour and the Chancellor's Office. The next day I read in the papers that Schröder had prevented me from taking the question of these jobs any further. While I was fighting for the rights of those who were dependent on casual earnings, the spin-doctors in the Chancellor's Office were busily feeding the press false information.

We held a crisis meeting in the Chancellor's Office and agreed to set the limit not, as the Chancellor had announced, at 300 but at 630 marks, which would at least ensure that women in part-time jobs were no worse off than they had been before. The following morning Schröder himself announced the new regulations. But the problem remained that the measure had not been adequately discussed and the assessments from the various relevant ministries were not yet available.

These mistakes made me very annoyed, since we had already devised schemes for subsequent developments. There were a number of further proposals on the table, some of them based on preliminary reports submitted by Fritz Scharpf, Joachim Mitschke and the Friedrich

* Insurance contributions were not payable on a monthly wage of under 630 marks.

Ebert Foundation. One suggestion was that earnings of less than 1,500 marks should be exempt, wholly or in part, from insurance contributions, so as to encourage the take-up of such casual jobs. These proposals would have solved the problem of these casual jobs, which would then have fallen into the larger category of jobs in the low-paid sector as a whole. In order to offset the lost insurance contributions the ecology duty could be raised. Or, put another way: the ecology duty would not be used as a way of reducing insurance contributions in general but in order to broaden the low-paid sector and make it financially more attractive.

Bodo Hombach, skilled in the arts of the spin-doctor, succeeded in presenting these ideas to the public in May 1999 as 'new'. An article in *Der Spiegel* under the title 'A Plan from Schröder's Drawer: A Radical Cure for Unemployment' reported on a comprehensive new scheme

> aimed at introducing a general tax allowance for insurance contributions in the case of low-paid workers, with a degressive reduction of this allowance up to a threshold beyond which full contributions would be paid. This proposal would have no time limit, nor would it be directed at any one or more specific groups. To this extent it would be the equivalent of a general reduction in taxation. The state would reimburse the welfare funds for the loss of the contributions previously paid by employers and employees, and employees would remain covered for social insurance.

So, thanks to Bodo Hombach, the work of the Friedrich Ebert Foundation has now finally been acknowledged, albeit rather late in the day.

The removal of the flat rate tax which the Chancellor had announced, without prior consultation, in the government statement did not present problems for the Federal Finance Minister alone. Because the *Länder* also derived income from this tax, there were arguments with the individual finance ministers as well, which went on for months and which, with the help and support of my old friend Heinz Schleusser, Finance Minister of North Rhine-Westphalia, I finally succeeded in settling.

The changes in the arrangements for those outside the national insurance system and the creation of a new category of low-paid workers were provoked by our answer to one basic question: Do we want to tolerate a situation in which more and more people are joining the ranks of the spurious so-called 'self-employed', go moonlighting or take casual jobs, thereby contributing nothing towards the cost of the welfare state while still able to claim welfare payments? It was going to require a lot of careful groundwork to ensure that people would agree to the proposed reforms.

Since this work was not properly coordinated, further mistakes were made. Before the members of the government team were announced, Gerhard Schröder gave an interview to the *Bild am Sonntag* in which the headline read: 'Official: Schröder says petrol is to be no more than six pfennigs dearer.' This figure of 6 pfennigs was not justified by any reckoning. Petrol prices had fallen by more than 10 pfennigs per litre over the previous year. For a government devoted to ecological issues we were making ourselves look ridiculous.

I was surprised that the opposition did not seize their opportunity – after all, one should always challenge the enemy on his own ground. Instead the opposition parties, which had put forward their own proposals for an ecology tax, decided that it would make a greater impression on the electors if they dismissed this modest step as merely a cheap way of raising money. Men like Schäuble, Repnik and Solms did not want to be reminded of their own reform plans.

These six pfennigs, however, also posed a problem for the government because we now had to introduce a new tax – electricity tax. Schröder's announcement had reduced the ecological tax reform to an empty shell. Fritz Scharpf enquired why the original plan to use the ecology tax to finance the new low-wage sector had been abandoned. He wrote a minute to this effect which I passed on both to the members of the parliamentary party and to the Chancellor's Office. But among the plethora of stipulations and decisions that various coordinators arrived at, this sensible proposal was for the present left on one side. Our work was further hampered by the fact that, as we had expected, the business world was up in arms against both reforms.

Our over-hasty actions and a lack of coordination had had the regrettable result of discrediting right at the beginning two of the central reform projects of the red-green coalition – reform of the ecology tax and the restructuring of the low-paid sector. A further difficulty for our public relations people was that our so-called 'modernizers' did not stand four-square behind these projects but proceeded to criticize them vehemently in the background. But it is impossible to win public approval for reform programmes if there are 'modernizers' in one's own ranks who use their authority to oppose these reforms.

A month after his first interview for the *Bild am Sonntag* Schröder gave a second, in November 1998, in which he was credited with declaring: 'Full pensions at 60'. This was another example of the Chancellor shooting from the hip. In fact, having regard to projected demographic developments, we had proposed in our paper that retirement age be lowered as soon as unemployment had fallen. Moreover it was obvious at a glance that such a measure was incapable of being financed.

The fickleness and forgetfulness of public opinion made it possible for us to lay this proposal at the door of Walter Riester, who was made to bear the brunt of the ensuing criticism over the following weeks.

Sooner or later, of course, it had to be admitted that the proposal could not be financed. But here too I wondered who had had the job of preparing the text of the Chancellor's interviews and checking their accuracy. Whoever these people were, they gave no impression of having followed the discussions that had gone on in SPD circles.

As a result of these mistakes over casual jobs, the ecology tax reform and nuclear energy policy, all of which could have been avoided if there had been more expert knowledge available in the Chancellor's Office and wider consultation, the spirit of optimism that accompanied the change of government took a series of perceptible blows. These mistakes also overshadowed the reform proposals that we had deliberately put in the forefront of the new government's programme in order to make clear to the working population that the new government had their interests at heart and was out to promote their cause. These proposals concerned the restoration of sick pay, the right to protection against summary dismissal, the reversal of the cuts in pensions and improvements in the health system.

The most difficult of our reform projects, however, was that for tax reform. And here I made a serious error in the course of the negotiations over the constitution of the coalition government. I had allowed the question to be brought forward in parliament with undue haste. While the negotiations were still going on, the finance ministers in both the federal and *Länder* governments had put forward a series of proposals that deviated from the original SPD plan and were to cause us a great deal of irritation. They opposed above all the plan to restrict the rate of depreciation, to tax disposal profits and to restrict losses on carry-over balances. We came under pressure from all sides not to pass the tax reform bill. Messrs Henkel, Stihl and Hundt, as ever, predicted the end of Western civilization and the demise of Germany.

I took a certain sporting pleasure in watching these arguments, since the tax bill was a genuinely Social-Democratic piece of legislation. It meant a gain for employees and their families of more than 20 billion marks, while medium-sized businesses, after a series of adjustments, ended up 5 billion marks better off. Big business, on the other hand, which used to boast that it had paid little or no tax over the years, now found itself facing a bill of more than 10 billion marks.

One who deserves special praise for her work in piloting the tax bill through parliament is Barbara Hendricks, my Minister of State. As former press spokeswoman for Heinz Schleusser, she had acquired a considerable competence in such matters and enjoyed the trust of the parliamentary party. In a marathon sitting she succeeded in piloting the measure through the various committees. As every proposal to withdraw tax concessions – there were over seventy in all – met with resistance in the discussions, one can imagine how much work she did.

On 10 February 1999 I was reporting at a press conference on the current position with regard to the tax reform bill, while at the same time Barbara Hendricks was pushing through a few changes in the Finance Committee. I was in the awkward position of not knowing what direction the discussions in the Finance Committee would take, and had no up-to-date minutes that would tell me how things stood on each individual point. So at certain moments, being unable to give precise information, I was forced to waffle. My opponents made the most of my discomfiture and began to spread rumours behind the scenes that the responsibilities of Finance Minister were obviously proving too onerous for me.

But in the last analysis the tax reform bill turned out to be a highly respectable measure, because it helped to bring more justice into the system, relieve workers' families and middle-ranking businesses of an excessive tax burden and do away with a number of unwarranted concessions. The unreasonably short period we had allowed for getting the bill through proved to be an advantage. In spite of losing the elections in Hesse, we managed to pass the bill through Bundestag and Bundesrat with the necessary majorities, since Hans Eichel, one of the outgoing ministers, was still a deputy for Hesse when the final vote was taken.

A particular chapter in the history of the tax reform bill centred on the taxation of the energy industry and the insurance industry. As was to be expected, the leaders of these two industries protested and gave grossly inflated figures of the effects the tax would have on their businesses. The Chancellor began to get nervous, worried that by taxing the energy industry too harshly, he might threaten his discussions on withdrawing from the nuclear energy programme. We were prepared to meet both industries, the insurance industry and the energy industry, half-way.

But these emendations to the bill unfortunately created the impression that provided one could lobby the Chancellor's Office forcefully enough, concessions would always be forthcoming. An additional source of confusion was that on one occasion the tax to be levied on the energy industry was calculated over a period of ten years, on another occasion over a period of four years. Naturally enough it was only the experts who noticed this. And of course this gave ignorant outsiders another chance to cause trouble by jibing that the Finance Ministry was not even in possession of the correct figures. The end of the affair was that after my resignation – surprise, surprise! – the energy industry came to the conclusion that the figures which the federal Finance Ministry had worked out in cooperation with the Finance Ministry of North Rhine-Westphalia were in fact correct.

The government's statement had one more surprise in store for me. The Chancellor said: 'We also intend to undertake a thorough review of business tax. Business earnings will in future be taxed at a maximum rate of 35 per cent.' The government's programme contained no such statement. In the amendment on which we were working there were proposals to reduce the rate of corporation tax on retained profits from 45 per cent to 40 per cent from 1 January 1999, and the maximum tax rate on industrial earnings from 47 per cent to 43 per cent from 1 January 2000. The figure of 35 per cent that the Chancellor had conjured up naturally put a question mark against the tax rates quoted in the amendment.

Critics were fully entitled to ask what was going on, when the tax bill referred to corporation tax for retained profits being lowered to 40 per cent and for business earnings to 43 per cent, while the Chancellor promised a maximum rate of 35 per cent across the board. No vote had been taken on the issue. When this figure of 35 per cent cropped up yet again, this time in the pages of the *Handelsblatt*, while we were still in the process of arguing for different figures, something in me snapped. Giving my indignation free rein, I protested that this was no way to conduct the affairs of government. The papers carried full details of what I said. By now, at the latest, alarm bells must have been ringing in the heads of all those who professed to have been totally taken aback by my resignation two weeks later.

Before the first tax reform was in place, a second was already announced. According to the programme for the year 2000 pensioners and unemployed would finance the reduction of business taxes. The proper course of action would have been, after the tax amendment bill, which was a real breakthrough, not to contemplate any further such bills for the present. If the need arose, further concerted action could be considered towards the end of the parliamentary term. Whatever the various arguments over the details of taxation policy, one rule prevails: it is not possible to go on proposing one series of amendments after another. To do so is to undermine the confidence of investors and consumers alike, and hinders economic development. Investors in particular need stable conditions within which to plan their activities.

A further point is that tax harmonization measures are being planned on a European scale. After these measures have been agreed upon, it will probably become necessary for us to introduce further tax amendments. Certain mistakes are evidently so attractive that people go on making them time and again.

In introducing the government's programme for the year 2000 Hans Eichel declared that a wealth tax would not be reintroduced. But in the government's programme we had promised to reintroduce just such a tax in the interests of a just distribution of wealth. Here I am bound to mention that in the course of the coalition negotiations this same Hans Eichel had repeatedly urged me to insist on the reintroduction of a tax on private wealth. As the proceeds from such a tax would find their way into the coffers of the respective *Länder*, Eichel wanted to use the money to supplement expenditure on education and research in the state of Hesse, and to promise this to the electorate during the campaign. As Schröder was opposed to the idea, I could not accede to Eichel's request.

Ironically, after the red-green coalition had lost the provincial elections in Hesse, the new Prime Minister, Roland Koch, called a press conference after one hundred days of his administration in order to take stock of the situation. The *Frankfurter Allgemeine Zeitung* carried the following report:

> The centre-piece of Koch's statement on the first hundred days of his administration was his education policy. The supplementary budget, together with the new school regulations and the change in the constitution of the universities, has rapidly created the conditions, as Koch put it, 'calculated to make Hesse paramount among the *Länder* as concerns education'. With the new school year, after the summer vacation, there will be an influx of new teachers such as has not been seen for twenty years. With 1,400 new teachers, through redeployment and with the help of additional funds which will facilitate the employment of supply teachers to the equivalent of 300 posts, Hesse will have created the equivalent of 2,000 new posts. There will also be a corresponding increase in the number of openings in teacher training.

While Hans Eichel was talking tirelessly in Bonn about the need for 'cuts', his successor in Hesse was adopting left-wing supply-side policies.

13

The Elections in Hesse

The provincial elections in Hesse are always something special for the SPD. Many are the times when they have produced a surprising result, such as the triumphant election of Walter Wallmann, which very few of us had expected.

On 7 February 1999 we were therefore prepared for anything. When I look back, I cannot help smiling to myself about Hans Eichel, who had constantly begged me to avoid providing any vicious shocks before the elections – by which he meant any programme of cuts. I could not resist pulling his leg. 'Hans,' I said, 'you're well aware what a Machiavellian character I am. One only gives vicious shocks at the beginning.'

When I tackled him over his change of mind after he had presented his programme of cuts, he was caught off guard and made out that it was only in January 1999 that he had asked me to avoid any unwelcome shocks. This was a pitiful response. The 1999 budget, as Eichel himself well knew, had been passed by the cabinet in January. The economy measures that I had introduced in November or December had passed through parliament and had set the course of the election campaign in Hesse. Why had it not occurred to Eichel, as Finance Minister in Bonn, that Richard Dewes, Reinhard Klimmt, Walter Momper and Manfred Stolpe could also expect, as he himself did, that an SPD government would not rock the boat unnecessarily in the course of their own election campaigns?

In the event, as far as the elections in Hesse were concerned, there was no opposition from Bonn on either economic or financial grounds. But opposition came from a totally unexpected quarter. Otto Schily had been charged with revising the citizenship laws. The coalition agreement on this subject read as follows:

> At the heart of our social integration policy will be the creation of a modern legal definition of the right of citizenship. In this connection we propose two specific relaxations in the present law:
>
> - Children born of foreign parents in Germany will receive German citizenship at birth if one parent was born here or immigrated to Germany as a minor up to the age of 14 and is in possession of a resident's permit;
> - Assuming they have not been convicted of any criminal act and that they can prove an ability to support themselves, the following may apply for citizenship: male and female foreigners who have legally lived in the country for eight years; male and female foreign minors, at least one of whose parents has an indefinite right of residence, and who have lived in Germany with this parent as a family for a period of five years; foreign spouses of German citizens after having lived in the country legally for three years and provided that the family has lived together as a family for at least two years.

In both these cases the acquisition of German citizenship does not involve the renunciation of the applicant's previous citizenship.

We also propose to expedite and simplify the process of naturalization by abandoning unnecessary bureaucratic procedures.

Barely had Schily set to work on redrafting this legislation than the CDU seized on the phrase 'dual nationality' as an electoral issue. It was an unfortunate choice of term, implying to many people that foreigners were being given more rights than Germans. There was a lot of passionate argument. Each man or woman must pledge their loyalty to one country, it was said: one could not allow foreigners just to pick out the bits they liked from the legislation of two different countries.

In times of high unemployment and cuts in welfare payments people are in any case less tolerant towards the claims of foreigners, and latent feelings of self-protection are likely to find expression in acts of open hostility towards them. Hostels housing asylum-seekers and refugees have been set on fire, and young foreigners have been attacked and killed by gangs of German youths. Germans who cannot find work see foreigners as taking their own jobs away from them, and at rates of pay far below the norm. This threatening mood is further exacerbated by the ruthless wage-dumping practices of many firms. I have often invited people to try and imagine for themselves what a German worker would feel like if he were pushed out of his job by a foreigner prepared to work for a third of his wages or less.

During my time as mayor of Saarbrücken families used to come to me who had been waiting years for a council flat, only to find that these flats were being used to accommodate asylum-seekers. Such decisions, forced on housing authorities by circumstances, give rise to xenophobia. Since, as a rule, foreign families have more children than German families, older Germans, in particular, work out how much these foreign families get each time there is an increase in child allowance. And if such increases are combined with cuts in pensions, it is not hard to imagine how senior citizens react.

I always used to listen carefully when my eighty-four-year-old mother discussed these matters with others of her age, so as to learn for myself how the older generation viewed decisions of this kind. I have therefore long been one of those in the SPD who have worked towards some kind of compromise between the major parties in this question of asylum-seekers.

As the foundation of the compromise that was eventually arrived at, Wolfgang Schäuble proposed a so-called 'third country' solution. When I look back on this time, I still consider my support of this compromise agreement justified. Too large an influx of foreigners makes their integration into society almost impossible. But I was sorry to see that many of my friends took a different view. The writer Günter Grass was one of them. The left wing of the SPD also disapproved of the proposed compromise. As well as the issue of integration I pointed out that an influx of foreigners affected chiefly the poorer, more unprotected elements in society. The well-off have nothing to fear. On the contrary, they profit from the situation by being able to employ such foreigners as cheap labour.

I am convinced that without the compromise agreement on asylum-seekers the SPD would have lost its ability to secure a majority over the country as a whole. Although it was reached at the beginning of the 1990s, the agreement also lay at the root of our success in the election of 1998. Given this background, I did not consider it wise to force the agreement through the Bundestag with our red-green majority. By its very nature the question of citizenship is one that must in its essentials meet with the approval of the vast majority of the population. I therefore pressed more and more strongly for us to embark on discussions with the CDU/CSU, the other large popular party.

But in the wake of our great success at the polls in September, a number of my friends were not willing to take up my suggestion. On a number of occasions I talked the matter over with Gerhard Schröder and Otto Schily, who were both of the opinion that the Greens would not join with the CDU/CSU in such an action.

In January the CDU/CSU had started collecting signatures for its own petition, appealing to people's instinctive xenophobia. No amount of fine words and sophistries could disguise their real intention. And they succeeded in their aim. One person after another, some of them SPD voters, turned up at the CDU's booths and asked 'where they could sign the list against the foreigners'. Others asked 'where they could sign against the Turks'.

Worried by these developments, I tried to interest Hans Eichel in trying to find a common solution with the CDU/CSU. But my idea made no impression – my friends in the party, he said, who were now seeking approval for the solution agreed by the coalition parties, would not be able to understand such a change of tactics. So I suggested to the party executive that we might call on the two main church organizations to act as a kind of adjudicator between the two big parties. Some liked the idea but in the end it was defeated by those who were of the opinion that just we and the Greens together should draw up the new citizenship law.

Just before the Hesse elections an uneasy feeling came over me. I knew what it would mean if, so soon after our success in the national election, we were to lose in a high-profile *Land* like Hesse. Hesse's economic record was better than that of either Baden-Württemberg or Bavaria. Eichel and his team had turned in a good performance. Since Hesse was governed by a red-green coalition, its economic performance provided evidence that gave the lie to the prejudice, widely held in bourgeois circles, that red-green was incapable of conducting a successful economic policy. Nevertheless I felt in the course of the election campaign how uncertain of themselves my own party colleagues were.

The crucial factor was that the CDU electors were far more strongly motivated than ours. Their campaign proved to be 100 per cent successful, despite the fact that there had been a good deal of internal party wrangling. Many members of the CDU/CSU saw the campaign as anti-foreigner, and therefore offensive; a few local branches of the party and other organizations even refused to have any truck with it. But as so often in politics, the end justified the means.

So the CDU/CSU were fully satisfied, and we lost Hesse. In comparison with the federal election, our share of the vote slightly declined: in the federal election we had polled 41.6 per cent, in the *Land* elections 39.4 per cent. As the Green vote collapsed, we did not have enough for a red-green coalition government. That we only lost by a small margin, compared with the national election, proves that, in spite of the mistakes made by the Chancellor's Office, our policies still commanded the support of a large proportion of the electorate. If, in the *Land* elections in Brandenburg, the Saarland, Saxony and Thuringia, the SPD had lost only 2.2 per cent of the vote, as in the national election, they would be in a strong position today. But in the intermediate period Schröder's government had embarked on a change of tack, and the electors, men and women alike, turned their backs on us.

Immediately after the elections in Hesse I made the necessary changes in my own policies – this time, quite deliberately, without telling Schröder. Relations between us had become strained and I was annoyed that some weeks before the elections he had shown himself increasingly more reluctant to accept my suggestions. I also wanted to avoid a series of endless arguments within the red-green coalition based on the attitude 'let's seize our opportunity'. We eventually reached a compromise along the lines proposed by the government of Rhineland-Palatinate, a coalition of the SPD and the Liberals.

The setback in Hesse was a blow to me. As Party Chairman of the SPD I felt responsible for what had happened. The fact that I had put forward suggestions well beforehand in order to prevent such a defeat was no excuse in my eyes for my inability to carry those suggestions through. Those on the left of the party also showed little sympathy for my actions, any more than they had over the compromise on the question of the asylum-seekers. And although the majorities in the Bundesrat had changed, those on the left were also angry with me for having made so quickly for the emergency exit.

14

Germany and France

As a Saarländer I have learnt from history that the reconciliation of France and Germany is the foundation of European unity. One of the constants in French foreign policy has always been to prevent the rise of a strong power in the centre of Europe. In François Mauriac's well-known words, spoken at the time of the division of Germany into East and West: 'I am so fond of Germany that I am delighted there are two of them.'

On the last occasion when I saw François Mitterrand, I asked him who in French history most greatly impressed him, expecting to be given a run-down of his long-term policies towards Germany and Europe. But his answer came like a shot. 'Mazarin', he replied – and I suddenly remembered that he had called his daughter Mazarine. Mazarin stood in the tradition of his mentor Richelieu, who lived in fear of the emergence of a powerful nation in the centre of Europe. But there was also a saying in France in 1635, 'Richelieu for war, Mazarin for peace.' Richelieu was capable of fierce hatred – Mazarin was incapable of hating. As a result of his successful negotiations at the Peace of Westphalia in 1648 and the Peace of the Pyrenees in 1659, he secured the hegemony of France over Europe.

In his book *De l'Allemagne, de la France* Mitterrand wrote:

I have a dream that, through their geographical position and their historical rivalry, Germany and France have been chosen by fate to lead the way in the creation of a new Europe. Once they have become aware of having preserved what I have no hesitation in calling an instinct for grandeur, they will realise that a united Europe is a project of which they are fully worthy.

This is something of which they must convince themselves from the outset. France has always faced the temptation to retreat into its shell, clinging to an epic illusion of a grandeur in isolation. Germany, on the other hand, has been torn between a role anchored in the unity of Europe and that of an unacknowledged heir of imperialist ambitions.

No doubt I shall be told that what I am describing is a utopia. But what is a utopia? Either it is an absurdity – in which case time will not be slow to deliver its verdict – or is it merely an anticipation of a reality that is capable of achievement. If at this moment, when everything seems possible in Europe, a supreme effort of will is made, that utopia will become reality.

Mitterrand set about fulfilling this classic French aim of preventing the rise of a strong central European power by forcing through the Treaty of Amsterdam, which provided for economic and currency union. I had repeatedly drawn attention to these historical connections in committee meetings of the party, pointing out that the German Bundesbank had become a powerful central European force. 'La Buba', as the Bundesbank was called in France, had become the central European bank and the other European states, including France, were forced to follow its decisions.

This was a situation that posed considerable problems, particularly after German reunification, when the Bundesbank raised the bank rate to a record 8.75 per cent in order to restore price stability after the post-reunification boom. By putting a brake on the national economy in this way, the Bank caused mass unemployment and plunged the economies not only of Germany but also of all the other European states into recession. In other words, the Bundesbank was, and had been for a long time, a powerful European institution answerable only to itself. As the confrontation between rival nation states had come to the end of the road, Mitterrand's policy was more sensible than that of Margaret Thatcher, who wanted to prevent German reunification. She wrote in her memoirs:

> I was also very much aware of another feature of the EC, which had been apparent from its earliest days, continued to shape its development and diminish Britain's capacity to influence events – namely, the close relationship between France and Germany. Although this relationship may have seemed to depend on personal rapport – between President Giscard and Chancellor Schmidt, or President Mitterand and Chancellor Kohl – the truth is that it was explicable more in terms of history and perceptions of long-term interest. France has long feared the power of Germany and has hoped that by superior Gallic intelligence power can be directed in ways favourable to French interests.

Elsewhere Lady Thatcher expressed similar reservations over a federal Europe, regarding it as all too likely, in such a federation, that a reunited Germany would assume the dominant role, since it would be too big simply to remain one country among many.

Lady Thatcher was quite consistent in her efforts to prevent the reunification of Germany, for her concern, central to the traditions of British foreign policy, was with the establishment and preservation of the balance of power in Europe.

Nor were Lady Thatcher's worries confined to Europe. The ninety-five-year-old American diplomat George F. Kennan constantly expressed his doubts as to whether a unified Germany in the centre of Europe was in fact desirable. In May 1999 Kennan wrote:

> My reasons for supporting the plan for a partition of Germany were not primarily based on a belief that we non-Germans were in any way morally superior but sprang from doubts whether the other European countries would be prepared to accept the prospect of Germany as a great power again in the very heart of the continent. As long as the other European countries do not feel at ease in the company of Germany, so long, *vice versa*, will the Germans not feel at their ease in their relations with the others.
>
> By attempting to set itself above the European Union and make itself the focus of European unity, and by casting Germany alongside the United States as the most powerful military power on the European continent, Nato is in my view committing a blunder of historical proportions. In so doing, Nato commanders are invoking the return of all the evil spirits that have haunted the history of modern Europe. If the price of rectifying this ghastly error is the sacrifice of German unity, then I for one would be prepared to pay that price.

I am firmly convinced that Mitterrand and Kohl have delivered the appropriate answer to Kennan's fears by pressing forward with European unity and intensifying collaboration between Germany and France.

If German foreign policy fails to learn this lesson, Europe will find itself facing immense problems. This is one reason why I view with alarm how Foreign Minister Joschka Fischer is tending to take his lead from Madeleine Albright, and Chancellor Schröder expresses over and over his admiration of Tony Blair. Franco-German relations have deteriorated markedly in recent years. Take, for example, Chirac's arbitrary decision to resume French nuclear weapons tests, or to convert a conscript army into a professional army, or of the argument over who should be President of the European Central Bank. We therefore considered it our duty to create conditions that would promote a renewed rapprochement between France and Germany. I made my own contribution to this movement by embarking on an extremely close collaboration with the late Dominique Strauss-Kahn, one-time French Economics and Finance Minister.

Strauss-Kahn was the son of an Alsatian Jewish father and a Tunisian mother. He grew up in Agadir and learned his German from his German nurse. I had seen him at various joint meetings with the Parti Socialiste but came to know him more intimately in the Saarland. His *chef du cabinet* was François Villeroy, a descendant of the famous pottery firm of Villeroy and Boch. The present head of the family, Claude Villeroy, gave a party in the ancestral castle for Strauss-Kahn and his charming wife Anne Sinclair, the well-known French television presenter. Strauss-Kahn and I quickly discovered that we shared the same basic opinions on economic questions. After my resignation he described me in an interview with the *Süddeutsche Zeitung* as his friend – a pleasant change from those who confine their political friendships to those who hold posts in government.

I also frequently spoke on the telephone with Lionel Jospin, whom I had got to know and respect at the time when he was still First Secretary of the Parti Socialiste. Through the good offices of my old friend André Bord, the former General Secretary of the Gaullist movement, I was also in contact with Jacques Chirac.

Gerhard Schröder clearly found it difficult to contribute anything to improving Franco-German relations. I thought it a mistake on his part not to have accepted the French President's invitation to take part in the celebrations to mark the end of the First World War. In my eyes it showed a lack of political instinct. At the Potsdam summit Chirac and Schröder strutted around calling each other '*mon cher Gérard*' and '*mein lieber Jacques*', like two young people who had just become engaged, but Schröder had failed to realize that the situation required that both the Gaullist President and the socialist Prime Minister had to be wooed with equal affection by the German Chancellor.

After the Potsdam summit I raised the matter with Schröder, who then invited Lionel Jospin and his wife to Quedlinburg in order to straighten the situation out. I often wondered at the time what Willy Brandt would have said to all this. I remembered his verdict on Kurt Schumacher: 'He does not have sufficient understanding of Europe or of the world at large.'

In the course of preliminary discussions over Agenda 2000 the two friends, Chirac and Schröder, found themselves at cross-purposes. Schröder had gone out of his way to express his annoyance over the huge sums of money that were being wasted in Europe, and following in the footsteps of Edmund Stoiber, he protested loudly at the excessive contributions the Germans were making to the European budget.

At the same time he had failed to try and reach a compromise solution with the French which would have been acceptable to a majority of European countries.

As one who enjoyed the most cordial of relationships with France, I could only marvel at the lack of coordination in the way the Chancellor's Office prepared for Agenda 2000. And there was a price to be paid. For in contrast to the bombastic public announcements, the actual results that came out of the discussions were meagre. The whole thing was a damp squib. The preparations for the Berlin summit were a classic example of how not to do things in Europe. *Der Spiegel*, normally well-disposed towards Schröder, wrote: 'Gerhard Schröder's presidency of the European council has ended as it began – with big words. The much-vaunted achievements have failed to materialize. The clear winners in the discussions on Agenda 2000 at the Berlin summit in March were France, with its agricultural subsidies, while Blair successfully defended his billion-pound rebate and Spain, Finland and Ireland received more in grants than had been expected.'

The publication of the joint manifesto, *The Third Way*, by Tony Blair and Gerhard Schröder, before the European elections was a serious miscalculation with regard to France. It had been prepared by Bodo Hombach at Schröder's behest behind my back. Before the French elections and Jospin's victory Jospin and I had issued a joint statement, published in *Le Monde*. Since we had enjoyed a friendly rapport before his victory, Jospin took it as a matter of course that we would continue to work together afterwards, and when we came to form a government in Bonn, our friends in France had high hopes for the future. With a socialist President in Paris and a social-democratic Chancellor in Bonn, many in the Parti Socialiste found the stage now set for the creation of the kind of Europe they had long envisaged.

But they quickly became disillusioned. *The Third Way* was received with a great deal of suspicion in Paris. It was a hodge-podge of platitudes, together with a re-hash of principles enunciated by Anthony Giddens which had been common knowledge in Europe for a long time. Its principal concern was with economic policy, and it claimed to offer a new, supply-driven political agenda for the left. Everybody could read into it what they wanted. In Germany it was regarded as tantamount to the rejection of the policies with which the SPD had won the national election.

The sociologist Friedhelm Hengsbach wrote:

The aim appears to be to induce in European social democrats a heady mixture of what is new, what is modern, what is adaptable and what is flexible. New compared with what? In what way modern? Adaptable to what? And why flexible? Replies to such questions are based on stereotyped references to things like changed physical circumstances, economic and social change, the growing pace of social and economic transformation and the increasing pressure of the forces of globalization. We are expected to regard such developments as natural events or acts of God. It does not appear to have occurred to the authors of this manifesto that these developments might be the result of mistaken policies or reflections of a deliberate change of political direction.

So once again the fires of the artificial conflict between 'modernizers' and 'traditionalists' were stoked up. The main protagonists in this pantomime, whether politicians or journalists, are distinguished by their total ignorance of the facts. Blair has made many speeches ringing with the tones of neoliberalism but has not carried through neoliberal policies. Instead he first set about raising the taxes payable by large businesses, as we in Germany also did when the government first took up office. Then he introduced a set of measures to deal with youth unemployment; education, health and the infrastructure were also among his priorities. Classes in schools were too big, hospital waiting-lists were growing longer and longer, and the decrepit London Underground system had become a danger to public safety. The Treasury talked of a tradition of under-investment by successive governments.

The principal stated aim of the Labour government was therefore the modernization of the school system, the National Health Service and the public infrastructure. The Prime Minister gave more money for schools and hospitals, restored a few of the trade union rights rescinded by the Conservatives, adopted a pro-European stance and signed up to the European Social Charter. One measure that he did take over from the Major administration was the annual raising of the duty on petrol in order to lower taxes elsewhere. Petrol prices in Great Britain are the highest in the European Community and would rouse a howl of protest in Germany. Self-styled 'modernizers' here would already be pronouncing the last rites over the economic corpse of Germany.

Despite this rejection of the policies of the Thatcher and Major eras voices have started to be heard asking where precisely the achievements of New Labour can be found. Under the heading 'The Irresponsible Resident of No. 10 Downing Street Trips Up', the *Handelsblatt* wrote on 20 July 1999:

It is taking a long time to deliver results. The modernization of the National Health Service has not taken off, and hospital waiting-lists have barely got any shorter. There is a shortage of doctors and nurses across the board, while demoralized staff complain about poor pay and long hours.

Nor are conditions any better in the schools. The government is making determined efforts to raise standards but is all too often frustrated by the lethargy of the teachers or too large classes. According to John Prescott, the minister in overall charge of transport policy, the privatized rail network is a 'national scandal' – a dismal picture of out-of-date track, old rolling stock, overcrowded carriages and late arrivals. The same features are threatening to bring the London Underground grinding to a halt.

And if you want to go abroad to avoid this chaos, you find yourself having to join the queue. A computerized system designed by Siemens for the British passport office could not handle the thousands of applications from people wanting to travel abroad – a fiasco for what Blair had proudly promoted as 'public–private partnership'.

Is this the model we ought to adopt in our search for a 'modern Germany'? Professor Jörg-Dietrich Hoppe, President of the German Medical Association, has warned us against going down the same road as the British National Health Service.

Something else to remember is that the Schröder–Blair paper was drafted by people with an inadequate grasp of Giddens's proposals for modernization. Basically Giddens makes four proposals.

Firstly, globalization requires nation states to collaborate more closely with each other. The Schröder–Blair declaration has virtually nothing to say on this subject. Giddens, on the other hand, inveighs persistently against worldwide market fundamentalism: 'The regulation of financial markets is the single most pressing issue in the world economy, in the wake of the Mexican crisis of 1994 and the succeeding troubles in South East Asia. Here as everywhere deregulation isn't the same as freedom, and a global commitment to free trade depends upon effective regulation rather than dispenses with the need for it.'

Giddens deduces, correctly, that of the daily currency transactions, amounting to 1 billion dollars per day, only 5 per cent involve trade. The remaining 95 per cent are speculative dealings and arbitrage transactions, because dealers who are used to investing huge sums are looking to make quick profits from exchange rate and interest rate fluctuations. These activities distort the signals that the markets give to long-term financial instruments and to trade. It would have helped matters if Blair, in particular, who a few months earlier had pressed for the reform of the Bretton Woods institutions, had insisted on at least mentioning this vital subject. There would have been no difficulty in referring here to the article that Strauss-Kahn and I had written for *Le Monde* and *Die Zeit*.

Giddens's second point concerns the equality of women at work and in society, which he regards as one of the greatest challenges to modernization. But Blair's and Schröder's scriptwriters make only trivial reference to this.

The third of Giddens's modernization projects is the ecological renewal of industrial society. The Blair–Schröder paper contains only commonplace statements like: 'We must combine responsibility for the environment with a modern market-economy initiative. As regards conservation, the latest technologies consume fewer resources, open new markets and create jobs.'

Lastly, Giddens considers the modernization of the welfare state, taking his lead from Scandinavian initiatives towards formulating an active employment policy. 'Back to work' is the English slogan, which implies the creation of opportunities for further education and training so that the unemployed can be offered new job possibilities.

Strictly speaking, the Blair–Schröder manifesto would be hardly worth mentioning, had it not come at a welcome moment in the fashionable ongoing public discussion on the subjects it raises. Benny Mikfeld, chairman of the Young Socialists, justifiably described it as a concoction of sociological banalities and restrained neoliberal polemics, while Heinz Putzhammer, representing the German trade union organization, said that the two authors had opened the necessary public debate on modernization by launching an historically blind attack on the welfare state.

Ralf Dahrendorf, for his part, spoke of an empty dogmatism full of glittering but hollow words which betokened nothing more than a will to power.

In the European elections Blair and Schröder suffered heavy losses, while Jospin, the 'traditionalist', emerged as the winner. In *Die Zeit* Roger De Weck wrote scornfully: 'The Frenchman gained people's confidence; the Englishman and the German frolicked around like a glamorous pair of media stars – David Copperfield and Claudia Schiffer. They are frequently to be seen in each other's company but where is the substance?'

Die Zeit joined in the game by quoting sections of the CDU's Godesberg Programme under the heading 'Confidential SPD Document':

A central feature of modern industry and commerce is a constant pressure towards increasing centralization and more and more mergers. Not only does big business determine the development of the economy and our standard of living – it also changes the whole structure of industry and society. Giant concerns that control billions of dollars and thousands of employees are not just forces in the economy but also dominate the lives of human beings. The dependence of workers and employees goes far beyond economic and material considerations. Through their cartels and their employers' organizations the captains of industry have gained a degree of control over the conduct of affairs of state that is no longer compatible with democratic principles. They are usurping the powers of the state. Economic power is becoming political power. This development is a challenge to all those for whom liberty and human dignity, justice and social security constitute the foundations of human society. The paramount obligation of an independent economic policy is therefore to rein in the power of big business. The state and society must not be allowed to become the prey of powerful pressure groups . . .

Common ownership is a legitimate form of public control which no modern state can do without. It serves to preserve freedom from the domination of powerful economic blocs. In the world of big business power has come to rest in the hands of managers who themselves are the servants of anonymous forces. As a result the voices of those in private industry have largely been drowned. The fundamental question today is that of economic power.

This was the proper answer to the pallid Schröder–Blair statement of principles, which in normal times would have been dismissed as an exercise in fashionable window-dressing and consigned to the waste basket. At the very moment when we needed a new pattern of Social-Democrat policies, a global conception of politics, we were presented with a demand that politics should impose on itself a self-denying ordinance. Yet only shortly before Giddens had maintained that globalization demanded not less politics but more.

Jospin disassociated himself from the Schröder–Blair declaration. Addressing his friends in the party who had gathered to celebrate their victory, he said: 'We are different, because we keep faith with ourselves. As a modern party of the left we shall follow our own path.' Furthermore he could not resist pointing to the superior economic statistics for France. In July 1999 *Manager-Magazin*, a journal free of any suspicion of massaging the data to suit the socialists' case, wrote:

It looks as though the German Chancellor could learn a thing or two from his comrades in France. French economic success cannot be dismissed as a seven-day wonder . . . Last year the French economy grew at a faster rate than at any time since 1989, and in 1999, for the second time running, the rate is expected to be one point higher than in Germany.

Particularly impressive is the improvement in the employment situation. At present some 300,000 people fewer are in employment in Germany than in 1994; in France, on the other hand, 750,000 new jobs were created over the same five years . . . Basically Jospin, like the red-green coalition in Bonn, is basing his policies on the principle of social justice, or increased demand. Since 1997 the minimum wage has risen, as have public sector pensions and school fees. In order to reduce government borrowing, taxes on businesses were raised, and since 1997 the self-employed and investors have also had to pay part of their insurance contributions . . . While setting out to balance the national budget, the government avoided introducing excessively harsh measures. This prudent course seems to many observers to be the secret of France's success.

Whose ears would not be burning after hearing this? After I had resigned from the government the collaboration between Dominique Strauss-Kahn and my successor Hans Eichel left a lot to be desired. The French gained the impression that there was an uncritical return on the part of the Germans to neoliberal supply-side policies, and that Hans Tietmeyer again had the final word.

On Franco-German relations in general the *Handelsblatt* wrote as follows:

The European election campaign has had strange results. At the end of May the social-democratic Prime Ministers met in Paris in order to promote the cause of a 'social Europe'. All was harmony and light between Premier Jospin, Chancellor Schröder and Prime Minister Blair. A week later came the first sign of discord – at the European summit in Cologne the concept of a 'social Europe' was quietly dropped with the undermining of the employment pact. Finally Schröder and Blair showed themselves in their true colours as radical liberals whose aim was to liberate the economy from the fetters of the state. The question of employment was no longer on the agenda. Europe was to become liberal, and only afterwards – maybe – social.

I cannot recall ever witnessing such an ideological U-turn, so foolhardy and so abrupt. But there was a snag – in so doing, Schröder forfeited his credibility with his electors and with his partners at home and abroad. One cannot take a man seriously who in the autumn of 1998 vents his wrath on those who show a lack of compassion for those left out in the cold, only to turn his back six months later on the whole principle of social democracy. One of the first consequences of this irresponsible, attention-seeking change of policy was a palpable cooling of Franco-German relations.

Nor was the attitude of the Green ministers in the Schröder government particularly conducive to promoting good relations with France. Itself a nuclear power, France gave a frosty reception to Fischer's demand for a renunciation of the right of first strike, while Trittin's diplomatic *faux pas* in Paris in January 1999 produced a howl of indignation. Trittin had announced Germany's intention to revoke the Hague treaties, pleading *force majeure*, without paying a single pfennig in compensation. The French had a fit.

In addition to the ill feeling provoked by political actions, there were resentments caused by decisions made outside the areas over which politicians had direct influence. For example there was the toing and froing in the negotiations between DASA and Aerospatiale, the agreement between the financial centres of London and Frankfurt, and the negotiations between Deutsche Telekom and France Telekom. Even when Hoechst merged with the French drugs giant Rhône-Poulenc, there were mutterings about a take-over. The French complained that Bonn had not provided any funds for a joint reconnaissance satellite. Conversely, Fischer claimed during the negotiations at Rambouillet that he had been hoodwinked by the French and the British.

However one chooses to look at such individual cases, the deterioration in Franco-German relations will have serious consequences for Europe as a whole. Whether one sets Anglo-Saxon culture above French culture is irrelevant. What counts in foreign policy are sober assessments of the situation and a clear definition of one's own interests. No country is so dependent on the achievement of European unity as Germany. And that unity can only be achieved in collaboration with France. Great Britain will continue to follow its own line for the foreseeable future.

Yet it had all started so encouragingly. Dominique Strauss-Kahn and I had set out in the clearest possible terms the reasons for the necessity for a European economic and financial policy:

> Europe has embarked on one of the most ambitious enterprises in its history – the creation of a common currency, the euro. The new currency opens up fresh possibilities for us to promote economic growth and employment, to confront the challenges of globalization, and to contribute to financial stability and development in the world . . . At the same time the pursuit of stability cannot be advanced as an excuse for national governments and banks failing to play their part in formulating economic policy and acknowledging their responsibility to provide employment . . .
>
> - The problem of unemployment must be tackled at the European level by the creation of a growth-oriented macroeconomic environment and the fulfilment to the greatest extent possible of our objectives in employment policy;
> - On the international level, building on the introduction of the euro

and acting in concert with our G-7 partners, we must stabilize the world economy against the knock-on effects of any untoward shocks. In traditional debates the protagonists of structural reform are still presented as the opponents of the advocates of macroeconomic control but this merely distracts attention from the political tasks that lie before us, since in order to wipe out unemployment, a dual strategy is required;

- We need a more effective policy mix in order to sustain non-inflationary economic growth and to maintain a climate of social peace. This requires the most efficient combination possible of wages and income development, fiscal policy and budgetary consolidation.

The rigid neoliberal insistence on the deregulation of the labour market has contributed more to the blocking of reforms than it has to the creation of jobs. We are convinced that Europe as a social model is a positive, not a negative step . . . Furthermore there is a need for a new transatlantic dialogue. The euro and the dollar will together cover the greater part of international financial transactions. This means that exchange-rate movements between the dollar and the euro will determine the course of the world economy . . . The Euro-11 group of nations must monitor exchange-rate movements and formulate a coherent joint approach. We also need to be in a position to maintain this approach *vis-à-vis* the markets and avail ourselves of those regulations which are designed to permit the operation of general guidelines for exchange rates.

This is of particular importance in the context of the introduction of the euro. The world's markets must be made aware that we would not welcome any substantial appreciation in the value of the euro . . . We should set out as a group to agree exchange-rate systems with countries in Asia and Latin America, as well as in central and eastern Europe, which have demonstrated their ability to maintain a convincing balance between flexibility and discipline. The European Union should seek to extend cooperation in the currency field to include the new applicants for admission to the Union.

Carlo Ciampi, Dominique Strauss-Kahn and I were of the opinion, as was Helmut Schmidt, that the International Monetary Fund (IMF) had come too much under the influence of the Federal Reserve and Wall Street. We therefore drew up plans to coordinate the way we should vote in the Bretton Woods institutions, in particular the IMF. This would have been a significant change. In particular it would enable the Europeans to prevent the Fund from being used to cover the risks of American investors with public money.

How accurately we had assessed the situation emerged from an article written in July 1999 in the *Deutsches Allgemeines Sonntagsblatt* by Werner Mayer-Larsen, in which he gave a character sketch of Larry Summers, the new American Treasury Secretary:

In terms of their economic and political beliefs, there is not a shred of difference between Rubin and Summers. They both demand open borders for the movement of capital and goods, deregulation and the disbandment of national bureaucracies but at the same time effective international institutions. Both men see the World Bank and the IMF as organs of American global policy, at least as long as there is no sign of a European management of this kind that demands to be taken seriously. A man like Lafontaine would have been the last person they wanted.

Rubin and Summers were not blind to the fact that Strauss-Kahn and I were out to establish a counterbalance to one-sided American policies that had regard only to American interests.

Together with Gordon Brown, whom we had invited to join our discussions, we agreed to coordinate our fiscal policies more closely. Ciampi, Strauss-Kahn and I, at least, were not impressed with the stability pact concluded by previous conservative governments. Massimo d'Alema, the Italian Premier, took a similar view. Consolidation is only possible in conditions of growth. Any attempt to consolidate in a recession is doomed to failure. I know of no example, anywhere in the world, where in conditions of recession it proved possible to consolidate budgets by the introduction of stricter economy measures.

At a Franco-German colloquium in Saarbrücken some time after my resignation I called it a scandal that participants at a Franco-German summit meeting could not converse in each other's language. Either they needed an interpreter or they talked in broken English. There were a few exceptions among the French – Roland Dumas, Pierre Chevènement and Dominique Strauss-Kahn all spoke excellent German. But on the German side the situation was pitiful. Nothing opens the way to a nation's culture like a knowledge of the language.

I therefore consider it necessary for us to create joint Franco-German institutions in order to train political and cultural elites better equipped to organize collaboration between the two countries. A Franco-German university, or a set of research institutes, staffed half by Frenchmen, half by Germans, would be a step in the right direction. I would even go so far as to propose the establishment of a bilingual Ecole Nationale d'Administration, in which, adopting the model of the ENA, the political and administrative personnel of both countries could be trained. Franco-German cooperation, of the kind enthusiastically called for at the Potsdam conference, needs to be put on a new footing if the interests of Europe are to be furthered.

The *Frankfurter Allgemeine Zeitung* had its own assessment of the Schröder–Blair manifesto:

What Schröder has to fear – probably to a greater extent than Blair – is the social-democratization of the people at large. The widespread anger at the removal of the tiny concession on casual earnings should not mislead us into thinking that the majority of Germans are wildly enthusiastic over the prospect of the age of the post-welfare state. That will come. That the Social Democrats cannot prevent it, and are well advised not to try, is a truth that the Schröder–Blair paper acknowledges. The most powerful leaders of the social-democratic parties have announced the end of the social-democratic age. But the age is taking its time in responding to the announcement.

The *Land* elections in Bremen and the European elections both showed that Schröder and Blair have good grounds for fearing the 'social-democratization of the people'. In Bremen the SPD polled 7.6 per cent less than at the general election. In view of the fact that previously it had done even worse, owing to the defection of a splinter group, the public's reaction was remarkable. The SPD were hailed as the real victors in Bremen, and several papers carried commentaries suggesting that the SPD could win again a second time.

But in the face of this decline of 7.6 per cent, compared with the general election, it was predictable that in the European elections, which traditionally show a poor turnout of SPD voters, we would lose by around 10 per cent. This is precisely what happened.

After the European elections I read in the papers that Gerhard Schröder had come to the conclusion that by delivering on our electoral promises concerning taxes, child allowance, pensions, health, protection against summary dismissal and sick pay, we had forfeited our economic competence. In the Bundestag debate on globalization in June 1999 Wolfgang Schäuble, a skilful tactician, stuck his knife in the wound and declared that Schröder had it in mind to break his electoral pledges to pensioners and the unemployed. The *Frankfurter Allgemeine Zeitung* reported: 'The conflict that arose from this situation must plunge everyone who is concerned to see a comprehensive modernization programme carried out in Germany into a state of despair. While the Social Democrats govern, the CDU opposition plays at social democracy, presenting itself as the protector of the little man and custodian of the sacred pension. Schäuble's words showed him to be closer at that moment to Lafontaine than Schröder was.

The results of the elections and the findings of the opinion polls showed Schäuble to be right. There is no way of driving social-democratism out of the public consciousness.

15

International Fiscal Policy

The liberalization of the world's capital markets in the 1980s was a political decision. It is important to emphasize this because so often the impression is given that it was a God-given development. It had become increasingly fashionable to justify decisions taken against the interests of the majority of the population by saying: 'If we don't do this, the markets will punish us' – meaning the international money markets. A revolution had taken place. Money was not exchanged on the international market in order to promote trade or investment but in order to make a speculative short-term profit. It was as though a worldwide casino had been opened, the difference being that instead of people investing their own money, hedge funds, in particular, borrowed money from the bank and used it to speculate in international investments. If anything went awry, it was not only the hedge funds that were in trouble but also the banks who had lent the money.

Hedge funds are highly speculative investment houses which gamble on macroeconomic developments and are in a position to deal over the short term with sums of money far in excess of their capital deposits.

In September 1998 Long Term Capital Management (LTCM), the star of the hedge funds, almost brought the world financial system grinding to a halt. They had bet exceptionally high sums of money in the casino. Their own capital amounted to a few billion dollars: at times they wagered up to 100 billion. When Russia became insolvent in August 1998, the value of its state securities fell drastically. LTCM and others were forced to sell so-called long positions, whose prices collapsed, resulting in a vicious circle of falling prices and dwindling bank balances. Almost all large hedge funds and all the big banks were involved, and the entire international financial and credit system was threatened with melt-down. Help arrived in the form of the Federal Reserve, which instructed a number of large banks to assist in keeping LTCM afloat. The situation was also helped by a rapid fall in interest rates in the USA.

When I read that Alan Greenspan and Bob Rubin were competing for the job of bank regulator, I quickly found an explanation. Both men had recognized that the regulation of American banks left a considerable amount to be desired. In Hong Kong hedge funds behaved even more outrageously, combining to speculate against the Hong Kong dollar. The banking world spoke of organized speculation. In view of the consequences of this irresponsible behaviour it would be more appropriate to speak of organized criminality.

In the wake of the crises in Mexico and Asia, and subsequently also in Brazil and South America as a whole, more and more politicians began to talk of the need to create a new world financial structure in which such scandalous developments would be avoided. Many years ago Alan Greenspan, who has far less confidence in the virtues of the market than his European colleagues, warned that the buoyancy of the markets might soon get out of control.

Most supporters of a deregulated global financial market overlook the fact that in these markets prices do not follow the laws of supply and demand but are based on predictions and expectations, together with various psychological factors. Price movements are therefore often irrational and can cause gross economic distortions. Since the concept of 'shareholder value' has come to dominate the banks' boardrooms, they have neglected their classical function. A person who is looking for a return of 15 per cent or more cannot do business with banks in their traditional form. In order to make 'a quick buck', one must enter the field of currency speculation. But to my surprise the social-democratic parties have paid scant heed to the political consequences of the deregulation of the international financial markets.

Nor did I myself have the slightest inkling, for many years, of the way the international financial markets behaved. Only with the discussions on globalization and the German national economy did I begin to take a closer interest in the subject. I came to see that social-democratic policies would in future only be viable if the world's financial markets changed their way of operating. Even the founding fathers of socialist and social-democratic parties realized that a society cannot be called just if profits are privatized but losses socialized.

That, however, is precisely what is happening in the international money markets. The most striking example is the crisis in Mexico.

American investors, in particular, had made speculative investments in order to reap high profits. When the peso came under pressure, the Mexican taxpayers had to bear the consequences and a cry for help went out to the International Monetary Fund. The Europeans, who are also members of the IMF, could do little more than nod their approval of whatever the Americans proposed.

But the International Monetary Fund administers the money, not of private investors, but of the international community, that is to say, taxpayers' money. This money was used to underwrite the financial risks of American investors and thereby avoid disastrous consequences for the American and international banking systems.

Put another way: high-risk speculation and irresponsible amounts of credit from the banks were made risk-free with taxpayers' money. Deregulation, regarded as a self-vindicating procedure, ends up with the destruction of the market economy, i.e. with the nationalization of the risks of depositors. And what happened in Mexico more or less repeated itself in Asia. Any social democrat worth his salt must take issue with the political problem that lies at the root of these developments. We cannot allow a situation to arise in which, worldwide, investors' losses are socialized while their profits remain privatized.

Interestingly enough, the same demand was made by conservative national and private banks, which had simply come to realize that such developments could no longer be tolerated. I received a letter from the Chairman of a London bank at this time, in which he told me that, although he had been a supporter of the liberalization and deregulation of the financial markets all his professional life, and had done his utmost to secure the acceptance of this principle in the international financial market, he was shocked to see over the last five years how the system had been abused by ruthless speculative investors who had no qualms about plunging national economies and whole nations into a state of crisis. Well-meaning politicians, he went on, who supported the processes of deregulation and liberalization, totally underestimate the effects of a deregulated worldwide financial system. Although, he concluded, the allocation of capital must be largely left to the market, a balance must be restored by the deliberate intervention of government in the markets.

There have long been demands for private moneylenders to share the risks inherent in their activities but in practice nothing has happened. According to the heads of government of the G-7 countries and their Finance Ministers, the recent crises in Asia, Latin America and Russia have made it clear that the international community must improve its procedures for avoiding and dealing with financial crises and for adapting them to a greater extent to the guidelines that control the workings of open capital markets.

At the G-7 conference in 1999 the heads of government also declared that the financial burden of serious crises such as those in South-East Asia and Latin America could no longer be borne entirely by public institutions such as the WMF and the World Bank, operating with taxpayers' money. Thus pressure must be brought to bear on private creditors to shoulder greater individual responsibility for the investment decisions they make. Decisions on granting credits must be based more on an assessment of the potential risks and returns of an investment, and no longer in the expectation that, if things go wrong, public money will be available to protect creditors from any unwelcome consequences. But again, little progress has been made in this direction.

A further possible means of putting a stop to international speculation would be to slow down the short-term movement of capital. The situation requires not deregulation but regulation.

Thus James Tobin, a Nobel prizewinner, suggested imposing a tax on the movement of capital in order to restrict such movements. Chile, for example, does this, and has declared the measure successful. In a whole series of speeches and discussions I constantly emphasized that the key to bringing worldwide financial speculation under control lay in the regulation of short-term movements of capital. In the beginning I was vehemently attacked by the apostles of the creed of supply-side policies but in May 1999 I discovered that Bob Rubin, the American Secretary of the Treasury, and Hans Tietmeyer, President of the Bundesbank, were both pleading for the control of short-term movements of capital. The criticism to which my ideas were subjected lacked all sense of balance and objectivity. Nowhere save in Germany was the supply-side credo of deregulation so passionately adhered to.

The *Frankfurter Allgemeine Zeitung* scoffed that we were gradually making ourselves look ridiculous. But the real vituperation began when, in order to stabilize exchange rates, we suggested a series of bands or zones, internationally agreed, in particular between the dollar, the euro and the yen. It was almost as though there had never been a successful European currency system with bands or zones for the various European currencies.

The origin of this proposal had been cunningly concealed. In 1994 a commission under Paul Volcker, a former Chairman of the Federal Reserve, had put forward the idea of currency zones. The members of the commission included financial experts from all over the world, among them Karl Otto Pöhl, former President of the Bundesbank. The commission had of course pointed out that a precondition for more stable exchange rates was a convergence of the corresponding economic policies, and it recommended that, on a national level, efforts should be made to ensure lasting growth, price stability and stable exchange rates through agreed monetary and fiscal policies. A Keynesian fiscal policy, the commission concluded, would contribute a great deal to the achievement of stability, while international collaboration between the industrialized nations should be further encouraged, with the aim of achieving a greater degree of macroeconomic convergence. In the medium term common goals for stability and growth need to be set, and the various economic cycles have to be synchronized.

Because Rubin and Greenspan were sceptical of the Volcker Commission's remedies, people in Germany frequently quoted them when criticizing my own proposals. I was interested to observe, however, that at the G-7 summit in Bonn in February 1999 the Americans did not reject the introduction of currency exchange zones as brusquely as the Germans maintained. The Americans still had in their minds the Plaza and Louvre Treaties, which pointed in the same direction and had been concluded at their express wish.

In the course of the interesting debate Greenspan and Rubin pronounced themselves rather to be in favour of close collaboration between the various central banks; one should beware, however, of making dogmatic commitments, and if the central banks were to intervene, it would have to be done by surprise. Public statements would only encourage speculation. In view of what had been happening throughout the world I found these arguments convincing.

Frictions arose when we read in the Annual Economic Review that the German government did not intend to support the introduction of currency zones. I was not able to correct this passage in the Review because the text was already printed and published. After the statements of recent weeks the declaration in the Review caused confusion. When I challenged the experts in the ministry, they explained that the term 'currency zones' came too close to a complex concept put forward by two American economists, Fred Bergsten and John Williamson, and was one we should deliberately avoid. The arguments were comprehensible to experts but difficult to convey to the public, and we were forced unnecessarily onto the defensive. Things improved somewhat when the Japanese Finance Minister, Kiichi Miyazawa, and his deputy, Eisuke Sakakibara, adopted our plan. The stabilization of exchange rates is, incidentally, also a concern of smaller emerging economies, which are becoming more and more dependent on the decisions of the financial markets.

In July 1999 the *Frankfurter Allgemeine Zeitung* published an article under the heading 'Argentinian Presidential Candidate Introduces Note of Discord – Negative Reaction from Wall Street to Discussion on Debt Moratorium'. The paper said:

> The high level of American share prices at the present time makes the financial markets very sensitive to the slightest suspicion of bad news. It only takes a casual remark from Eduardo Duhalde, candidate for the Argentinian presidency, to cast a shadow over the basically positive atmosphere on the stock exchange produced by good quarterly results from American industries. If he wins the election, says Duhalde, he intends to press, with the support of the Pope, for a one-year moratorium on Argentina's foreign debts. Wall Street then recalled that one-fifth of America's trade with Latin America is with Argentina, and that Argentina is the third-largest economy in the region. An early reaction was to increase the risk premium on the shares of banks which traded extensively with Latin American countries.

At the same time press agencies were reporting that Goldman Sachs had invited both Argentinian presidential candidates and their prospective Finance Ministers to New York in order to reassure investors. But is it really the job of a Wall Street company to invite Argentinian politicians to New York in order to warn them that a future President of their country would be well advised to take account of opinions on Wall Street? As I read this report, I saw the face of the cool, smiling Bob Rubin in front of me. He had been Chairman of Goldman Sachs before becoming Treasury Secretary.

The real reason for Rubin's appeal to Wall Street lies in the fact that the consumer boom in the USA is to be traced to the overvaluation of shares on the stock exchange. There is thus a broad consensus in the country between government, central bank and political parties to avoid anything that might bring the high-flying Dow Jones crashing to the ground. Interestingly enough it is not only the Democrats, who have always been funded by Wall Street, who support this policy but also the Republicans, who are traditionally funded by industry. But since the concept of shareholder value has come to dominate industry and the salaries of American industrial bosses have been geared to shareholder value, the Republicans too have had to take notice of the interests of Wall Street.

The *Süddeutsche Zeitung* wrote under the heading 'President For Sale': 'It would be naive to think that a candidate or a party could collect millions of dollars solely in order to defend its own ideals and programmes . . . An election campaign run on US dollars leaves a future President of the United States no choice but to show his gratitude later. In the last analysis it is the citizens who pay, and the price gets higher and higher.' To which needs to be added, that the highest price is paid by the citizens of those countries which are the principal sufferers at times of international financial crisis – the men and women of South-East Asia, Russia and South America.

The problem of the exchange rates between dollar, euro and yen cropped up again a few weeks after I resigned my position in the government. German neoliberals complained that the euro had become too weak, although our exports profited considerably from this situation. Then we read that the Japanese central bank was intervening in the currency market. This step was justified by Eisuke Sakakibara on the ground that an overly strong yen was threatening Japan's economic recovery. The Japanese had apparently set themselves a specific aim, namely to hold the yen at a rate of 120 to the dollar. In September this rate began to rise again, with investors banking on a recovery of the Japanese economy. Whereupon the Japanese central bank intervened once more.

It was with a certain *schadenfreude* that I watched the members of the European Central Bank entangling themselves in contradictions when they were asked whether they too had a fixed rate of exchange in mind as part of their monetary policy. The European Central Bank, indeed, had strongly criticized the German Finance Minister's statements on the setting of exchange rates. It is, of course, only as it should be that a national bank should in the first instance guarantee price stability within its own national boundaries. But it is equally clear that it cannot stand idly by and watch while the exaggerated reactions of the money markets lead to negative economic consequences at home. In fact it was only a matter of time before the European Central Bank also had to admit that it could not remain entirely indifferent to the exchange rate.

All this came into the open in June 1999. The European Central Bank confirmed that it had intervened in the markets at the request of the Japanese. It had bought euros and sold yen, with the result that the yen weakened from 123 to the euro to 125. On 21 July the Japanese central bank intervened again to prevent a rise in the rate of the yen to the dollar. The Federal Reserve also became involved, buying dollars for yen by arrangement with the Japanese central bank. While the dust was still settling on the verbal battles over the stabilization of exchange rates, the biggest central banks had the good sense to work together to actually achieve this stabilization. This was precisely what we had demanded.

The greatest wrath that the disciples of neoliberalism showered on my head, however, was when I challenged a taboo by daring to recommend that the European national banks should reduce their interest rates. True, a number of chief economists of German merchant banks had already demanded cuts in interest rates. But after I argued along the same lines, they withdrew and made out that I was talking the euro down. They had come to recognize, correctly, that with falling exports a strong euro was not in Europe's interest. They also realized that, as a rule, falls in interest rates do not result in a stronger currency. But as I had been made the bogeyman of the orthodox thinkers, everybody agreed that it was I, Oskar Lafontaine, who was to blame for the weak euro.

In fact the value of the euro was a direct reflection of economic developments in America and in Europe. The American economy was booming, whereas in Europe it was down in the dumps. Consequently interest rates were higher in America and potential yields more attractive. So investors preferred to go into dollars rather than into euros.

The investment bank Lehman Brothers recently put forward another argument. They pointed out that the growing number of cross-border takeovers and mergers was having a growing influence on exchange rates; the rate of the euro to the dollar was the most markedly affected by this, and might partly explain the present weakness of the euro, because more European firms are buying up American firms than vice versa. If such a deal is for cash, this will produce an additional demand for dollars, because one result of the announcement of a takeover is generally to make the firm that is taken over more attractive to investors. The increased interest in the shares of this firm will then lead to further movements of capital, which in their turn will result in changes in interest rates.

After my resignation the euro strengthened for a while, then fell back further and further. When I introduced Horst Ehmke's book *The Euro-Coup* in Frankfurt, I took the opportunity to mock my adversaries by telling my audience how frustrated I was to see that in spite of my resignation the euro was still falling. It was a blow to my self-esteem, I complained ironically: I had grossly overrated my influence – so had my opponents.

There were two amusing moments during the G-7 summit in Bonn in February 1999. On one occasion Hans Tietmeyer felt moved to make the extravagant claim that it was not only nominal interest rates that were at a record low but also real interest rates. The bank rate was 3.3 per cent at the time. I offered to wager with him that he was wrong, because I had the graph of interest rate movements firmly in my head, and knew that we did have lower real interest rates in earlier years. There was a good deal of grinning and smirking among the other G-7 members when Tietmeyer declined to accept my wager.

There was a still more amusing episode. When the Americans asked Wim Duisenberg what could be done to encourage consumer spending in the European countries, he gave the usual answer: monetary policy had played its part, national budgets had to be consolidated and labour markets needed structural reform. This was too much for Paul Martin, the Canadian Finance Minister. He had heard this old yarn time and again, he fumed: the Finance Ministers complain that the European stability pact leaves them no room for manoeuvre, while those in charge of monetary policy say that they have tried everything but that the only way out of the situation lies in the structural reform of the labour markets. Since the Americans had stimulated their economy through a fiscal and monetary policy of expansion, there was no way they were going to be convinced by the arguments of Tietmeyer and Duisenberg. Both sides were obviously on the defensive.

Kiichi Miyazawa, Dominique Strauss-Kahn and I smiled. At the press conference that followed, I suggested that my position and that of the Americans were in fact not so far apart, adding that my repeated call for a strengthening of domestic demand in European countries had the unreserved support of the Americans.

When Tietmeyer then delivered the profound observation that the essential factor was the expectations of the investors, the journalists present grinned because they saw their prejudices confirmed and that Tietmeyer had taken me down a peg again. It is somehow impossible to get across to those committed to supply-side policies that a man who intends to open a shop or a pub somewhere first has to ask whether he will attract a sufficient number of customers. The neoliberals are convinced that investors will gain confidence if welfare benefits are cut, economies are made in public expenditure and wage restraint is exercised.

A different picture was emerging on the European front. The collaboration between Strauss-Kahn and myself had succeeded in liberating the two strongest economies in the Euro-zone from the grip of orthodoxy. We frequently discussed with each other how we could persuade the European Central Bank to follow the American example and pursue an expansive monetary policy. We openly promised to adhere to the stability pact so as not to provide national banks with an excuse not to lower interest rates. By the end of 1998 all the economic indicators pointed to the need for a cut in interest rates. After my demand for such a cut had been roundly criticized, the European national banks settled at the end of December on a rate of 3 per cent.

On that same day I travelled to Ottawa and Washington for initial discussions with Paul Martin, Canadian Finance Minister, and Bob

Rubin, American Treasury Secretary. Referring to the pointless discussion on the stability pact, I said to the journalists accompanying me on the plane: '3 per cent is 3 per cent for the base rate too.' The fact that, in spite of noisy pronouncements to the contrary, interest rates had in fact been cut and my demand vindicated on economic grounds, earned me no friends – a situation in which I frequently found myself. The business journals that had claimed to possess superior knowledge and previously rejected my plea for a reduction in interest rates as being without foundation, now changed their tune and maintained that mine was an opinion they had always shared. At the same time they were on the look-out for the next opportunity to parade their prejudices and dislikes where I was concerned.

Although I could see no point in the childish insistence that Finance Ministers should not make statements on monetary policy lest they compromise the independence of the national banks, I sought to continue the debate in private. In a confidential discussion with Wim Duisenberg I said that in my view the banks should do more, pointing out that in America the short-term real interest rate at the time of recession was nil and not 2.3 per cent, as stated by the European Central Bank in its report of March 1999. He replied that, if the recession continued and provided there was no threat to price stability, more could certainly be done. He confirmed this intention by deciding on 8 April 1999 to cut base rate to 2.5 per cent.

The European Bank came under immediate attack from the German apostles of neoliberalism, who were afraid of a change of monetary paradigm to match the pattern of the American Federal Reserve. But such a change is in fact a primary condition for reducing the incidence of unemployment in Europe. Therefore it is not something to be afraid of but something to be looked forward to. My predecessor Theo Waigel gave an immediate response. 'The European Central Bank has spent its ammunition', he wrote. 'Monetary policy can no longer be accused of putting the brakes on the economy.'

But one must not lose sight of the fact that even a short-term real interest rate of 1.6 per cent is still not comparable with a rate of 0 per cent. This was the rate decided upon by the Federal Reserve in 1992 and 1993 in order to stimulate growth and employment. At this time unemployment in the USA and in Germany were at the same level. Later the figure fell in America but continued to rise in Germany.

My radical criticism of the mistaken monetary policy of the European central banks, led by the German Bundesbank, was, and still is, used to paint a picture of me as a one-man band. To counter this, I would like to quote, in addition to Paul Krugman (see p. 27), the words of Gavyn Davies, chief economist of Goldman Sachs in London:

The Federal Reserve, the European Central Bank and probably the Bank of Japan as well, must shoulder their global responsibility. Up to now they have failed to do so, preferring to concentrate on domestic issues. If the global monetary conditions are out of balance, it may happen that the Fed is forced to act, although it may have no wish to do so. I am convinced that over the past three years global monetary policy has been too restrictive. In the last two years the Bundesbank has been pursuing a monetary policy that has been far too restrictive . . . It did not adjust promptly enough to falling rates of inflation but instead continued to fight the battles of the 70s and 80s. The Fed did not make this mistake.

And there is another area in which the European Central Bank was a source of disappointment to me, namely its manifest lack of transparency. A modern central bank ought not to shroud its policies in a blanket of secrecy. But this is precisely what the European Central Bank is doing, which makes it difficult for us to blend it into our democratic procedures.

Wim Duisenberg once observed: 'It is normal for politicians to express their opinions from time to time on the interest rate policies of those charged with defending the status of the currency. But it is equally normal for us not to listen.' As long as one takes such remarks seriously, one might as well give up the ghost. Although Duisenberg does not care a fig for politicians' views on monetary policy, I hold to my opinion. Duisenberg was no less intelligent as Dutch Finance Minister than he is today as President of the European Bank. If the value of the currency is regarded as a more important issue than employment, the banks will become more important than democratically elected governments. If a 'stability culture' of this kind becomes established, the unemployed in Europe will have a long and hard road ahead of them.

That all traces of economic common sense in Germany have not yet been lost, can be gleaned from a report published by the IFO Institute in July 1999. This report points out that impulses for the consolidation of the economy come in the first instance from monetary policy; that a low rate for the euro will assist exports; and that a rise in real wages will strengthen the domestic economy. This is just the economic development we aimed for during the government's first months in office.

In March 1999 the *Handelsblatt* wrote: 'A mood of optimism has taken hold . . . This positive view of future trends derives from people's expectation that their financial situation will continue to improve over the coming twelve months . . . If this favourable domestic climate persists, one of those to profit will undoubtedly be the German retail trade, for it has been shown that in the past there has always been a statistically demonstrable correlation between a trend towards retail consumption and the actual behaviour of consumers.' But then the paper goes on to stress the need for a freeze on wages and pensions and for continued cuts in public spending.

In addition to monetary policy, a central subject of discussions at European level was taxation policy. France and Germany agreed that a greater degree of tax harmonization was necessary. We had reached a position that was unacceptable to European workers. In the European rush to reduce taxes, taxes on money, that is on interest, personal wealth and business profits, were steadily falling, whereas income tax, excise duties and welfare contributions were continually rising. The workers were the losers in the European race to reduce taxes, and the one-sided development of the tax system also had a detrimental effect on the economy.

The confused taxation systems at present in operation in Europe encourage tax evasion on a massive scale. Some of the German merchant banks played their part in tracking offenders down. Directors were convicted and banks were made to pay large fines. The Amsterdam Treaty did not go far enough. Tax harmonization should have been formulated more precisely and made more binding. Those countries that profit from tax dumping, like Luxemburg and Ireland, persist in trying to delay such a harmonization. Worst of all is Great Britain. When I put forward the case for such harmonization, supported with logical economic arguments, the *Sun* called me the most dangerous man in Europe. A little later Dominique Strauss-Kahn and I, together with Joschka Fischer and the Belgian finance minister Jean-Jacques Viseur, were dubbed 'Gauleiters'.

New Labour's reaction to these outbursts was chicken-hearted. Developments will show that the British economy will suffer in the long run if Britain does not join the euro. And it remains a fact that since the Thatcherite reforms the British economy is among the weakest in the European Community.

In the European Finance Ministers' club Dominique Strauss-Kahn and I received particularly strong support from Carlo Ciampi, for many years President of the Italian state bank and later the country's President, who shared our economic views to a large extent. Ciampi is the most charming and witty of men and exudes a real human warmth. One little episode shows him at his most characteristic. President Chirac and the other heads of state present had been arguing for hours over how long Duisenberg's term of office should be and when Claude Trichet, Chirac's favoured candidate, should succeed Duisenberg as President of the European Central Bank. Ciampi got to his feet, and all the others looked at him in surprise, wondering what pearls of wisdom he was about to offer. 'Why not elect me?' he said. 'I'm already 77!'

Strauss-Kahn, Ciampi and I had set ourselves the task of interpreting the rigid rules of the stability pact according to the laws of economic reason. The stability pact was the brain-child of the proponents of supply-side orthodoxy, and Hans Tietmeyer, former President of the Bundesbank, had played a major role in getting the pact accepted. No one challenged him more vigorously than Helmut Schmidt. Schmidt reminded Tietmeyer that it was he, Schmidt, who had drafted the Lambsdorff paper on the turn-round of the economy. But what happened in practice was that government borrowing rose fourfold, taxes and welfare contributions became higher than they had ever been, and unemployment reached an unprecedented level.

In 1990, as Chancellor Kohl's personal adviser on matters concerning the currency union between East and West Germany, Tietmeyer shared responsibility for the grave errors that were made and for the utopian promises that were given. Helmut Schmidt reminded Tietmeyer that he had been one of the principal forces behind the Bundesbank's decision to raise interest rates in 1990, as a result of which unemployment rose over the whole of Europe. He also shared responsibility for the improper refusal to realign the Deutschmark exchange rates within the European currency system, a realignment which had been made necessary by the raising of interest rates. The Bundesbank had pushed through the Maastricht convergence criteria without any public explanation of why the overall debt of any single participating state should not exceed 60 per cent of its current GDP.

Similarly no economic justification had been offered for the decision that the annual credit to which a member state was entitled should not exceed 3 per cent of its GDP. If a state succeeds in making large-scale savings, it can take up larger credits without affecting the financing of private economic investments. In Helmut Schmidt's own words:

> If a nation saves only little, or nothing at all, then even 4 per cent as the limit for government borrowing is far too high. In America the rate for private savers is around 4 per cent, in Germany it is around 11 per cent and in Japan over 16 per cent, yet theoretically even Japan, on the basis of the 3-per-cent criterion, would not today be allowed to join the euro. In a buoyant economy the figure may be allowed to drop slightly under 3 per cent, whereas in conditions of recession the threshold is too high. Article 104c of the treaty must therefore be interpreted flexibly.

Helmut Schmidt's contribution to the debate in 1996 still retains its relevance today. In America the savings quotient has since fallen. That is to say, the Americans are spending more than they are saving. Because they are running budget surpluses, foreigners are subsidizing the private sector. In 1998 private households in Germany saved a total of 266 billion Deutschmarks. Private wealth was assessed at 4.5 billion Deutschmarks, and cash reserves came to 5.7 billion Deutschmarks. This private wealth will be inherited by the next generation. Who is going to explain to the new government champions of saving that the high levels of saving in private households and businesses must be put to economic use, and that the man who uses in the form of loans what has been saved in the past is not living at the expense of our children's futures?

The problem in public finances is that the proportion spent on interest is too high, which restricts the state's freedom of manoeuvre. We need an upturn in the economy for the state to regain this freedom. The problem for the Social Democrats is the unequal distribution of wealth. In the context of the national finances it is the workers and their children who pay the taxes while the well-to-do and their children pocket the interest, which is often not taxed.

A further point made by Helmut Schmidt, still relevant today, is that, whereas in previous decades the left had developed its economic and social criteria in a national framework, the age of globalization requires the modernization and adaptation of these criteria. We require a political response to the challenges of a world no longer organized in terms of nation states, as Habermas put it. It is not the 'markets', so-called, that will have to make the decisions that will determine the course of our society but democratically elected parliaments and governments. Step by step, consolidated, worldwide policies based on cross-border cooperation must provide the answer to the processes of globalization.

Seen in terms of this historical claim, the role played by Helmut Schmidt needs to be reassessed, as much by the left as by others. If one accepts the organizatory principle of the markets, Schmidt was the first to recognize the challenges that would face a post-national world order. In 1975, in company with Giscard d'Estaing, he organized the first economic summit of the world's biggest industrial nations in Rambouillet. Both men were in agreement that the great economic problems confronting the world could only be solved by international cooperation. In the wake of the collapse of Bretton Woods they created the European currency system. While the European left was still concerned with Vietnam, Nicaragua and the Third World, Schmidt gave the first Social-Democrat reactions to the new situation created by the deregulation of the world's financial markets.

In his book *Globalization* Schmidt wrote: 'As in international maritime traffic, slowly but surely, certain universally accepted navigational rules and safety regulations have come to be adopted – and to a far greater extent in aviation – so also international movements of money and capital need rules. They need to be monitored and made subject to codes of conduct.'

At the moment, Schmidt went on, it had not yet been felt necessary, but he would not be surprised if an attempt were made to return to a system of fixed interest rates, at least between dollar, yen and euro. In the USA shares were vastly over-valued, and the blame for driving rates up lay with psychopaths – 30-year-old traders and 40-year-old managers who lacked any world perspective and any sense of responsibility for the consequences of their actions.

Together with the controllers of merchant and investment banks, fund managers have a greater influence on the development of the world economy than do elected governments and parliaments. As a first step, organized speculation must be countered by the coordinated intervention of the national banks. Short-term movements of capital must be regulated. As in a dam, the inflow must remain open but the outflow must be controlled.

16

My Resignation

On 10 March 1999 we held our first cabinet meeting to discuss the plans of the various departments. I had asked Gerhard Schröder several times not to keep just to the items on the agenda. This way, admittedly, cabinet meetings were always over quickly. But it seemed to me far more important, in view of the repeated blunders and the persistent lack of proper cooperation between different departments, that ministers should report in advance on their plans and intentions. As far as possible these plans should be made available to the cabinet before the press got hold of them and made them public knowledge. My experience as Prime Minister of the Saarland had taught me that this was the best way to secure prompt cooperation between departments and with the parliamentary party.

Schröder opened the proceedings himself, then turned to Jürgen Trittin. Reports had appeared in the papers that Trittin was drafting a new anti-smog bill. Schröder used the occasion to warn Trittin expressly not to embark on any further initiatives that would have a negative effect on the economy. Trittin, who had often been forced to suffer public indignities at the Chancellor's hands, put up a feeble defence of his plans, promising at the same time to secure the agreement of the other ministries before making his plan public.

After this Schröder turned to Christine Bergmann, who was reported in the newspapers to have under consideration a more flexible organization of study leave. Here too the Chancellor sensed the danger that business circles would find something for which to criticize his government, and he concluded his remarks by saying that the country could not be governed against the interests of the business community and that there was no way in which he would accept policies directed against those interests.

In the discussion that followed I tried to take the heat out of the situation by confirming that criticism of employers' federations created a bad atmosphere not only in business circles but also among workers and the self-employed. Schröder was right, I added, to remind us not to go too far.

There was no doubt in my mind that a Social-Democrat government would take decisions that would be highly unwelcome to the captains of industry. But it also went without saying that we had to engage in discussions with business leaders and introduce our reforms at an appropriate pace. I drew attention to the fact that industry would gain from the reduction in wage-added costs and that tax reforms would save smaller companies some 5 billion Deutschmarks. As was to be expected, the next day the papers were full of the cabinet meeting, especially the *Bild-Zeitung*.

The *Bild*'s informant, whoever he was, had evidently passed on the information that the Chancellor's criticisms were also aimed at me – which was untrue. On the paper's front page, in the familiar large letters, was the headline 'Schröder Threatens To Resign'. Below this, in slightly smaller letters, came the statement: 'I will not accept a policy that is directed against the interests of the business community. A moment will come when I can no longer assume responsibility for such a policy.' The report then went on to say that the Chancellor's criticism was aimed at his Finance Minister and Party Chairman.

But Schröder had not uttered a word of criticism against me during the meeting. To be sure, he cannot have failed to notice that for some while the gulf between us had been growing wider, and he is one of these people who have a well-developed sense of when to go onto the offensive. It had long been my policy to parry any attack by Schröder with an immediate counterattack of my own. I had also asked for an assurance that any criticisms we might make of each other should be made in confidence, not in public.

After the cabinet meeting I had a session with the representatives of the left-wing group of the parliamentary party. As we were in the course of debating the political decisions that had to be taken over the coming months, the article in *Bild* on Schröder's alleged threat to resign was handed to me. I asked my press spokeswoman, Dagmar Wiebusch, who was also present, to call Uwe-Karsten Heye, the government spokesman, and insist that the Chancellor deny the report. When she returned, she replied that Heye was already in the process of issuing a denial on all television channels.

That this was a direct challenge to the Chancellor was a thought that did not occur to Schröder. A half-hearted denial from Heye was no longer sufficient. It was, after all, not an everyday occurrence that the papers should report that the Chancellor had threatened to resign because he did not like the policies of his Finance Minister and Party Chairman. The following morning I decided to bring forward the moment of my resignation, which I had originally planned to coincide with the election of the Federal President. I no longer had any desire to be a member of a cabinet that could not produce the necessary degree of cooperation and in which the leading figure betrayed his obligation to support his ministers, above all in public.

The American sociologist Norman Birnbaum summed up the first four months of our administration:

> Nobody had been more alarmed at the initial courage demonstrated by the new government than the Chancellor's office itself. With its totally uncritical attitude towards Tony Blair's empty patter about a 'third way', and ignoring the economic and social costs of Clinton's employment programme, the Chancellery allowed itself to be plunged into a state of panic by the one Social Democrat who derived his legitimacy from the electors, not from the captains of the German economy and that of the world as a whole. The international elite of multinational concerns now controls not only the means of economic production but also the political power to influence the formation of public opinion. Rarely in a democratic country has a prominent politician been subjected to such a concerted attack as here Oskar Lafontaine. His colleagues have shown the utmost disloyalty towards him.

The more observant journalists, however, had long observed that there was method in all this. Whenever one of his policies came unstuck, as with the taxation of casual earnings, the ecology tax, pensions, and the reform of corporation tax, the Chancellor would assert his authority and make it clear that accountability for these errors of judgement rested with others.

The magazine *Stern*, which had put its weight behind Schröder's candidature for the chancellorship, wrote:

> Some of the papers made certain Bolshie elements in the SPD parliamentary party and the trade unions responsible for putting the brakes on the reform policies of the red-green coalition, and for causing the seasonally adjusted unemployment figures to show a slight rise. Everyone else is to blame but the shining knight himself. *Die Woche* had an article headed 'Chancellor in Chaos'. It should really have been called 'The Chaotic Chancellor'. For in social policy, the key area for the restoration of the country's well-being, Schröder has not only no coherent plan, no blueprint, but often little idea in which direction to go. Hardly

a day goes by without the would-be modernizer getting his facts mixed up.

Over the succeeding months Walter Riester was systematically bullied. To avoid being misunderstood, let me say at once that there are bound to be stormy debates in cabinet meetings, and it is naturally the responsibility of the head of the government to criticize as and where he sees fit. But constant leaking to the press, to the detriment of his colleagues, even those who thought they would have their opportunity to shine if others were taken out of the limelight, is in the last analysis intolerable. The next cabinet meeting could not have avoided leading to violent exchanges between Gerhard Schröder and myself, which would then naturally have been fed to the press, bedecked with the appropriate garnish.

To be fair I must add that some weeks earlier Schröder had suggested that he relieve me of the leadership of the parliamentary party. He had come to the view, as I had also, that my duties as Finance Minister were making it increasingly difficult for me to discharge my responsibilities as Party Chairman with the wholeheartedness that the present time demanded. Peter Struck had been kept informed of the idea and approved of it.

Those commentators are wrong, therefore, who concluded after my resignation that my retirement from politics had been Schröder's aim all along. In the first place it was my own decision whether to remain Party Chairman or not, and also whether I should retain my seat in the Bundestag. On the other hand had I taken on the leadership of the parliamentary party, it would have had the result that many would have welcomed, namely that in the dual function of Party Chairman and parliamentary leader I would have had an even greater influence on the policies of the coalition government than before.

But for weeks I had been firmly convinced that, given our divergent political views and our different methods of working, the only solution was for one or other of us to resign. And that, as things stood, could only mean me. Gerhard Schröder was our leading candidate for Chancellor, and our constitution says that it is the Chancellor, not the Party Chairman, who lays down the political guidelines. I was certain that, after my resignation, Schröder would also lay claim to the office of Party Chairman.

This seemed to offer the chance of a new start. I hoped that, as Party Chairman, Schröder would seek a dialogue with the party and give up his former habit of polishing his own image at the expense of the party. This was the only way, as I saw it, that we could arrive at a coherent set of Social-Democratic policies.

I then dictated three short letters to my long-serving secretary Hilde Lauer. The first read:

> To Gerhard Schröder:
> Dear Herr Bundeskanzler,
> I hereby tender my resignation from the office of Finance Minister.
> With best wishes,

The second was to Wolfgang Thierse, President of the Bundestag:

> Dear Herr Bundestagspräsident,
> I hereby resign my seat as a member of the German Bundestag.
> With best wishes,

(The resignation was then officially entered in the records of the Bundestag.)

The third letter was addressed to the members of the Executive of the Social Democratic Party:

> Dear Colleagues,
> I hereby announce my resignation from the office of Chairman of the Social Democratic Party. I express my thanks to you and to the members of the party for your trust and for your generous cooperation. I wish you all success in your efforts in the pursuit of freedom, justice and solidarity.
> Yours sincerely,
> Oskar Lafontaine

This last letter was the hardest to write. It is not every day, after all, that the Chairman of the Social Democratic Party resigns. Schumacher and Ollenhauer both died in office, while Brandt resigned because he felt towards the end that he did not have the full support of the party, and because they would not agree to the appointment of Margarita Mathiopoulos as his press spokeswoman.

In his memoirs Hans-Jochen Vogel quoted several reasons why he had not put himself forward again as a candidate in 1991. 'On the one hand,' Vogel wrote,

> the time seemed ripe for the younger generation to take over. If I had been nominated, my term would not have expired until after the Bundestag elections, by which time I would have been over seventy, and those from among whom my successor would be chosen would also be that much older. Moreover I did not feel that my strength was inexhaustible, and no thought was more unwelcome to me than that others might detect a decline in my powers of concentration or a loss of energy.

What the party needed, after three successive defeats in the federal elections, was a radical change of leadership. Its political programme was thoroughly up to date. Now was the time for a new leader to take the party forward and make clear that the transitional phase is over, and that the Social Democrats have the strength to challenge the conservatives and defeat them. Such a move, coming especially after the recent defeat at the polls, would demonstrate that the party was capable of governing.

Björn Engholm withdrew his candidacy because he had made false statements to the committee investigating the Barschel affair as to when he had first become aware of Barschel's wheeler-dealing. Rudolf Scharping was rejected at the party conference in Mannheim.

My decision to relinquish the position of Chairman of the SPD caused me a great deal of agonizing. I had joined the party in 1966. Never in my wildest dreams had I imagined that twenty-nine years later I would be Party Chairman. As the years went by, my life became more and more closely bound up with the party. For me, as for the other members, the party is both a home and a family. Still today people are looking for the warmth and sense of security that a family can offer. The Social Democratic Party, above all, which was suppressed by Bismarck and banned by Hitler, has a tradition of giving its members the feeling that they have joined a community of men and women who are there to help each other. This is the tradition that led to the adoption of 'comrade' as their way of addressing each other. The spiritual roots of the party lie in the ideals of solidarity and human sympathy. How often do we find ourselves failing to fulfil these ideals through our indifference or our selfishness.

I would wish to have my period as Chairman of the SPD judged according to whether during this time we achieved a greater degree of togetherness. We succeeded in taking a united team and a firm body of principles into the elections of 1998. The government's programme was approved by a large majority, and the election of the party's nominee for Chancellor, together with the choice of the government team, took place without any arguments. The result was a historic victory, victory by a large margin. With hopes high I looked forward to standing side by side with Gerhard Schröder and bringing in our programme of reforms to deal with the neoliberalism that had hitherto dominated the scene. These hopes were shattered, and I came to realize that I had to go, because it was to Gerhard Schröder that the electorate had given its vote of confidence. I had plumbed the depths.

Around four o'clock in the afternoon I got into my car and drove to Saarbrücken. While I was on the *autobahn*, a call came through from Marianne Duden, the Chancellor's secretary, who told me that the

Chancellor wanted to speak to me. I replied that my decision had been taken and nothing would be changed. My regards to the Bundeskanzler, I concluded.

When the press agencies got hold of the news, a number of television teams made their way to my house on the hill and set up camp there. They stayed for five or six days. I had given no reasons for my resignation. I needed some breathing space and wanted to reveal my reasons in such a way as to cause the least possible damage to the party. A man who has suffered a painful parting is quite literally speechless. He has no desire to speak but wants just to regain his composure and step back from the scene for a while.

But our news media do not have a shred of sympathy for a man in such a situation. They all proceeded to clamour that the public had a right to learn the reasons for my resignation. I had naively assumed that, before I actually resigned, the public must have followed television news programmes and reports in the papers, and could have hardly failed to notice that the Chancellor and the Party Chairman were increasingly at loggerheads. But I was wrong. Even the sensational leader in the *Bild-Zeitung* about the infamous cabinet meeting when the Chancellor himself had threatened to resign had not stuck in people's memories. Television teams continued to besiege my house, impervious to the effects of their behaviour. Rumours were launched, and gleefully recycled, that I had been speculating with the euro or on the stock market, or that I had been an informant for the Stasi.

By Sunday 14 August I was at my wit's end. Finally I called Norbert Klein, a journalist with the ARD whom I had known for many years, and told him I was prepared to make a brief statement on television. The interview ran as follows:

Question: **Herr Lafontaine, what was your principal motive for resigning? Everybody is waiting for an answer to this question.**

Answer: I first needed to stand back and look at my decision objectively. Anybody who can comprehend the significance of such a step will, I think, understand that.

The first thing I should like to say is that my decision has nothing to do with the political direction taken by the government over recent months. We are proud of having kept many of our promises – something new in politics. Hitherto the electors were all too often disappointed to find that pledges that had been made were not kept. We looked for policies that would promote social justice, policies for workers and for families. We have launched such policies, and they have been widely welcomed. The reason for my resignation was the lack of team spirit that we have displayed in recent months. Without teamwork there is no hope of achieving success. Teamwork requires members of the team to show consideration for each other and back each other up, if necessary in public, so that team spirit governs the work of government.

Let me give you an example. While we were reducing the tax burden on smaller businesses by 5 billion Deutschmarks, our team was arguing over whether we were pursuing an anti-business policy. Whatever is that supposed to mean? If the team no longer plays effectively together, one must find other players. That is what underlies the step I took. It is known who the members of the new team are going to be. I wish them and their captain Gerhard Schröder all success.

Question: What has this to do with the team's captain?

I side-stepped the question and replied:

The question that will certainly be asked is, why is it only now that I am speaking out in public? As I said, I needed a little time. Above all, I wanted to avoid turning a statement into a self-justification. I also wanted to offer an example of how to avoid exonerating oneself at the expense of others. So let me say again: the mistakes that were made, were made by all of us, and I think that is an approach which everybody can accept. In the days when I was Party Chairman it annoyed me when members who had resigned or retired made comments prejudicial to the interests of the party. As we all know, such comments are eagerly seized on by the outside world.

One more explanation, this time for the party itself. As can be imagined, mine was not an easy step to take. I have been a member of this party for thirty-three years, and for thirty of those years I have held leading positions. That is longer than many other politicians. The party is part of my life. Since the attempt on my life I have naturally asked myself repeatedly how I can reconcile this burden with the demands of my family and of my private life in general. And after many years I have made my decision in favour of my private life, for all the reasons I have given.

I hope the party will understand my move. And I should like here and now to express my gratitude for all the confidence that has been shown in me – all the affection, I might even say. It gave me strength over many years to undertake this arduous work. I wish the party continued success and shall follow its progress with the keenest interest. For I belong to this party.

And there is one thing we must never forget. The human heart is not yet traded on the stock exchange. But it has a position. It beats on the left.

Thank you.'

As can be imagined, this statement, the meaning of which, especially with its reference to teamwork, was clear enough, was not what the scandalmongering press had been expecting. What they would have liked was for me to declare war on Gerhard Schröder at once and attack the policies of the red-green coalition. But the war in Kosovo had not yet broken out, nor was there as yet any Schröder–Blair declaration of principles or any programme for the year 2000. Besides that, many journalists were annoyed that a politician had resigned of his own free will, without being forced to do so by the press. One underestimates the media's bloodlust at one's peril.

Journalists had often boasted in my presence of how they had brought about the demise of this or that politician by forcing him out of office. They now wanted to pay me back by portraying my resignation – which should be a natural option in a democracy if a politician comes to the conclusion that he cannot go on doing his work properly under the prevailing circumstances – as an act of treachery. Then, still not satisfied, a few went so far as to deny me the right to express my views on political issues in public.

It was a matter of regret to me that so many of my friends in the party did not understand why I had resigned. Those on the left of the party, in particular, complained that I had left them in the lurch. The question was now more rarely asked as to whether I had felt that I did not enjoy sufficient support. The subject of what would now happen to those on the left occupied Claus Koch in an article in the *Süddeutsche Zeitung*:

One can understand why many of the Party Chairman's friends are angry with him. His resignation will establish a benchmark for all the resignations that will soon follow. Others will have to go one better. That one from their own ranks should hold up the party and demonstrate so spectacularly the embarrassing situation in which it finds itself, is to the party faithful an improper way of behaving. The whole party has let itself down. And when Klaus Zwickel talks of the cowardice of this 'traitor', it is the 'traitor' who has exposed the cowardice of the Social Democrats, including their left wing, rather than the other way round.

Lafontaine's resignation clearly demonstrates that for the foreseeable future there is no alternative to a unified, consensus politics, and that the Blair–Schröder line has won the day. Lafontaine has declared the SPD to be morally bankrupt. A year ago it might have been possible to hold a left-of-centre position; today the right wing under Schröder is in clear control. The centre is always on the right. Anyone who still persists in living left-wing lies, Lafontaine is saying, is condemned to a life of careerism under the arch-careerist Schröder. Those on the left of the party must be made to realize that having once been misled by their leader with bogus pseudo-policies, they have now been written off by Lafontaine as well. Given that this was a highly political resignation, he had no alternative.

I had no intention of declaring the left wing morally bankrupt. But I did want to use my resignation to make the party think again about the direction it was going. The Schröder–Blair declaration and the programme for the year 2000 make it clear that a reassessment of the party's course is unavoidable.

During these days my mind often went back to the time when Willy Brandt resigned from the chairmanship of the party. The ostensible reason was his proposal to appoint Margarita Mathiopoulos, a politically independent Greek woman, as party spokesperson. But in reality those on the right of the party had been plotting his downfall for a long time. *Der Spiegel* reported that Hans Apel, former SPD Finance Minister, punning on the name of the car manufacturer, recommended a BMW – letters standing for '*Brandt muss weg*': 'Brandt Must Go!' *Bild* characteristically made insinuations about Brandt's well-known weakness for the female sex and showed photos of him with various attractive women with whom his name had been linked from time to time. Even the *Frankfurter Rundschau* carried the headline 'Brandt's Dalliance With a Hellene'.

In his farewell speech Brandt referred once again to the argument within the party: 'Some of the things I was forced to listen to and to read gave me such a shock that I cannot bring myself to repeat them here. It had nothing to do with washing dirty linen in public. And I must ask you to remember that the SPD is a European party and is beginning to have an influence in efforts to bring about a better understanding between nations. We cannot leave xenophobic utterances unchallenged. We must counter them in such a way that even philistines can see where we stand.'

At the same time Brandt did write in his memoirs of the *bonhomie* that characterized his farewell party. 'The ceremony to mark my formal retirement was held at an extraordinary party conference in the Beethovenhalle in Bonn in June 1987. Bouquets of flowers were everywhere and compliments abounded. I did not look back in anger but in gratitude for many enjoyable years, looking confidently and optimistically towards the future. It was a happy farewell.'

But I have never believed this. I knew the old man too well. In reality – he was, after all, the greatest Chairman of the party in the twentieth century – he laid down his office with a heavy heart.

In contrast to Willy Brandt, who had to put up with a lot of unpleasant mud-slinging, I got off relatively lightly. My wife and I had decided not to answer the telephone during the first few days. Instead the answering machine took the strain. Many of our friends called to ask for explanations. Bundestag deputies, officials and ordinary party members wrote me touching letters. Egon Bahr, for instance, wrote: 'You must have gone through hell. I wish you a speedy recovery from your wounds and a period of tranquillity in which to regain your strength and tackle new challenges.' I was grateful to Bahr for this.

Leading politicians of other parties wrote or telephoned – Helmut Kohl, Wolfgang Schäuble and Norbert Blüm of the CDU, Hans Dietrich Genscher and Günter Rexrodt of the FDP, and Antje Vollmer of the Greens. On one of our answering machines there was a message saying that Joschka Fischer wanted to talk to me but I heard no more. Gregor Gysi of the PDS also called, as did Hans Modrow, for whom I had gained considerable respect during the time when he was Chairman of the SED in Dresden in the days of the old GDR.

The first representative of our allied socialist parties in Europe to call was my old friend Alfonso Guerra, from Spain. Guerra had for many years been Deputy Prime Minister in the government of Felipe Gonzales, with whom he had built up the Spanish Socialist Party since 1974. During the Franco era he had been a bookseller in his home town of Seville – which is also Gonzalez's home town. The bookstore is still there, now under the name of Antonio Machado, a writer and poet who came to a miserable end in 1939 in France, after the Civil War. A fellow-Saarlander, Gustav Regler, has written about him in his autobiography, *The Ear of Malchus*. Machado is Guerra's favourite author. It is his custom at Christmas and New Year to send his friends serious works of literature. Over the years I have developed a close friendship with him. When my son Carl Maurice was born, Guerra was the first to write.

After many years together with Gonzalez, Guerra fell out with

him over matters of economic and finance policy and also over fundamental questions of ideology, and in January 1991 he retired from
politics. He was deeply disappointed that I had resigned, especially
since only a few weeks earlier my wife and I had been in Madrid to
launch the Spanish translation of our book *Don't Be Afraid of Globalization*. The launch, which had been organized by my old friend
Dieter Koniecki, director of the Friedrich Ebert Bureau in Madrid,
was a great success. Over 900 people were present, the great majority
of whom took heart from the fact that a German Finance Minister
and his wife had delivered such a broadside against the apostles of
neoliberalism.

Dominique Strauss-Kahn called from Paris, conveyed Lionel Jospin's
best wishes and wanted to know what had led to my resignation. I
told him what I had already told others, that a ship cannot have two
captains, each of whom wants to steer his own course. Strauss-Kahn
invited me and my wife to stay with him in Paris. A call also came
from Jack Lang, the long-serving French Minister of Culture, who had
helped us in the Bundestag elections. He wanted to know whether I
would consider becoming President of the European Commission, since
I no longer held any office that would prevent me taking on such a job.
I told him that I had only recently resolved to spend more time with
my family. But I could not resist adding the comment that I was sure
the German Chancellor would be highly delighted to hear of the suggestion.

At the end of 1998 reports surfaced in the press that I was interested
in becoming President of the European Commission. There was not a
word of truth in the reports. The only way I could rescue myself was
to reply that what I really wanted was to become Pope. But now that
the story was really in circulation, Strauss-Kahn called me in Berlin
and said that France would support me if I really did want to become
President of the Commission. I suggested he take on the job himself.
Since we were both pulling in the same direction as far as European
economic and finance policy was concerned, I would have considered
him an ideal choice. Gerhard Schröder also told me around this time
that he would nominate me for President of the Commission if I wanted
him to do so.

I also received a cordial letter from Bob Rubin in the United States,
expressing his appreciation of my efforts to promote growth and employment in Europe and thanking me for my cooperation.

Among the many demonstrations of friendship that came from the
other social-democratic parties in Europe, I should like to mention a
letter from Hans Fischer, President of the Austrian National Assem-
bly. Fischer wrote:

The fact that you felt driven to take such a radical step suggests to me that you were facing very difficult problems and had to make fundamental decisions. Even with the benefit of hindsight it is not possible to judge whether your decision was right (maybe it was inevitable) unless we are in full knowledge of your motives and of the circumstances in which it was taken. I am sure, however, that you turned over all the considerations in your mind. I can also imagine that it was not only the decision itself that was hard to make but that it was, and still remains, difficult to come to terms with the immense changes that will flow from it.

It was particularly refreshing to receive a telephone call from Helmut Kohl. First the former Chancellor assured me of his respect and sympathy. Then he enquired whether it was true that we had bought a farmhouse. I replied that we were negotiating to buy one but that a final agreement had not yet been signed. If the deal came off, said Kohl, he would present me with a bullock. Or would I prefer a lion, or a tiger, he asked. Somewhat bewildered, I asked him what he expected me to do with such an animal. Probing still further, he wanted to know whether I had any idea what young lions and tigers cost. This question too left me at a loss. Then he told me that they cost around 250 marks each, and that they were so cheap because more and more zoos in Germany were now able to rear big cats without difficulty.

As to my ignorance of what these big cats cost, Kohl rounded off his telephone call by saying: 'I always knew you had no idea about real life!' In taking leave of each other, we agreed to drink a glass of wine together some day.

I relate this conversation at length as an example to the uninitiated of how the wily old Helmut Kohl used to try to tie people up in knots. As nobody subsequently denied, he had been grossly underrated during his time in office. I always admired the skill with which he brushed off the humiliations he suffered at the hands of the press during his early years, and when it became my turn to be a victim of the media, I used to remind myself that Kohl had been far more shabbily treated over many years.

After my resignation Gerhard Schröder showed that he was capable of action. He reacted by issuing a statement to the effect that the government's work had to go on and that he would appoint a successor as swiftly as possible. At the same time he indicated in discussions with senior members of the party that he was prepared to take over the chairmanship of the party himself. His ambivalent attitude towards this position emerged when he said: 'It was the gates of the Chancellery that I rattled, not those of the Ollenhauer House [the party headquarters of the SPD].'

17

The War in Kosovo

On 23 March 1999, twelve days after my resignation, NATO made a decision to attack Yugoslavia in order to force President Milošević to put a stop to the murders and expulsions in Kosovo. Schröder made a statement on television. He said: 'This evening NATO began air strikes against military targets in Yugoslavia. The aim of these attacks is to prevent further systematic abuses of human rights and prevent a human disaster in Kosovo . . . The military action is not directed against the Yugoslav people. I wish to make this clear, particularly to our Yugoslav fellow-citizens. We shall do everything in our power to avoid casualties among the civilian population.'

As we now know, none of these aims was achieved. NATO proved unable to prevent a human disaster in Kosovo or to avoid casualties among the civilian population of Serbia. It was inevitable that the war, during which the Serbian economy and infrastructure were destroyed, should also be aimed at the Serbian people. While the war was still on, I began to doubt whether I had been right to give up the chairmanship of the party as well as resigning as Finance Minister. Willy Brandt's policy of peace and *détente* had been for me, as for many others, one of the principal reasons why I had joined the SPD. Right from the beginning I found it hard to agree with Schröder's policy over Kosovo.

After the victory of the red-green coalition in the general election the Kohl government sought our agreement to a resolution passed by the previous parliament to contribute a German contingent to the multinational stand-by NATO force. As Chairman of the Social Democratic Party, I raised the question in the course of the discussions as to whether such a resolution automatically meant that there would be no further political consultations before a military attack was ordered. The replies given by Defence Minister Volker Rühe on one side and Foreign Minister Klaus Kinkel on the other were different. Whereas Rühe said that once the resolution had been passed, there would no longer be any political possibility of preventing a NATO attack, Kinkel said the opposite. Wolfgang Schäuble was visibly embarrassed and stared out of the window. I insisted on a clear answer.

That same day I demanded from the Foreign Ministry a written statement that the Bundestag's decision would not automatically trigger military action. This meant that, before an attack was launched, there would be a further opportunity for discussions on whether, with the troops at stand-by, the order to attack should be given. Having been given this assurance, I put my name to the Bundestag resolution as chairman of the Social Democratic Party.

After all the preparations and all the initiatives launched by European governments and the United States, it would not have been right at this stage to exercise a veto, especially as the Kohl government was still in office. Instead I insisted, while the negotiations were taking place at Rambouillet, that before Germany gave its consent to a military attack, there should be a detailed discussion in the cabinet of the strategies that had been planned. I took the view that it was not possible to agree to military intervention without being informed beforehand of the overall strategy and its likely effects. During the negotiations at Rambouillet Fischer told the cabinet that NATO was determined, if the negotiations should fail, to commence air strikes. Recalling the statement made by the Foreign Ministry, I realized immediately that the situation again demanded a political decision.

After Fischer had finished his speech, Schröder turned to him and Scharping and said: 'When we reach that point, we'll talk about it on the telephone.' When I heard this, I protested that this was not the proper way to do things. If Germany, for the first time, was going to join a war, I said, there must at least be a meeting of the cabinet, to be followed by a cabinet decision. Going to war on the basis of a telephone call, I added, was hardly the proper procedure. Turning directly to Schröder, I said that it must surely be also in his own interest to have the weight of the whole government behind him at such a moment.

Joschka Fischer supported me and Schröder was soon convinced. A provisional date for a cabinet meeting was agreed upon but this point was never reached, because NATO did not want to intervene immediately after the Rambouillet negotiations.

Thus before my resignation as Finance Minister military strategies and NATO plans were not discussed any further. I can therefore pass judgement on them only in retrospect. The whole of NATO's military involvement could in any case only be justified on the basis that Milošević would quickly sign the agreement. If, on the other hand, this was highly unlikely – and there was a great deal of evidence to support this – the action taken by NATO was irresponsible.

In the frequent discussions that had taken place in the ranks of the SPD over the acceptability of such military interventions, Christoph Zöpel once put forward the view that military strikes designed to prevent the infringement of human rights were more in the nature of police actions. This is one way of looking at it. But what would one think of a police force which, learning that a band of criminals was on the way from A to B in order to pillage and murder, sent a force to A in order to destroy the infrastructure there? Those responsible would soon be sent packing. But in the case of cross-border police actions things are evidently different.

There was one unpardonable omission on my part. I failed to study the text of the agreement drawn up in Rambouillet but relied on the Foreign Minister. Annex B of this agreement, which dealt with the stationing of NATO forces with unrestricted right of movement in the whole of Yugoslavia, only came to my attention later in the press. There was no discussion in the cabinet over whether someone may be legitimately compelled to sign a treaty while under the threat of military force. Rudolf Augstein put his finger on it. 'In Rambouillet,' he wrote, 'the United States laid down military conditions which no educated Serbian could have accepted.'

When the attacks began, I felt relieved that I was no longer a member of the government. It is always hard to say in retrospect how one would have reacted to a given set of circumstances. But since I had already firmly decided to resign, I assume people will believe me when I say that, under the given conditions, I could equally well have taken our entry into the war as my reason for resigning. Even if one regarded military intervention as inevitable, the way NATO set about it, both politically and militarily, was reckless and irresponsible.

In the first few days of the war I blamed myself for having failed, out of a misplaced sense of loyalty, to make an issue of it earlier within the party. I had banked too long on the probability that NATO would not carry out its threats. It would have been only with an explicit resolution from the party in my hands that I might have been able to influence the course of events. I doubt whether even such a resolution would have sufficed. Probably only if I had been Chancellor could I have prevented the war from starting. I would have insisted on receiving the approval of Russia, China and the whole Security Council and refused to give my consent to military action which, instead of putting an end to the murdering and pillaging, had the very opposite effect.

Doubtless public opinion would initially have been strongly opposed to Germany following its own independent course in this way. But a politician must learn to weather such storms and stand up for his principles. Our manifesto makes it quite clear: 'NATO is and remains a defensive alliance. The monopoly of power to enforce the maintenance of peace in the world lies exclusively with the United Nations. Actions by NATO which go beyond its remit for the exercise of collective defence require a mandate from the United Nations or from the Organization for Security and Cooperation in Europe.'

The joint coalition agreement was even more specific: 'Participation of German forces in operations to preserve peace and international security is dependent on compliance with international law and adherence to the terms of the German constitution. The new German government will do all it can to preserve the United Nations' monopoly of military power and to strengthen the authority of the Secretary General.' Never had I dreamt that within a matter of months all these intentions would have been consigned to history.

On 1 May 1999 I addressed the traditional meeting of the German Trade Union Congress in Saarbrücken. The event aroused considerable attention. The press were expecting me to settle my account with Schröder and his government. Many of my friends in the party and colleagues in the trade unions were interested to hear what I had to say about the war in Kosovo. The last thing in my mind was to give the impression that I had a ready-made answer but at the same time I wanted to make it clear that I condemned the NATO action. Here is what I said:

> If I take this opportunity today to state my position with regard to the war in Yugoslavia, I would first remind you that this is not the only war taking place in the world today. In many countries scattered across the globe everyday life is dominated by misery and poverty, persecution and murder. Think of Africa, think of Algeria, think of Ethiopia, think of the Sudan, think of Ruanda, think of Congo, think of Asia, and think too of the persecuted Kurds. Turkey is a member of NATO. Think of Tibet and its persecuted people, think of Afghanistan and of the many other countries where grave injustices are being perpetrated and people made to suffer.
>
> But today I should like to concern myself with Yugoslavia. I need to approach the subject with some delicacy, because no one can offer patent, straightforward solutions. At the forefront of our minds, however, should be the question, how can we most rapidly alleviate the suffering of the people there? How can peace be most speedily restored?

It is not a matter of saving face, as I have read in various quarters. It is purely and simply a question of human suffering, of the preservation of human life. Naturally we all have in mind the people of Kosovo, those driven from their homes and killed in cold blood. But let us also remember the people of Serbia, who live in a state of fear under the constant threat of being bombed. Think too of those army deserters who are being hunted down for not wanting to take part in the war . . .

We have all learnt in the meantime that many mistakes have been made in Yugoslavia, some of which go back years. We often hear that Germany ought not to pursue an independent course. But I must remind you that Germany went its own way at the very beginning when, against the opposition of Paris, London and Washington, it pushed through the official recognition of the separate Yugoslav states because the concepts of freedom and self-determination were misinterpreted. Freedom and self-determination are incompatible with ethnic expulsions – that is where the misinterpretation starts. Freedom and self-determination are inconceivable – indeed, lie beyond the bounds of human experience – unless they are linked with solidarity and human compassion.

It was therefore a mistake to encourage this political particularism, which rested on the principle of ethnicity, let alone to give it official recognition. It had also been a mistake some years earlier for the Croats to be allowed to drive out the Serbs in the aftermath of the NATO bombing of Krajina. This too is something we must keep in mind when we talk about the war in Yugoslavia.

It would be wrong to think that it is only one of the ethnic groups in multinational Yugoslavia that has been subjected to ethnic cleansing. The Serbs too have suffered. I often hear people say: NATO has somehow to save face. It has to win – there is no going back. Nietzsche wrote in *Thus Spake Zarathustra*: 'Let your peace be a victory.' But I ask: A victory for whom? What does 'saving face' mean when we contemplate all the human suffering that has been endured in this war?

I demanded an immediate stop to the bombing and the resumption of political negotiations.

NATO bombed Yugoslavia for seventy-eight days and seventy-eight nights. Its planes flew 36,000 sorties. They left a ruined country – villages razed to the ground, schools destroyed, along with hospitals, factories, bridges, powerhouses and pumping stations. This, together with the human cost in lives and expulsions, is the legacy of the war. The embarrassing haggling over how to apportion the costs of reconstruction has begun. The European Commission has estimated that a total of 60 billion Deutschmarks is needed to rebuild the crippled Yugoslavia. The Americans, who bore the brunt of the costs of the war, say that it is now the Europeans' turn. Hans Eichel at once announced that there would be no tax increases to help pay for the war.

Theo Waigel had had no such qualms. When, after the Gulf War, he received a bill from Washington for 13 billion Deutschmarks, he simply increased value added tax.

Immediately after the end of hostilities it became clear that armistice was not the same as peace. In earlier speeches I had always included the sentence 'Peace cannot grow on bomb sites.' The Serbs were now expelled from Kosovo. General Wesley Clark, the NATO Supreme Commander, had to guarantee the Serbs protection from Albanian acts of revenge. 'NATO is prepared', he said, 'to re-intervene militarily in Yugoslavia in order to prevent serious abuses of human rights.' It is probably impossible for outsiders like us to imagine what it means, after all the atrocities that have been committed, for Albanians and Serbs to have to live together again.

This war has changed Germany, and I hope we learn the proper lessons from it. Significantly there were hardly any peace demonstrations. The PDS mounted a few protest meetings, particularly in Berlin, but there was nothing on a large scale. This is not surprising, since the two big organizations whose policies and traditions require them to promote the cause of peace and oppose war – the SPD and the trade unions – had no wish to undermine the position of the Schröder government.

I was also angry about the part played by the Greens. I had wanted a red-green coalition because I hoped to get the support of the Greens for a foreign policy built on the need to find a peaceful solution. But the Greens had in the meantime dropped the word pacifism from their vocabulary. Questions with a pacifist slant raised in meetings of their parliamentary party were frowned upon. In one discussion on the war in Kosovo an analogy was drawn with converts to Catholicism. Saul became Paul, exchanging one creed, one set of beliefs, for a new set, which he then defended with even stronger conviction. The old anti-war slogan '*Frieden schaffen ohne Waffen*' ('Make peace without weapons') was turned into '*Frieden schaffen mit aller Gewalt*' ('Make peace with all the force you can muster').

Joschka Fischer had once said: 'I look forward to the day when our party has enough pacifists to be able to pursue an alternative, peace-oriented foreign policy without recourse to an army.' During the war in Kosovo he said: 'I have learnt not only "No more war" but also "No more Auschwitz". The bombs are necessary in order to put a stop to the activities of the "Serbian SS".' Scharping spoke of 'a glimpse of the unspeakable German past with its genocide, its eugenics and its concentration camps', and went on: 'If we deny horror its name, we denigrate those stricken by it and treat them like mere ciphers.' Day in, day out he showed us images of horror on our television screens – gruesome pictures of massacred Albanians.

In contrast to the government's view of the situation the writer Peter Handke commented: 'We want to prevent a new Auschwitz, but now NATO has created a new Auschwitz of its own . . . Then it was gas chambers and a bullet in the back of the neck. Today it is a computerized flick of a switch from a height of 5,000 metres.'

I was relieved to find CDU politicians warning of the danger of playing up the moral significance of the German contribution to the war in Kosovo. To exaggerate the moral justification for the war is political dynamite. People who argue like Scharping and Fischer can no longer explain why they do not also intervene militarily in many other parts of the world where murders and expulsions are taking place. There are considered and objective arguments for concluding that it is not feasible to do so. But when asked why they do not intervene in other parts of the world, those who occupy the moral high ground have no answer. If we were to set out to punish abuses of human rights wherever they occurred, as we did in Kosovo, we should end up by dropping bombs on half the world.

Everybody has the right, of course, to change their opinion. But a radical change of attitude is always accompanied by the danger of exaggeration. To equate the terrible events in Kosovo with Auschwitz, and turn 'No more war' into 'No more Auschwitz', is just such an exaggeration. The propaganda machine made the Serbs the bad guys and the Albanians the good guys. But does not 'No more Auschwitz' also mean that never again can an entire people be portrayed as the one and only source of evil?

Even though Fischer subsequently reversed his stance, when I think back, I cannot approve of the role he played during the conflict in Kosovo. To be sure, he did change his mind at an early stage and succeed at the party conference of the Greens in Bielefeld in getting the motion passed that military force is on occasion necessary to bring about peace. But he had signed the coalition agreement and promised to support the United Nations as the sole arbiter of the use of force. Was it necessary for him to be party to so many serious mistakes, despite the fact that, as Foreign Minister, he had the opportunity and the authority to stand out against them?

It was unforgivable on his part to follow the Americans and push the United Nations to one side. If one adopts a policy of peace, then one must strengthen the authority of international law, not weaken it. But that is precisely what happened in the war in Kosovo. It was unpardonable not to have brought Russia into the process. Schröder's behaviour towards Primakov was totally out of place. Only after they had thrown out the baby with the bath water did Schröder and Fischer come to realize that no peace is possible in Europe without Russia.

We need a concerted European plan of action in our foreign and security policy. At the very least Germany and France must pull together as they did in the good old days of Giscard and Schmidt, or Mitterrand and Kohl.

But Schröder cannot find a proper accommodation with the French. Moreover the 'cohabitation' between Chirac and Jospin is hardly conducive to effective political action in France. Tony Blair has little to contribute to the establishment of a European plan of action. He has to deal with the traditional British antipathy towards Europe and spends his energy on infotainment and public relations exercises.

Nor must one forget that China was brought only occasionally into the discussions, in spite of the fact that, as a nuclear power, China has a right of veto in the Security Council. The bombing of the Chinese embassy in Belgrade further exacerbated the situation. At the same time it must be conceded that Schröder struck the right note on his visit to China and succeeded in bringing about an improvement in China's relations with Europe.

The disastrous war in Kosovo has given us the opportunity to rethink the terms of NATO involvement in out-of-area problems. Too many questions remain unanswered if the alliance is to be given such responsibilities. No explanation is needed if troops are called upon to defend their own families and their own country. Similarly justification may be found for their deployment in another country within the framework of a mutual assistance pact. But why should they risk their lives as mediators or policemen in a civil war that was taking place in a foreign country? In response to questions, soldiers from the German contingent in the NATO force in Kosovo said that they had felt no sense of hatred towards their adversaries, as they might have done if it had been their own country that had been attacked.

Doubts were expressed over the use of air strikes. The NATO commanders needed to avoid casualties among their contingents. Air raids minimized the risks for their own soldiers but increased the danger for the Albanians and the Serbs. A policy of intervention that shielded the lives of their own soldiers but exposed others to greater threat was unacceptable. Put more bluntly – to kill innocent people in the name of the defence of human rights is not justifiable even if such tragic events are described as collateral damage.

This is yet another example of how treacherous language can be in times of war, and of the old saying that the first casualty of war is truth. Can anyone imagine that Jamie Shea, the NATO spokesman – whose cheerful, matter-of-fact manner made me shudder – would have referred to the death of his own wife and children as 'collateral damage'?

Ulrich Beck wrote:

> All this only goes to show how great is the confusion wrought by globalisation in the field of society and politics. The extent to which people arrogate to themselves the right to inflict on the world a militarized humanism in the name of human rights is alarming. A claim of authority to attack other states on moral grounds could turn into a latter-day crusade on behalf of human rights. In a world full of dictators it is an invitation to wage endless war, a warrant for the abuse of power. And this in a technocratic age when doctors would have us believe, in a society exposed to global risks, that the effects of war can be contained.

Václav Havel took the opposite view. In an essay called 'Kosovo and the End of the Nation State', he wrote:

> The bombing of Yugoslavia, for which there was no mandate from the United Nations, put human rights above the rights of the nation . . . But this did not happen in an irresponsible manner, as an act of aggression or an infringement of international law. On the contrary. It was done out of a respect for law, a law higher than that which protects the sovereignty of states.
>   The Alliance acted out of respect for human rights, in response to the dictates of conscience as well as to the provisions of international legal documents. This 'higher law' has its taproots outside the empirical world. For whereas a state is the work of man, man is the work of God.

Put in another way: NATO was entitled to break international law because it acted as an instrument of the 'higher law' of God. It does not take much imagination to see what suddenly becomes possible in Asia or in Africa or in South America if military forces invade in the name of the 'higher law of God'.

In the course of the war in Kosovo NATO celebrated the fiftieth anniversary of its foundation. From the beginning it had never seen itself merely as a military alliance but also as a community pledged to the defence of certain values. This can be seen from the text of the Atlantic Treaty itself, where the signatories commit themselves to defend the fundamental values of democratic freedom and the rule of law. Specifically they undertake

(1)   To act in accordance with the charter of the United Nations;
(2)   To settle every international dispute in which they are involved by peaceful means;
(3)   Not to endanger peace, international security or justice;
(4)   To refrain from the threat of force and the use of force in their international relations.

NATO jettisoned each and every one of these pledges in the war in Kosovo. Force was used without the required mandate from the United Nations. The military action taken was a clear breach of international law and contrary to the commitments undertaken in the Treaty.

Modern laws on the conduct of war are based on the Geneva Conventions of 1949 and the supplementary protocols of 1977, which are basically recognized as part of the common law of the various nations. The first of these protocols states that neither the civilian population as a whole nor individual civilians may be made an object of attack. The use of force with the primary aim of spreading fear among the civilian population is forbidden. But precisely this was the purpose of the NATO bombardment.

At the beginning the German government could count on the support of the vast majority of the population for the deployment of German troops in Kosovo. But as the days went by, opinion began to change. There were increasing signs that, rather than reducing the incidence of abuses of human rights, the war was actually increasing it.

By the time of the European elections the mood had changed. The majority of the German people was now opposed to the actions of NATO. At a time when the question of cutting pensions and unemployment benefit was again being discussed, people found it incredible that we should be bombing roads, bridges, railway tracks, power stations and waterworks in Yugoslavia, only to rebuild everything with hard-pressed taxpayers' money the moment the attacks stopped.

The destruction of the Yugoslav economy and infrastructure was a direct consequence of NATO strategy. When we look back, we cannot but ask ourselves where we are going if international law is callously broken and the constitution is stretched almost to breaking-point, while we seek justification, explicitly or implicitly, in victor's justice. In a world in which justice prevails, no one can be at one and the same time both prosecutor, judge and hangman. If one behaves in this way, one need not be surprised when others follow suit. The war in Kosovo was a step backwards for the international community.

If one takes these policies to their logical conclusion, one would first have to change the names of our Defence Ministries back to what they used to be – War Ministries. The war in Kosovo was certainly not a defensive war. The argument that we had to defend human rights is false from the beginning. One does not defend human rights by killing innocent people.

Zbigniew Brzezinski, the former White House security adviser, expressed the view that western European states, and also central European states to an increasing degree, had largely become American protectorates and dependencies, a situation which in the long run would be healthy neither for America nor for Europe.

Alongside the world's one superpower we need a strong, united Europe. America can easily slip into the danger, as Helmut Schmidt put it, of ruthlessly promoting its own interests in response to domestic pressure. A common European defence and security policy, as our experience in Kosovo has again shown, is today more necessary than ever.

18

The Medium is
the Message

To observe that the nature of politics and political activity has undergone radical changes in recent times is to state the obvious. Our society has become a media society. It is therefore a suitable moment to
reflect on the consequences that the arrival of the media society has
had for politics.

In my opinion these consequences have been highly detrimental.
And lest this be seen as merely a personal quirk of judgement on my
part, let me quote Wolfgang Schäuble. 'Political activity in the age of
the media,' wrote Schäuble,

> is conducted under the permanent glare of the lights and is thus under
> permanent pressure to produce results. This has nothing to do with the
> natural openness of democratic government. It represents the transfor-
> mation of normal political processes into a series of events conducted
> under the television lights. Particularly in the case of discussions of
> complex questions, which need to allow time for reflection and the con-
> sidered advancement of reasoned solutions, situations are artificially
> dramatized and their significance played down in the public perception.
> If the assembled politicians cannot deliver a positive message, the occa-
> sion is deemed a failure, or the discussion is adjourned, which amounts
> to a semi-failure.
>
> The modern infotainment culture cherishes the short headline, the
> catchy title, or at the most a five-line report, which cannot convey the
> complexity of the subject. Success in politics lies in the way things are
> presented, not in their substance. Content is dispensable. Television has
> left deep marks on our political culture, not all of which have proved to
> be of benefit. There is a concentration on personalities and scandals,

which leads to an unbalanced perception of political events. Television is an intrusive medium which invades the individual's privacy and often ends up by stripping him of all vestige of personal dignity.

The media, particularly television, change our perceptions and thereby us as persons. The objection is often heard that all depends on the use we make of the media. But this is a highly questionable view, not least because it assumes that we have complete control over the workings of technology. This is an illusion.

We can, of course, take part in a religious service via television. But all we get is a picture, and the picture-book effect is the very opposite of what we are seeking to experience, namely the reality of being actually present in church. We must also remember that, as long as films could only be seen in a cinema, it was a communal experience. Today we watch television programmes in the privacy of the home, with family or friends, or frequently alone. The lonelier a person is, the longer he sits in front of the television. 'Millions upon millions,' wrote Günther Anders, 'there they sit, each cut off from the rest yet like all the others – hermits in their cells, not, however, renouncing the world but anxious at all costs not to miss a scrap of that world. There is no surer way of depriving a human being of his humanity than by pretending to preserve the freedom of his personality and the rights of his individuality.'

What does it mean to experience war live on one's own television screen? The Yugoslav poet Charles Simic wrote:

> The bombardment of cities is one of the great spectacles of the late twentieth century. This is even truer today, in the television age, than it was in the days of radio and newspapers, when much was still left to the imagination. Now we can sit in our living rooms with a cool beer and a packet of potato crisps and watch the bombing of Baghdad or Belgrade every evening. I am sure that the bombing of Hiroshima or Dresden would have been shown live on television if the technology had been available. There we sit in our slippers, watching such horrors night after night.

Here too, as with a church service, we have the illusion of actually being present. But we are not present – we are at home, drinking beer and munching crisps. Our perception of the terrible events happening before our eyes is changed. So too is our judgement. The Gulf War came across as a war game conducted between computers.

Nor did this change of perception fail to influence politicians. 'Today', wrote the French philosopher Paul Virilio,

American technology has become for Clinton a kind of Wonderland. Like a child in the playground who is afraid of being laughed at by the others for being soft, the President shows off all his wonderful toys and demonstrates to the world how they work. What happened in Iraq was repeated in Kosovo. On the one hand the world's superpower had to demonstrate its humanity and compassion, on the other it needed to lend credibility to its assertion of global domination. So it displayed its military arsenal – not only cruise missiles and F-117s, which had already been used in Iraq, but also the B-2 bomber, which costs roughly the equivalent of the gross domestic product of Albania.

What is far worse, however, is that television pictures give the impression that war is controllable. Those who take part in war via television cannot but have a fundamentally different view of war from our parents, who have experienced the horrors of war on the battlefield or in the air-raid bunker.

Nor does television change only our perception and our experience. More and more, by their choice of what to show, the media are affecting political decisions. 'Foreign policy by NBC', the Americans call it.

Horst Grabert, former Head of Chancery under Willy Brandt and in 1984 German Ambassador to Yugoslavia, had his answer to those who justified the war in Kosovo with the slogan 'No more Auschwitz'. 'Krajina is closer to Central Europe than Kosovo', Grabert wrote.

> But hardly any of those who raise their voices today in protest against the war in Kosovo were to be heard talking of human rights when some 220,000 Serbs were expelled from territories in which they had been living since the days of Maria Theresa. What kind of morality is it that chooses to ignore such events but uses the present situation as a pretext for military intervention? This is an accusation I level at political leaders, not at peoples. People are morally affected by the expulsions in Kosovo because they are personally confronted by them in the media. They could not be equally affected by events in Krajina because the media carried few, if any, reports on the situation at that time.

Must it not give us food for thought when a decision on whether to go to war depends on television coverage?

Henry Kissinger had his own view:

> This is how it comes about that politicians see foreign policy as an aspect of domestic policy, with which it is linked by ideological objectives. Consequently strategic long-term goals get pushed into the background. The West embarked on its intervention in Kosovo in part, at least, as a response to public indignation and the pictures of columns of refugees that we saw on our television screens night after night. On the

other hand a similar fear of the images of the corpses of allied service-
men caused them to set out on a military strategy which had the perverse effect of only adding to the suffering of the people in whose name
they claimed the war was being fought.

While Rudolf Scharping was showing pictures of murdered Albanians on television day after day, I was thinking of my wife. She had
founded an organization known by the acronym INTACT (International Action Against the Circumcision of Girls and Women). The
word circumcision sounds harmless enough. But female circumcision
means torture, because the sexual organs remain horribly disfigured
to the end of the woman's life. The operation is irreversible. Between
130 million and 150 million women in the world are circumcised,
victims of the abuse of the human right of protection from bodily
harm. Only in exceptional cases is the operation carried out under
expert medical supervision – generally it takes place in primitive huts
under catastrophic hygienic conditions and is performed by traditional
healers, midwives or barbers, without anaesthetic. It often takes half
an hour, and several women are needed to hold the girl down while
the operation is going on. Two million young girls are circumcised
every year, 5 to 10 per cent of whom die as a direct result – 100,000 to
200,000 a year. I found myself wondering what would happen if these
gruesome pictures were shown on our television screens every day.

But not only do the media change our perception and influence our
decisions – they also mould the personalities of those we see on our
screens. Those who constantly appear on television tend to narcissistic
modes of behaviour. This narcissism was defined by the psychotherap-
ist Alexander Lowen as both a psychological and a cultural condition.
'On the individual level,' wrote Lowen,

> it is a personality disorder characterized by an exaggerated cultivation
> of one's image at the expense of one's real self. Narcissistically inclined
> individuals attach more importance to the way they appear to others
> than to the way they themselves feel. They will deny emotions that con-
> tradict the image of themselves that they want to create. Since they act
> without emotion, they tend to entice and manipulate others and fight to
> acquire power and domination. They are egoists, concentrating exclu-
> sively on their own interests, but they lack the true values of the self,
> namely self-expression, composure, dignity and integrity.
>
> On the cultural plane narcissism is characterized by a loss of humane
> values – a lack of interest in one's environment, in the quality of life, in
> one's fellow men and women. A society that sacrifices the natural envir-
> onment to the thirst for power and profit shows that it has become
> insensitive to human needs. When wealth is ranked more highly than

wisdom, when recognition is more highly admired than dignity, when success takes precedence over self-esteem, then that culture is over-valuing the 'image' and has become narcissistic.

I had long been intrigued by the question of how Ronald Reagan, who was hardly an intellectual high-flyer, could become President of the United States. The answer is that in the age of the media he sold politics as infotainment. And he was outstandingly successful at it. With his years as a film actor behind him he knew how to project himself on television to his best advantage. So skilfully did he address the nation on television that many of his audience, including myself, were taken in by the deception. Because I could see no manuscript, I assumed he was speaking extempore, and I was impressed. Then someone explained to me that there was a teleprompter, not visible on the screen, from which he read off his speech, giving the impression he was speaking without notes.

The viewers fell for the trick. I find that significant. I myself have spoken at many meetings, large and small, and quickly established a rapport with my audience. But on television, depending on which part of the speech was being shown, everything looked quite different – often it did not look effective at all. A speaker who wants to reach his audience must stay close to what he says, laying bare his emotions and seeking to carry his listeners with him. But on television, particularly with the short extracts that are usually shown, everything comes across quite differently.

The words of Walter Benjamin in his famous essay on the reproductibility of the work of art are relevant here: 'Even with the most perfect of reproductions there is one thing missing – the here-and-now of the work of art, its unique presence in the place to which it belongs. The here-and-now of the original is what defines the concept of authenticity . . . And the whole sphere of authenticity lies beyond the scope of reproductibility, whether technical or any other kind.'

Some may wonder about my recourse to the concept of the work of art in this connection. But as far back as Classical Antiquity we find references to the art of rhetoric. Maybe it does not come naturally to talk today of 'the art of speaking'. But it is an ability that should be especially appreciated at a time when all that television news has to offer is half-sentences or, if we are lucky, two or three complete sentences.

Watching flamenco dancing on a video made me realize how inadequately such musical experiences are conveyed on mechanical equipment. For many years, when the papers assumed I was in Tuscany, I was in fact in Spain, and very often in Andalucia. It was not only the

Alhambra, the *mesquita* in Cordoba, Seville and Ronda that fasci-
nated me but also flamenco dancing. Flamenco is the constant search
for a shared emotion expressed by the performer through song and
dance on behalf of his or her audience. Its objective is not the enthusiastic applause of listeners and spectators but the establishment of a
direct communication with an intimate gathering in which each person present feels himself individually addressed. For centuries it was a
purely vocal art but it is incomplete without the interjected calls and
clapping from the spectators. Its climax comes when what the singer
feels in his heart coincides with what he sings.

The loss of authenticity to which Benjamin refers was something
that caused me, and, I am sure, many of my fellow-politicians, a great
deal of heart-searching. Pompous declarations became the order of
the day, because it was no longer a matter of winning over one's listeners in parliamentary debates. What now matters above all is to cut
a good figure and make a favourable impression on the thousands of
viewers one does not know and cannot see.

Such a situation was ready-made for Ronald Reagan. Bill Clinton is
cast in the same mould. Like Reagan, he is always in a good mood and
there is always an encouraging smile of quiet optimism on his face.
Both men have become successful role models among politicians. Not
everyone can muster a permanent smile but for many it has become
second nature. On the other hand it can be embarrassing if such a
smile becomes so deeply entrenched that it is still on display when the
speaker is talking of sad or tragic events. During the war in Kosovo I
was always irritated by the constant grin on the face of Jamie Shea, the
NATO spokesman. Someone called his press conferences 'dazzling sales
talk'.

Tony Blair, too, is a politician made for television. He is good-look-
ing, smiles cheerfully and optimistically and is blessed with the rhetorical gifts of an accomplished preacher. The *Frankfurter Allgemeine
Zeitung* described him as representing a marketing campaign rather
than a political campaign.

Jean Baudrillard once complained that the political class no longer
had any 'specific character'. 'Their element is no longer that of decision and action,' he wrote, 'but that of the video game. Their interventions have become more and more restricted to the calculation of special
effects. They have lost their political aura and could easily be replaced
in the eyes of the masses by sportsmen or show-biz personalities – that
is to say, by professional entertainers.'

That is a damning criticism of the work of our politicians in today's
world. But does not the current organization of society positively com-
pel politics to be conducted according to the rules of television and

television commercials? And what are the consequences? Political matters are dealt with in haste because there is a perpetual rotation of images and subjects. It is important to look one's best in the daily news programmes. It is equally important to be favourably reported in the following morning's papers, especially the tabloids. In this way politics becomes a media event, divorced from anything that smacks of long-term planning.

Thus Bill Clinton came into office with the intention of initiating reforms in the fields of social policy, health and education. He ended up with policies that correspond to the tentative neoliberal measures put forward by the Republicans. Nor does his foreign policy suggest any coherent overall strategy. Sporadic air strikes against Iraq, Sudan and Afghanistan, and his similar decision over the war in Kosovo, demonstrate that.

It was natural that it should be Tony Blair who always leapt to President Clinton's aid. General de Gaulle called Britain the Americans' bridgehead in Europe. At the same time Blair has succeeded, with the help of his spin-doctors in Europe, in giving the impression of forging a completely new kind of social-democrat politics, freed from the shackles of tradition.

To what extent the development of this image has been helped by the interest of German employers' organizations in portraying Great Britain as a model for neoliberal policies, is a question still to be answered. It remains a fact, however, that the actual decisions taken by the Blair government in the field of domestic policy are the very opposite of what was dangled before the electorate during the election campaign. Whatever the Blair administration does is labelled 'New This' and 'Modern That', and is then ready to be packaged and sold. 'New Labour, New Europe, New Everything' – up goes up the ironical cry, even in Downing Street.

Maybe this sort of politics is inevitable in our media-driven society. But it is a sort of politics to which I can find no access – nor do I wish to do so. What we need today is something that will last, not something that is over and forgotten tomorrow. To be sure, there is no way in election campaigns to avoid following the rules of advertising. But must promises be made only to be broken once the election is over? In the field of taxation policy, for instance, we have seen how Bush, Chirac and Kohl all fell into this trap. That is why I was insistent that the SPD should avoid making such mistakes.

Political success does not lie in programme ratings or personality points. It lies, for me, in attempting to bring about, often through hard, relentless work, improvements in the living conditions of our fellow men and women.

19

Flexibility

Whenever the directors of a national central bank are asked why unemployment in Europe cannot be cured, they reply: 'Monetary policy has done its job. It is only structural reforms in the labour markets that will lead to higher growth and increased employment.' This is also the standard answer given by the European Central Bank when asked why unemployment in Europe is so high. No single word characterizes better the false direction taken by politics at the end of the twentieth century than that of the 'flexibility' of the labour markets.

Indeed, the term 'labour market' itself implies that there are workers, i.e. men and women, who offer themselves for sale in a market where potential customers, i.e. employers, buy their services. But men and women are not commodities. To apply to human beings terms which properly apply only to objects, shows how humane values have become degraded. It has always disturbed me to hear people, even my friends in the trade unions, talk of the 'labour market', albeit without any trace of a pejorative meaning. And if in the heat of the moment I catch myself using the term, it annoys me. It is incompatible with the concept of human dignity.

Moreover if the word 'flexible' is added to the equation, the situation becomes even more questionable, for it implies that the terms of employment – that is, the conditions under which men and women earn their living – can be changed at will, with human beings being treated like goods for sale or sums of money.

This is where we see the effects of globalization at their most glaring. Globalization is used as a weapon with which to attack the achievements of a social market economy, the welfare state. Workers in Europe are told that they must face worldwide competition. Employers point to countries in which there is no minimum wage and where employees work round the clock for a wage that is only a fraction of that earned by European workers. There are no trade unions in these countries and children are also made to work. Therefore, say the neoliberals, we in Europe must be more flexible. They do not demand more night shifts, more weekend working, more overtime and lower wages – they just talk of 'flexibility', a word that has a modern ring that conceals the true reality.

It is worth noting that proposals for flexible working come as a rule from groups in society that would never dream of accepting part-time or flexible working themselves, such as boards of directors or university professors with guaranteed tenure. Standard employment practices, which guarantee a worker's social security and provide him with a framework within which he can plan his life, are one of the most important achievements of modern society. The central political question is, what form will the employer–employee relationship take in future? This is the point at which one has to decide whether compassion and humane values are to remain the foundations of modern society or not. If traditional working practices are going to increasingly give way to flexible working conditions, it will make inroads into social life as we know it.

Max Weber spoke of man's need for a context within which to arrange his life. The American sociologist Richard Sennett went so far as to posit that fixed working conditions help to form character by promoting values such as loyalty and a sense of mutual commitment and by enabling people to set themselves long-term objectives. On the other hand, argued Sennett, flexible working practices, in the absence of any counter-influence, can lead to a disintegration of character and a loss of self-esteem. A reduction in welfare provision and the removal of protection from summary dismissal combine to produce a sense of insecurity and a fear of losing control of one's own life. Such developments tend to lead to short-lived friendships and a decline in one's involvement in the affairs of the local community. They also leave their mark on family life. Whereas family ties depend on settled conditions, flexibility and mobility make for restlessness and a tendency to avoid long-term commitments.

The retention of one's occupation is also important, and to lose one's links with that occupation is often a painful experience. When German reunification came about in 1990, it was not only the material aspirations of the East Germans that were not fulfilled. The complaint was frequently heard that the impact on working practices and the loss of a guaranteed job in one's chosen field resulted in a feeling of inadequacy and redundance. People talked of a devaluation of their skills and abilities, a development that cannot be categorized solely in economic or business terms.

The subject of the conditions under which people work has become one of today's most pressing social problems. And it is a problem to which those on the left must have a different solution from that put forward by neoliberal so-called 'modernizers'. One cannot avoid the problem by pointing out that a pensioner can supplement his pension by taking on casual jobs, or that a mother is free to earn some extra pocket money after her family has grown up and left home. Such cases do not strike at the heart of the issue. The pensioner will normally have had a regular job which gave him a sense of identity, while the housewife received her sense of identity from raising her children and attending to the needs of the family. What is at stake is the replacement of regular terms and conditions of work by casual agreements and short-term contracts.

In Germany today there are 27.7 million people in full-time employment. But the number of those in permanent jobs is shrinking; 3.9 million are already on short-term contracts. There is also a boom in part-time work. In 1998 there were 575,000 workers on temporary loan; five years earlier the figure had been 266,000. Many hope to use such a job as a springboard to permanent employment.

Then there are the low-paid workers – those in the so-called 630-mark jobs – whose numbers are calculated to lie between 3 and 6 million and who represent a broad swathe of low-paid workers comparable to that in the United States. In addition there are the bogus self-employed, who get neither unemployment benefit if they lose their job nor a pension, and who have no job security. A person dismissed for being sick or too old has recourse only to welfare. The law of the jungle prevails.

Certain specialists, such as graduates in information studies, are much sought-after. They earn a great deal of money and are naturally in a position to take out private insurance against losing their job. But those on low earnings envy those who receive a regular monthly income as full-time workers or employees. Classic self-employed groups such as doctors, lawyers and architects are not left to their own resources but are organized in guilds or professional associations which come to the aid of their members in time of need. But the newer self-employed, especially those on very low wages, have nowhere to turn. It is therefore a good thing that the trade unions have now begun to take up their cause. The argument that money is saved through the non-payment of insurance contributions does not hold water. What the employer saves, society pays out in the form of welfare as soon as one of these low-paid workers loses his job.

It was therefore appropriate that, immediately after coming to power, the new red-green coalition government should have set out to limit the abuses inherent in the principle of flexible working. It was also justified to put an end to the process by which an increasing number of people were evading their obligation to pay social security contributions. The social security system serves to maintain social cohesion and is there to provide help for those who find themselves in difficulties through no fault of their own. But this help is not the responsibility of just one section of the population. At the foundation of the welfare state rests the obligation of all citizens to provide solidarity and assistance to their fellows by means of the national insurance system.

The neoliberal view that private insurance schemes are preferable to that run by the state is a relapse into nineteenth-century ways of thinking, attitudes particular, by and large, to those classes which do not expect to find themselves in a state of material or existential hardship. But it was conspicuous that in the frontal attack on the new proposals for dealing with the low-paid and those on casual earnings, only the Minister for Employment and a handful of members of the parliamentary party voted the other way. The government did not succeed in making it clear that what was at stake was the issue of social cohesion. Even a modern society cannot afford to sacrifice tried and tested methods that have been built up in the field of labour relations over many years, and in the last analysis good relations, built on binding commitments, form the basis of any democratic state. A job-hopper society, in which many people are compelled to move from one job to another, in one place after another, without protection from a welfare system, is not a humane society.

Investigations have shown that the nature of casual jobs in the media has led people to play safe and cut out any potentially offensive material to anticipate the possible intervention of the censor. They are, after all, anxious to keep their jobs. One can observe a similar effect in the field of education throughout Europe. Young teachers are engaged on vague terms and are given vague job profiles. As a result they are condemned to a specific type of conformism. The same trend can be seen in research. If this trend to temporary appointments continues, the day will come when society discovers that economic censorship can be worse than political censorship and can have far-reaching social consequences. Sociologists are already talking of a mentality of uncertainty.

The organization of the labour market is also bound up with freedom and democracy. To be free, a person must have a proper job. A person on a temporary contract always has to keep one eye on those who hold in their hands the course of his or her future career. There is an air of subordination, even of toadying – though at first sight the mechanisms of censorship cannot be recognized as such.

In an article in the *Süddeutsche Zeitung* Claus Koch drew attention to the loss of a sense of responsibility that accompanies the introduction of flexible working practices:

> There is a type of German male that one comes across ever more rarely – the gaunt, sinewy worker, born into the world of machines and the working practices they impose, thus committed to their service and the rationality of their organization but at the same time determined in his acts of rebellion. The epitome of accountability . . . But today's society, built on service industries, has no use for such a morality of responsibility because this authority presupposes experience, and thus rests on permanence, durability. Such values are unwelcome to the slick, self-promoting operators of today.

A discussion paper distributed to members of Gerhard Schröder's economic advisory group, published in September 1997, still recognized these connections. 'We reject the path of conservative ideologies, i.e. the path that leads to conformity with the forces of a globalized economy by dismantling labour agreements and social relationships. The signs of social erosion are unmistakable in the USA and are becoming increasingly so in Great Britain. The much-trumpeted synthesis of a modern, state-of-the-art economy and social integration is nowhere to be seen.'

And the writers go on:

> We must therefore adjust the parameters within which the factor of labour can be put to its most efficient use. But given the strong external pressure for change, and given also the loss of the traditional sense of security, people will only be able to comprehend the mobility and flexibility that are being demanded of them if they can be certain that their livelihood is not under threat. Only within a 'corridor of security' will it be possible for old, entrenched positions to be given up and new challenges accepted.

The authors of this paper were far ahead of Bodo Hombach and Peter Mandelson.

20

The Third Way is a Route to Nowhere

After my resignation the reaction of the press was almost unanimous. Now at last, they said, Schröder had the chance to push through his programme of 'modernization'. For too long he had given way to Lafontaine and the party bosses.

Der Spiegel wrote:

> Schröder is now set on creating a radical change of mood. Flushed with a new sense of optimism, the modernizers of the SPD are about to embark on their new projects, with the support of the Greens, who at their meeting last Friday enthusiastically endorsed the adoption of a neoliberal philosophy under the following headings:
>
> (1) Part One of the tax reforms is to be put into effect. But at the same time, from 1 January 2000 industry will profit considerably from a reform of corporation tax. Families will benefit in accordance with the decision of the Supreme Court;
>
> (2) Schröder and his colleagues are banking on the success of the Alliance for Employment initiative and the consensus on energy policy. Now that bogeyman Lafontaine has gone, Schröder can count on the cooperation of the industrialists;
>
> (3) Properly formulated and costed plans are to be submitted for reform measures in the other areas of the economy that have been targeted – health, pensions and low pay. At last the Chancellor is poised to deliver what he promised after the chaos of his first hundred days in office – less haste, more thoroughness.

Lobbyists and employers' associations were jubilant at Lafontaine's departure, as though they were celebrating a second victory of capitalism over a planned economy. 'This is one of the happiest days of my business career,' raved Hans Schreiber, President of the Confederation of Executives in the Insurance Industry. 'Lafontaine was a destroyer of capital and a destroyer of jobs.' Hans-Olaf Henkel, on behalf of the industrialists, added: 'The Chancellor has managed to shake off one of his shackles. Now he has got just one left – Environment Minister Trittin.' Shares on the Stock Exchange soared. Within seven minutes the euro gained two cents against the dollar. In the first fifteen minutes' trading on Friday the DAX rose 300 points compared with the previous day – a rise of 6 per cent. Two cheers for Schröder.

The London *Sun* also gave vent to its delight at my departure, behaving as though it had been brought about by their own stupid headlines.

I was reminded of a passage in Dostoevsky, one of my favourite authors:

> There are different kinds of opponent. Not with all of them can one discuss the point at issue. A few days ago I heard the following story, said to be an ancient fable of Indian origin. Once upon a time a pig got into an argument with a lion and challenged him to a duel. But when he got home, the pig began to feel afraid. The animals discussed what was the best thing to do, then said: 'Look, pig, there's a cesspit nearby. Go and wallow in it before you arrive for the duel.' The pig did as he had been told. The lion arrived, sniffed, puckered its nose and went away. For a long while afterwards the pig boasted that the lion had been too afraid of him to engage in a duel.

If it had only been a question of the smell of the cesspit – to retain Dostoevsky's image – I would not have declined to fight. For over thirty years I had been fighting such duels and had often had such smells in my nose. Far from scaring me off, opposition only served to make me redouble my efforts. At the time of the Alliance for Employment I often had difficulty in stopping myself from laughing at what was going on. The economic views expressed by the employers' spokesmen were to me, as everybody knows in the meantime, foolish in the extreme. I took great pleasure in putting economic data in front of them which were guaranteed to worry them, at least for a while. In the face of my analysis of the social circumstances, and given my demand that we should turn our backs on the policies of neoliberalism, I could hardly have failed to expect to meet with tough opposition to my policies.

The ultimate reason for my resignation was that Gerhard Schröder had been given a mandate by the country's electorate, and the Chairman of the Social-Democratic Party cannot go out of his way to seek a confrontation on fundamental issues with a social-democratic Chancellor. With a mixture of amazement and anger I watched, after I had resigned, as Schröder set out to lead the party up the garden path by the so-called 'Third Way'. I came to the conclusion that a number of the leading figures in the SPD, the new Party Chairman at their head, had failed to grasp why, and by what means, we had won the election. In March 1999 Herbert Mai, Secretary of the Transport Workers Union, to which I also belong, wrote a worried letter to his members:

> Comrades:
> Developments and events in the past few weeks have provoked a debate over whether the new government should change direction and bring in policies which favour the interests of the business world to a greater extent than before. Pressure to do so has been brought to bear by employers' organizations and particular industries, supported by tendentious arguments published in conservative papers and journals.
> In such a situation, to take sides in a contest between SPD and the Greens to offer employers ever-lower tax rates in ever-decreasing intervals, combined with further advances in deregulation, carries with it the risk that the government will become increasingly dependent on decisions taken in meetings of business associations and industrial confederations, or in the boardrooms of individual concerns.
> The outcome of the federal election of 27 September 1998 was a clear rejection of the continued adherence by CDU/CSU and FDP to predominantly supply-side policies in economics, taxation, social and employment policy. The SPD and the Greens together won a parliamentary majority because both parties promised to set employment policy at the heart of their reforms, thereby putting a stop to the redistribution of wealth from the poor to the rich and working for a higher degree of social justice.

Lest Mai's statement be dismissed as the prejudiced utterance of a dyed-in-the-wool 'traditionalist', we can turn to the evidence of the Allensbach Institute for Demoscopy, published in June 1999 in the *Frankfurter Allgemeine Sonntagszeitung* under the heading 'Are the Social Democrats' Plans Losing Their Shine?' The Institute came to the conclusion that it was not the government's guiding principles that the electors rejected but their actual policies:

> With the disastrous *Land* elections that the SPD has suffered in the course of the year, the electorate has been passing a negative verdict on the party which had emerged as the jubilant victors in the national election only a few months earlier. More and more people expect the SPD to go on losing support. When one adds to this the Chancellor's clear dissociation, in his joint manifesto with Tony Blair, from the SPD's earlier programme and at the same time from his own policies over his

first nine months, one has the impression that, so slight is the attraction exercised these days by social-democrat ideas that even the Chairman of the party sees little hope of putting them into effect.

Not that traditional social-democrat values are simply out of fashion with the voters. People attach great importance to a strong state that cares for its citizens through a highly developed welfare system sustained by ideals of equality. The outcome of the election was a vote for the retention of the welfare state against the former government's policies aimed at its reform. Contrary to what was often assumed, people were not voting primarily for a set of new faces.

More self-dependence, less state – that is a message which people associate with the expectation of an increasingly divided society, more detachment and egoism, growing unemployment and insecurity, and less protection for the disadvantaged and for minorities. But it is not only the principle of a strong state and a comprehensive social network that meets with the approval of a broad spectrum of the population: it is also the ideal of equality among men, an ideal which is a firmly established principle in the philosophy of social democracy. The broad majority of the population feel that a country develops better when it not only offers equality of opportunity but also strives to promote equality of achievement. The growing criticism of the government is therefore not to be attributed to a declining confidence in the traditional values of social democracy.

In the summer of 1999 the government insisted that wage increases, if granted at all, should be limited to the rate of inflation, in order to reduce unemployment. This overlooked the fact that unemployment had risen dramatically in Germany precisely at the time when wage rates were most rapidly falling, i.e. over the last twenty years. Dieter Schulte, Chairman of the Trade Unions Federation, was moved to remark: 'There are good suggestions, bad suggestions and crazy suggestions. The suggestion to confine wage rises to the rate of inflation belongs without doubt to the last category.'

Matthias Brodkorb, leader of the Young Socialists in the province of Mecklenburg-Vorpommern, took a similar attitude, scoffing that what the 'modernizers' were putting forward as new proposals were gradually approaching the ridiculous. 'We demand that the employers make common cause with us,' he said. 'In 1998 alone their profits rose by 30.5 per cent. We propose that increases in profits be similarly linked to the rate of inflation.'

These were exactly my own sentiments. Since German reunification the value of shares has risen year in, year out. The DAX* stands at an all-time high. Business profits have exploded and there are more mil-

---

* Deutscher Aktienindex, the German stock exchange share index.

lionaires than ever. Huge fortunes are inherited year after year. According to the union that represents workers in the internal revenue, over 800 billion marks are spirited away into tax havens abroad. The IMF has put the total amount of such tax evasion in the world as a whole at 7 trillion dollars. While real wages are stagnating or falling, the government goes on prattling about a wage freeze. Earning money, i.e. work, is becoming less and less worthwhile. Owning money, on the other hand, is becoming more and more profitable. What has led to this crazy state of affairs and the equally crazy proposals for dealing with it?

We must remember that as early as 1982 the Kohl government noticed that all was not well with our society. They promised a change in moral values – more decency, more community spirit, more social cohesion. They also promised, of course, to make society more expressive of conservative values.

But when their period of office came to an end, things were seen to have got no better. On the contrary. People talk today of having to push others out of the way in order to get on. Bullying and intimidation are on the increase. Fine-sounding values like liberality and individualism are used to conceal self-interest and self-advancement, and sociologists lament the decay of humane values. When policies like those of the Kohl administration are built on the principles of market forces and deregulation, the social consensus is bound to be at risk.

Before the Bundestag election we were talking of the fragmentation of society. We were fully aware that it was not politics alone that was responsible for the change in social values. If, as a consequence of growing prosperity, traditional ties such as those to family, church or trade union become weaker, social norms and values will change. The homogeneity which used to characterize classes and groupings in society will splinter and lead to a multiplicity of new social entities, while habits and modes of behaviour undergo corresponding changes.

The mass media, especially television, play their own influential part in helping to turn relativity into non-commitment, pluralism into the philosophy of 'one thing is as good as another'. Liberality – better called licence – preaches a gospel of 'anything goes'. There is nothing to choose between one thing and another. Values are calculated by reference to the numbers of viewers – so-called ratings. What is going through the mind of those people who, for the sake of a few pence and without a trace of embarrassment, reveal their innermost secrets in endless chat-shows before scandal-hungry audiences? What is the attraction of the many films which aestheticize or glorify violence? And to what extent does politics bear a responsibility for this situation?

The individualistic, neoliberal concept of freedom, ironically, carries the seeds of its own destruction. It fails to recognize that individual freedom can only flourish so long as it is anchored in social solidarity. A conception of freedom that emphasizes the individual at the expense of the solidarity of society will only drive people apart.

The liberal politician Alexis de Tocqueville saw such a situation coming.

> Let me imagine the various ways in which despotism could manifest itself. I envisage a host of people, all more or less alike and in similar situations, who move round and round in a circle without pause in search of trivial, everyday little pleasures which fill their lives. Each stands alone, isolated, heedless of the fate of all the others. As far as he is concerned, the human race consists simply of his family and those around him. He stands side by side with his fellow-men but he does not see them. He touches them but he does not feel them. He exists solely in and for himself.

The threat of totalitarianism, whatever form or shape it may take, has by no means been lifted. Some see a danger in the nature of certain developments in modern information society which recall the fears of de Tocqueville. As long as alienated individuals and disaffected social groups are satisfied, or at least pacified, by the flood of shallow entertainment and spin-doctored news items drilled into them on their television screens, there is always the possibility that absolute political power will fall into the hands of those who exercise unfettered dominion over people's minds via the media. The election of the media mogul Silvio Berlusconi as Italian Prime Minister was a warning signal.

At the end of the twentieth century the political ideology of neoliberalism is the expression of a *Zeitgeist* that worships the individualization of society. The FDP, for example, basks in the confident expectation that it is the party of the future. In the case of the FDP this *fata morgana* is not difficult to understand: any party that has stood for years on the verge of collapse needs to bolster up its self-confidence with the illusion of a rosy future waiting round the corner. But the blind enthusiasm with which neoliberals and 'modernizers' set about cutting welfare benefits evidently prevented them from soberly discussing the problems that arise in a self-centred society ruled by the principle of 'each man for himself'.

For if it is correct – and there is much to indicate that it is – that a society which has abandoned the ideal of solidarity is more likely to fall victim to authoritarian forms of society – see, for instance, the success of extreme right-wing groups in recent *Land* elections – then in the last analysis an unregulated *laissez-faire* politics will undermine the social basis of individual freedom.

Seen against this background, the discussions going on between the Young Socialists and the Greens are quite extraordinary. In all recent elections the FDP has discovered how 'enthusiastic' the electors really are about their proposals. And the social reality in the more liberal Anglo-Saxon democracies can hardly be a mystery to the Young Socialists and the Greens.

Although there is today a large degree of correspondence between the democratic structures in western Europe and those in North America, European countries have developed in their own way. They have their own historical traditions and a different political culture. The tradition of individual freedom in the United States is widely admired throughout the world. But it has its dark side.

A glance at the history of emigration from the Old World to the New in the nineteenth century shows immediately how strong the attraction of the United States was to the anarchist wing of the European working-class movement. It is one of the ironies of history that it should be this traditional anarchic tendency in American society that had its most lasting influence in that very area of activity in which the immigrants could have done without it – in the economy. American communitarists have recently been making their compatriots aware of the extent to which the anarchic tendency endemic in the Anglo-Saxon conception of the market economy has hindered the development of a sense of community and social solidarity.

In his classic plea for 'strong democracy' Benjamin Barber maintained that the anarchistic disposition was highly sensitive to sources of public authority and control – such as the state, the majority, or even the exercise of the law – but was totally blind to the agents of private coercion, such as the stock market or the forces of anarchy.

It would assuredly be no bad thing for the Europeans if they were less firmly fixated on the state in certain areas of social life. Nor would it do any harm if their political representatives were to off-load some of their responsibilities on to society itself. That people hold their elected representatives accountable for everything that goes wrong, is the natural reaction to the way these representatives claim the credit for everything that goes well. A culture of democratic participation assumes that civil society will shoulder part of the responsibility. The fixation of European society on the state hinders the development of that pioneer spirit of adventure and enterprise so characteristic of American society. But the other side of the coin is that that pioneer spirit does little to encourage social cohesion and a general feeling of social well-being. Instead there is a deep-seated anti-state attitude in economic life which paralyses political activity.

No other area of social life is more utterly dominated by the urge to self-advancement than that of the economy. There is no cause for surprise when one observes that those to whom any hint of libertarianism in society is anathema, and who are among the first to talk of the need for law and order, are prepared to defend the anarchic state of our economy without reservation.

But what happens if profits fall? Then a different kind of truth comes into operation. Industrialists apparently have two kinds of truth at their disposal, one for good times, the other for bad times. If a business is doing well, it puts out a case for non-intervention by the state – no subsidies to potential competitors, no ecological levies, no additional social burdens. But when times are bad, they sing a different tune. They demand subsidies. And if the business goes bankrupt, it is the state that picks up the tab for the workers made redundant.

But at least everybody is agreed that a 'free' market can only be created within a fixed framework which regulates the movement of goods and the conduct of the economy. What is in dispute is the extent of this regulation. Politics is judged by different criteria from economics. Its aim is the well-being of the community, not the promotion of private profit. True, high unemployment demands action on the political front. But as long as appropriate regulations for the conduct of a market economy are not in place, any economic policy is bound to fail.

This is not meant as a justification for introducing a whole raft of new regulations. There would be no point in forcing the economy into a bureaucratic strait-jacket of rules and regulations and throttling its dynamic forces. But wherever the market economy produces undesirable social consequences, it is the function of politics to remedy the situation. It is a platitude often forgotten that it is not the responsibility of society to serve the interests of the economy but the economy that has the duty to serve the interests of society. Yet those who remind the world of this fact are often dismissed as yesterday's men, traditionalists who have not moved with the times, for the national debate on the development of the economy and the future of society is dominated by the one-sided neoliberal views of the employers' organizations.

In her study of 1996 with the title 'The Terror of the Economy', Viviane Forrester complained that people had lost the ability to view the current economic and social order in other than rigid, oversimplified categories. Forrester's critique of the one-dimensional free enterprise social order characteristic of the end of the twentieth century reads like a confirmation of de Tocqueville's vision of the future, in which the powers that be will relieve the masses of the responsibility to think for themselves and avoid giving them any precise information, so that they can the more easily be manipulated and controlled. If the national debate were decided less by the material interests of one social group and more by focused thought and the accuracy of the information adduced, such ideological one-sidedness would not survive. Maybe Forrester tends to overstate her case but her analysis strikes at the heart of the matter.

It must be conceded that the employers' organizations have chosen a propitious moment to launch an ideological offensive. There has been no better time since the Second World War for such an initiative than the last few years. When the Iron Curtain between East and West was lifted, so too was an economic barrier. Nothing now stood in the way of economic globalization. Globalization inevitably offered a new challenge to western European countries, above all to Germany, whose economy depends on the export trade. Under the new conditions of increased global competition industry has had to adapt its working practices to meet the demands of a new age.

But Germany has the most competitive export trade of the highly developed nations of the world. In order to maintain this lead, we must invest. We need good schools and universities, well-equipped research facilities and a sound infrastructure – roads, railways and telecommunications. The future lies in the hands of the country with the highest energy productivity and the most environmentally friendly technology. The ailing British economy is paying for what Gordon Brown called 'the tradition of under-investment in the state'. Rolls-Royce and Rover have been bought up by German motor-car manufacturers.* Imagine what the reaction would be in Germany if Mercedes, BMW or Volkswagen had been taken over by British firms. The British process of dismantling the welfare state is another example of a senseless economic policy.

In *The Third Way* Schröder and Blair went so far as to write: 'We do not rule out deficit spending – during a cyclical downturn it makes sense to let the automatic stabilisers work. And borrowing to finance higher government investment, in strict accordance with the Golden Rule, can play a key role in strengthening the supply side of the economy.'

But if the welfare state is abandoned, there are no automatic stabilizers left, and the tradition of under-investment will spread to the private sector. The deregulated global financial market offers profit margins in the area of speculative investment which far exceed those of domestic industries. Financial investments have thus grown more quickly than those in manufacturing. This is the reason for the decline

* This refers to the situation as it was in 1999.

in investment in the European Community since the middle of the 1970s.

At the same time conditions in the international financial market not only affect investment quotas but cause significant changes in management cultures. More and more businesses are raising capital via the stock exchange. As a result they are increasingly dependent on the short-term interests of their shareholders, which means in turn that decisions are taken on the basis of short-term considerations and variable costs. A large proportion of these variable costs consists of wage costs. From enjoying worker participation for decades, with the right to share in the decision-making process, the worker was now reduced to the level of a wage statistic.

Eighth March 1996 became known in the international financial markets as 'Black Friday'. The Dow-Jones plunged and European and other stock exchanges followed suit. The panic had been caused by the news that unemployment in the USA had fallen by an unexpectedly large number. The American government had announced that in the previous month of February 705,000 new jobs had been created. *Le Monde* reported curtly on 12 March that the stock exchange was prone to react sensitively to 'any item of bad news'.

Such was the situation in a nutshell. Daniel Goeudevert wrote: 'It is a perverse situation when a firm announces that it is laying off workers and then stock exchange prices rise.' Rising share prices is just what shareholders are looking for. Small wonder that it should be precisely at such times of high unemployment that companies make huge profits on the stock exchange.

Justifiable as it is to question the logic that compels firms to dismiss staff in order to keep up the price of their shares, it would be absurd to blame businessmen for seeking to make a profit. Profit is the purpose of economic activity. Nor is there any sense in condemning all rationalization. It serves to raise productivity, and productivity is an important factor in economic strength. Rationalization is also a precondition for short working hours and satisfactory wage-levels. Rationalized and consolidated production processes are for many firms the only hope for survival in the world of tough global competition. Other firms, whose businesses are doing well, seek in this way to increase their share of the market by making special offers. Others, again, are only concerned with raising their profit margins. According to the rules of a 'free' market economy there is nothing improper about all this. Why, after all, should a private firm employ workers it does not need? It is the job of the politicians to ensure that the procedures of the private market economy run smoothly within a basic framework which compels those within it to have regard to social and ecological considerations.

But Germany today is still dominated by an ideological climate in which anyone who accepts such a responsibility is immediately criticized for lacking 'modernity'. Employers' organizations add their own gloss to the situation. By their constant complaints about Germany being no longer competitive, 'so that we are forced to transfer our production abroad', they create a climate unconducive to the taking of decisions that have regard to the public interest. Indeed, the way in which the public is frequently misled by the propagation of false facts and inconsistent arguments borders on a deliberate policy of deception.

The policies of neoliberalism would never have conquered the ideological high ground with such ease if they had not employed the rhetoric of public service and social commitment. For a long while the heart of this ideology was a total faith in the blessings that came with unfettered economic growth, and anyone who queried this faith on ecological grounds was palmed off with the shibboleth that growth guaranteed more jobs. After it had become obvious that the economy could well grow without providing more jobs, a new principle had to be discovered for the employers to demonstrate their concern for the common weal. This new principle stated, 'the greater the profits, the lower the unemployment'. And there is indeed a correlation between unemployment and profits.

But there are two different ways of expressing this correlation. One is that a firm will not expand and take on more workers if it is not making a profit. The other is that a firm can raise its profits by laying off workers. In an economy without the corresponding social obligations profits as such are far from being a guarantee of employment. So why mislead the public with half-truths? Nobody can seriously doubt that employers too contribute to the general good by following their own interests. But what is good for business is not always good for everybody in society.

The importance that business attaches to the systematic influencing of public opinion in its own interests can be measured by the dramatic rise in the number of lobby groups. Consultancy firms earn considerable sums of money these days by manipulating people's opinions and influencing political decision-takers. In the face of the sophisticated techniques employed by these skilful operators working on behalf of sectional interests, genuine arguments concerned with public issues often get pushed into the background. Say what one will about politics, be it justified or unjustified, one principle remains unshakeable – in a democratic society the public good is the ultimate arbiter. So central is this principle, and so powerfully does it affect the behaviour of politicians, that even the most corrupt cannot entirely escape its attraction.

Globalization, with its demands and potential consequences, leads to a sense of insecurity, both in business and in society. This is the starting-point for the ideological offensive of neoliberalism. Globalization is turned into an ogre, the alarming prospect of whose domination makes people more willing to make concessions. Germany, one of the strongest nations in the world, is given a bad image, in the interests of lowering corporation tax, scaling down the welfare state and enforcing wage restraint.

As well as globalization the collapse of communism has given a fillip to the neoliberal cause. The unconditional surrender of socialist economies and social orders put an end to the East–West conflict, leaving democracy and the market economy the undisputed victors.

Cynics sometimes become nostalgic when they think back to the days of the Cold War. How convenient was that polarization into East and West, a clear division of the world into two spheres of influence – the West ruled by capitalism, the East by socialism! A comparison with the frightening eastern model was in itself enough to establish the legitimacy of the western democracies. Now, however, these democracies had to seek their justification within themselves, in their own aims and values.

An 'Iron Curtain' had protected western labour markets from the competition of eastern manpower, and the processes of global competition had shown the superiority of a social market economy over a command economy. Those living in the West saw their ever-increasing affluence as a law of nature. To be sure, prosperity had its price – the ceaseless destruction of nature and the ruthless exploitation of the natural resources of Third World countries. But only part of this price had to be paid by the West, while the West's efforts to alleviate misery and starvation in the poor countries that supplied those natural resources remained modest.

The collapse of the Berlin Wall caught the West off guard. It had not been expected to be so sudden. Only today can we see in its totality all that has changed. The Cold War was sustained by the arms race, an uninterrupted process of rearmament conducted with all available technological means and at massive expense. It rested on the ideological conflict between two different philosophies and two different economic systems. If it had not entrenched itself behind walls and barbed wire, the eastern bloc, lagging far behind the West, would have had to declare itself bankrupt years earlier. The full extent of the bankruptcy only came to light with the collapse of the Wall. Since that time, with a few exceptions, it has been the system of the free-market economy that has prevailed, and the organization of society has been governed by its laws the whole world over.

If one were to draw a straight line to represent the East–West conflict between rival economic and social orders, at the right-hand end of the line would be capitalism in its Anglo-American form, and at the left-hand end would be communism with its Stalinist structures. In between would be a broad stretch in which elements from both systems jostled side by side. The so-called 'convergence theoreticians' of the 1950s thought that the East–West conflict would fade away as the two economic systems moved closer together. Such illusions were also cultivated by the search on the part of democratic socialists for a 'Third Way', a middle path that would synthesize the advantages of the two extreme systems while discarding their disadvantages. A free market economy and a democratic social order were to combine in a system of social security.

Now that the East–West conflict is history, it has become clear that the dissolution of the old socialist system did not lead to the disappearance of global competition between the two systems. That competition goes on – in a more democratic, more relaxed, less threatening manner than before but no less vigorous, no less ideological. The balance, moreover, has shifted. With the collapse of communism it is now the social market economy that occupies the left-hand end of the spectrum. The Anglo-American conception of a market economy now finds itself confronting the European version of a social market economy.

As long as the social market economy occupied the middle ground on the line that joined the two extremes in the global competition, it was comparatively rarely under attack. It is as though the driving forces behind the systems at each end of the line had passed it by and left it relatively unscathed. The existence of communism created a breathing-space for the social market economy, which had contributed in no small measure to the 'victory' of capitalism. In the face of the standard of living and the social security enjoyed by the West, 'real existing socialism', as the rulers of the GDR wanted their system to be known, lost what little attractiveness it had left.

The honeymoon period is now over for the social market economy. The neoliberals of all countries have joined forces and are preparing to attack. Those who do not join in dismantling the welfare state will suffer at the hands of the financial markets. With the prospect of yields of 15 per cent there is no room for wage increases. All sense of embarrassment at the inequalities in the distribution of income has vanished. Wall Street is astonished when the Deutsche Bank pays five directors 335 million marks in salaries and bonuses over a period of five years. In this age of shareholder value the worker has become a mere cost factor.

We must therefore mount a vigorous offensive on behalf of the social market economy, developing it and bringing it up to date so that it can meet the challenges of the future – including ecological challenges. We must construct a model European welfare state capable of facing up to global competition and superior to the example presented by capitalism in its Anglo-Saxon form.

It is only to be expected that in the ideologically highly charged atmosphere of 'market radicalism' generated by the neoliberals, a reform programme put forward by the social democrats should meet with resistance. An alternative solution, either on a small or a large scale, is lacking. The proponents of neoliberalism concluded from the collapse of communism that any alternative to the market economy in its present form would be doomed to failure. That is what the American historian Francis Fukuyama would have us believe when he proclaimed that the disintegration of the Eastern bloc signified 'the end of history'. Conjuring up 'the end of history' was like performing an act of neoliberal exorcism. The evil spirit must once and for all be driven out of the minds of the left – the evil spirit of utopianism.

It is remarkable how many are enthusiastically joining the ranks of the exorcists and conceiving history as moving only in one direction, a direction to which there is no alternative. In 1995 a French scholar by the name of Jean-François Kahn wrote a book on the subject with the revealing title *The Single Thought*. Forty years earlier Leszek Kolakovski, a Polish philosopher, had published a work on the same subject called *Man With No Alternative*. It was a cry of protest against the suppression of free thought under Stalin, against the concept of the dictatorship of the proletariat, a conception which had similarly meant the end of history.

One-dimensional thinking cannot survive for long. It is incompatible with freedom. The question is: how long, in a technological world pulsating with hitherto unsuspected potentialities, will the crazy idea persist that there are no social alternatives? What is holding German intellectuals back? In France and the USA, for example, there is a public debate on the economic situation and its social consequences. But the Germans seem for some reason to be holding back. Have the epoch-making events of 1989–90 left them so shattered that they need time to catch their breath? Have some had the wind taken out of their sails by the fulfilment of their long-cherished desire to live to see the reunification of their beloved country? Others, perhaps, feel unsure of themselves because their predictions of how history would develop have been proven wrong and their utopias destroyed.

Or is it merely an attack of *fin-de-siècle* melancholy that is preventing German intellectuals from speaking out – and this, of all times, at a moment of profound technological and economic change as we enter a new millennium. Today more than ever before we need a sense of direction in a country in which 4 million unemployed are anxiously looking for an alternative political culture to that of conservative *laissez-faire*. We need a culture that not only rewards the urge towards greater and greater profits and is not driven solely by an insatiable desire for material possessions. We need a more democratic culture with more social participation, a culture that attaches more importance to education and knowledge, more value to the quality of life and a sense of community.

This silence on the part of our left-wing intellectuals, which, compared with their former shrillness, almost amounts to intellectual capitulation, has perhaps another, more general explanation. There is a cultural process at work in which original thought is being increasingly crushed under the weight of conformity, of reproduction and repetition. If there is one single characteristic that distinguishes the course of modern civilization, it is the fantastic development of reproductive technology. That this development has now reached man himself, making possible the cloning of human beings, is both logical in itself and symbolic of our age. That an artificial figure like Michael Jackson could become the idol of the teenagers of today is a natural expression of this symbolism. There is no better term to capture the essence of our age than that of 'the media society', for as the word itself says, the media are the means of reproduction, the agents of cultural cloning.

Back in 1936 Walter Benjamin published his famous essay 'The Work of Art in the Age of its Technical Reproducibility', in which he predicted the direction in which technology would lead. He saw that much of what could be said about the reproduction of the work of art, with its consequent loss of authenticity and profundity, could as well be applied to the reproduction of politics. 'The crisis facing the democracies', he wrote, 'can be understood as a crisis in the conditions in which man as a political animal has to function . . . The influence and effectiveness of modern art becomes the greater the more it allies itself with the processes of reproduction and the less it talks in terms of originality and uniqueness.'

Benjamin's argument could equally well be applied to the field of politics to read: 'The influence and effectiveness of modern politics becomes the greater the more account it takes of the power of reproducibility.' It is not complex relationships or long-term strategies, not originality or profundity, not truth and substance that offer the best possibilities for reproduction but superficial impressions, shallow theatricality.

Politicians adjust themselves to the system. If reproducibility is the criterion of 'modern times', the modern politician will follow the rules and conduct politics as a media event. But there is a price to be paid. The contents matter less than the packaging. Firm outlines become blurred, commitments are withdrawn, arbitrariness spreads its influence. And as intellectual content recedes, so arbitrariness takes over. In many areas 'modern' has become a synonym for 'arbitrary'.

But there are signs that the left wing is waking up. The instant success of Viviane Forrester's book in France – the *Neue Zürcher Zeitung* called it 'the first step for a long time to win back the field of social criticism for the left wing' – suggests that a broad alliance of middle-class values and left-wing intellectuals is still – or perhaps again – possible, in Germany as well.

An alliance of this kind between the majority of the population and the intellectuals has usually shown itself in the past to offer the most fertile soil for thoroughgoing social reforms. Opinion polls show a growing identification with values that were formerly thought of as left-wing. 'Modernizers' would have us believe that terms like 'left-wing' and 'right-wing' mean little to people nowadays. But the polls prove otherwise. In fact, even the experts could not identify certain values as 'left-wing' or 'right-wing' with greater confidence than the majority of the population at large. Nevertheless these polls do allow us to conclude that there is a broad measure of support in Germany for left-wing policies which put an emphasis on social values.

People have come to understand that the welfare state is in need of reform. They were prepared, and still are, to accept certain limitations. There was the time, for instance, when Norbert Blüm made annual savings of 98 billion marks by cutting pensions and unemployment benefit. People will accept reforms in the welfare state provided they are carried out fairly. Reductions in welfare benefit lead to disputes over a just distribution of wealth, and at such moments policies are needed that respect the principle of social justice.

In the USA, where inequality of incomes and living standards has increased dramatically in the past two decades, Richard Freeman, one of the country's leading experts on labour and employment matters, coined the term 'apartheid economy', pointing out that all the economic advantages of neoliberal 'Reaganomics' had accrued to the upper 5 per cent of the population. All the rest had suffered as a result of these policies, and the poorest had suffered most. Freeman even talked in terms of a potential new class struggle.

What is true of America is doubly true of Europe. Left-wing governments came to power in Europe because the electors rejected neoliberal policies of social indifference. If politicians turn a deaf ear to the cries of distress from their countrymen and fail to remedy the situation, the mood of protest will seek other outlets. Radical parties will become more popular if the social-democratic governments of Europe fritter away their unique chance to present their electorates with a social-democratic model of society in opposition to that of neoliberalism, which has only resulted in a series of dramatic financial and currency crises.

There is an urgent need for a greater sense of community spirit, above all in economic life. This is precisely the objective and the commitment of democratic left-wing parties. Let us remember that originally the word 'socialism' meant not a system of production but simply the urge to channel the efforts of individual men and women in such a way as to serve the interests of the community – society – as a whole.

In addition to the familiar causes, most of them social, that have led to the loss of community spirit, the forces of globalization have played a considerable part in distracting attention from the need of the economy to serve the whole community. Under the conditions of global economic competition there is little scope for the intervention of national governments. National economies in their traditional form, which were concerned to strike a balance between the various individual economic interests within their own national framework in the interests of the nation as a whole, have become increasingly incapable of dealing with the situation in the face of the growing internationalization of the markets. With global competition each enterprise fights for its own cause alone, and all that matters is success. That is all there is to it. There is no democratically legitimized authority that can mediate in order to reach a supranational balance of interests.

Any attempt to inculcate an element of what might be called communal spirit into international economic relations cannot restrict itself to mere appeals to the moral conscience of those involved. What is really required is the introduction of an element of regulation into the system. And the enforcement of that regulation in a global market can undoubtedly only be carried out from a position of strength. No individual European country has that power but the European Union certainly does.

The first thing is for the members of the European Union to agree on a common economic and fiscal policy. Germany must press more strongly for a more comprehensive coordination of tax rates, while the trade unions need to be more forthright in seeking to consolidate a wages policy for the Union as a whole. A commitment to the adoption of a European Social Chapter as a means of combating unemployment is only the first step towards the establishment of a model European welfare state.

The development of such a model would not only have the advantage of strengthening the position of the social market economy – as opposed to that of 'pure' capitalism – in the global competition between rival systems and putting in place the regulations necessary for the establishment of a power base in the global market. It would also prove to be the catalyst for the creation of a supranational structure within which a kind of 'national Europeanism' could emerge. Many people do not have a feeling of Europeanness in their blood. The Union is to them a marriage of convenience, made in order to secure specific advantages in areas such as those of economy and defence. The concept of a unified Europe occurs only as a vision in the speeches of idealistic politicians. The real situation we confront is dominated by the sober truth that the instruments of national politics are no longer adequate to deal with the demands of a globalized economy.

A sense of belonging grows from a shared area of experience. But how can this experience be nurtured as long as Europe is little more than a common market-place? Consumerism alone is not strong enough to create a lasting sense of belonging – quite apart from the fact that with the loosening of the social framework more and more people are coming to see the world of consumerism as an area of experience from which they are excluded. Increased social hardship has also resulted from the removal of all hindrances to competition in the wake of globalization, as well as from the measures which almost all states have found themselves forced to undertake in order to meet the Maastricht criteria.

It is idle to speculate whether it would have made better sense to promote the unification of Europe in other fields before adopting a common currency. The time for such a decision has past. Developments must be left to take their course. However, we cannot allow the adoption of a single currency to lead to a subsequent weakening of social policy. The population would not accept a European unity purchased at such a price, and rightly so. A single currency as a catalyst of future development will only prove its worth to the extent that it stimulates and accelerates individual initiatives directed towards the consolidation of European unity – initiatives in the fields of taxation policy and employment policy, in the establishment of a unified economic policy and ultimately of a unified social policy. If the peoples of Europe are to acquire a sense of belonging and combine to create a European nation, Europe must succeed as a democratic project, a project sustained by the ideal of social justice.

The fact that we have not made much progress towards our goal is due to the absence of a European identity. To establish this identity step by step is an intellectual and cultural challenge. The market cannot do so. Conceptions of society based on economic blueprints contradict the essence of Western culture. They reduce human beings, with their desire for freedom and dignity, to the status of objects that have to be adapted to the prevailing conditions of the capitalist system. The adaptation of political policies to what are claimed to be economic imperatives is not a Third Way. It is a route to nowhere.

21

A Glimpse of the Future

In June 1999 Eckhard Fuhr published an article in the *Frankfurter Allgemeine Zeitung* entitled 'Change of Position'. He wrote:

> If the Christian Democrats were in power, many observers would have less difficulty in assessing the significance of the political events of the last few months. At last, friends of the government would have said, things are happening for which we have been waiting far too long. In a radically changed political situation Germany is proving herself to be a reliable member of the Western Alliance in the war in Kosovo. No longer does she claim a special role as a result of her history or take refuge behind the defences of moral neutrality.
>
> In domestic affairs too reforms are at last being put in place about whose general direction there can be no argument – a review of public finances without the fear of savage cuts in welfare benefits but with the long-term prospect of a balanced budget, lowering the level of pensions ... In party political terms, at least, it is difficult to see what the tactical position is. It is as though two opposing armies had marched past each other in the fog and ended up in the enemy camp, where they completely lost their bearings. Without any long-winded, heart-searching debates the Social Democrats have moved as far as one could imagine from their traditional positions and their old political logic.

It is true – the opposing armies find themselves occupying their enemies' positions. The SPD Programme 2000 became the CDU Programme 2000. The CDU won provincial elections one after the other without raising a finger – disillusioned with their party, masses of SPD electors simply did not trouble to vote. The red-green coalition's Programme 2000 showed how the opponents had switched ends. Industry was to enjoy 8 billion marks in tax concessions, most of the cost being borne by pensioners and the unemployed. The reintroduction of a private wealth tax and an increase in inheritance tax were both rejected by the Chancellor and his Finance Minister. Apparently pensioners and the long-term unemployed are better off than the well-to-do and their heirs.

Anthony Giddens was of the opinion that the redistribution of wealth should always form part of the social-democrat agenda, and that inheritance tax should be kept high to prevent too many privileges being passed from one generation to another. Addressing the same subject, Werner Perger wrote in *Die Zeit*:

> This is without doubt the reform strategy with the greatest risk of failure. Schröder knows that he has wasted too much time already. All the more ambitious is his programme. The least we could have expected about the nature and extent of his plans would have been a hint in his declaration of policy on taking office – the first wasted opportunity. But at that time the new Chancellor, still flushed with success, was not yet willing to withdraw his election pledges.

This goes to the heart of the matter. At the same time it is strange to find Werner Perger obviously enjoying the spectacle of a Chancellor reneging on his election pledges – as though in a democracy parties were not expected to tell the voters before the election what they proposed to do after the election. In our election manifesto we had not made any promises we could not keep – rather, we had made the entire programme subject to financial considerations. We had, however, with the poorest pensioners in mind, branded the pension cuts introduced by the Kohl administration as thoroughly obscene and pledged to avoid a total dismantling of the welfare system. 'Schröder is now forced to try and win back the people's trust which he put at risk with his silent capitulation to Lafontaine and the party executive, and which he had already forfeited to a large extent – in no small measure by indulging in the eclectic confusions of the so-called Third Way.'

But is breaking election promises really the best way to gain people's confidence? And who are these supporters of 'the eclectic confusions of the so-called Third Way'? It is the same old story. Those who enjoy wealth and a high income but pay virtually no tax and do not live under the threat of unemployment are those who are most vocal in their demand for the reform of pensions and unemployment benefit and for the curtailment of the rights of employees. Particularly strident are the voices of politicians, professors, journalists, self-employed businessmen, bureaucrats and others who have not the slightest inkling of what it means to survive on a pension of 1,250 marks a month, on unemployment benefit of 1,000 marks a month or on welfare benefit of 800 marks. Nor do they realize that a shop assistant or an unskilled worker often has to make do on a net income of around 2,000 marks a month.

So that there should be no doubt about what the government's policy would be with Gerhard Schröder as Chancellor and myself as Party Chairman, we had worked out a detailed plan of campaign. And leaving aside a few bureaucratic blunders, most of them due to a lack of coordination in the Chancellor's Office, we did indeed fulfil a considerable number of our pledges during the first few months of our administration. In the fields of taxation, retirement and health policy, sick pay and summary dismissal, and through our efforts to put a stop to the continued erosion of insurance and welfare benefits, we put measures in place exactly as we had said we would before the election.

In particular we had made the rejection of neoliberalism a central plank of our economic, fiscal and social policies. We did not only seek to make cuts in corporation tax but aimed to reduce the tax burden on the population as a whole. We wanted to see the reinstatement of workers' rights to job security and severance pay, not continual cuts in benefit payments. And in place of repeated pleas for wage restraint we demanded that all workers and employees should have their fair share of the growth of the nation's prosperity through bonuses geared to productivity.

It was only to be expected that these new policies would meet with stiff resistance on the part of those groups in society who had profited most under the Kohl administration. Newspaper publishers were bound to protest over proposed changes in the system of casual labour which had worked to their advantage for so long. Naturally there was resistance to our new taxation policies from the insurance industry and the electricity companies. And it was no surprise that there was opposition from foreign currency dealers to the measures put forward by the French Finance Minister Strauss-Kahn, the Japanese Finance Minister Miyazawa and myself to curb the activities of international currency speculators.

But the only hope of success for social-democratic policies is for them to remain credible and to face head-on the challenge of private interest groups. If such policies lose their credibility – or, even worse, if their protagonists begin to do the opposite of what they had promised before the election – then the Social Democratic Party will forfeit the allegiance of its voters even more rapidly than the parties of conservatism.

In the above-mentioned article Eckhard Fuhr also wrote: 'Lafontaine's resignation as Party Chairman and Finance Minister marks the failure of his attempt to take the European Union to the left, against the neoliberal mainstream of European politics. There are many in the SPD who do not want to see it as a failure. But there is nobody outside the immediate ranks of the party prepared to take up the banner of Social Democracy à la Lafontaine.' To mount just such a rebellion against the neoliberal mainstream was what characterized the whole thrust of my work as Chairman of the Social Democratic Party.

The political challenge facing the Social Democrats is to bring under control a capitalist system that is running wild, justifying itself by appeals to what it claims are the cast-iron laws of economics. We live in an age of neo-conservatism. This conservative revolution will have us believe that it is progressive, rational and scientific. It has elevated an economic law – a law that generates its own logic and operates according to the law of the market and the principle of the survival of the fittest – into an unyielding social rule. It glorifies the power of the financial markets, capitalism in its purest form, which acknowledges nothing but the law of maximum profits.

Padded with scientific jargon and supported by the media, neoliberalism has become a kind of conservative ideology masquerading as the embodiment of 'the end of all ideologies' and 'the end of history'. The call for less state turns increasingly into a call for less democracy. Democratic political decisions are replaced by the demands of the market, and, as history has shown, many adapt to the claims of the prevailing *Zeitgeist*.

In the autumn of 1999 the SPD stood once again at the parting of the ways. As at the time before the party conference in Mannheim in 1995, the polls showed the party approaching the 30 per cent mark. And again as in the pre-Mannheim days, it has to face the question of whether to submit to the neoliberal *Zeitgeist* or not. But the difference is that today it is the strongest party. And the Chairman of the party is the Chancellor.

Before the Mannheim Conference Hans-Jochen Vogel had urged Gerhard Schröder to stand against Rudolf Scharping as the party's nominee for the chancellorship. 'But the question repeatedly arises,' he wrote, 'of how he would use the power which he is seeking. One wonders whether his own television appearances are not more important to him than the interests of the party, which cannot allow itself to be turned into a trampoline on which people can jump up and down as they like. To judge from Schröder's behaviour so far, he has not only caused considerable harm to the party but has also damaged himself.'

Today Schröder is trying to change the policies of the SPD from above. But a change of course ordered from above is not true to the traditions of the SPD, which has always seen itself as a democratic grass-roots party sustained by a political programme. It would be only right and proper, therefore, if Gerhard Schröder would explain to the coming party conference what lies behind his new line and why he has chosen not to adhere to the government programme that was approved by so large a majority. The Schröder–Blair declaration is a repository of commonplace observations and vague intentions which is quite unsuitable as the starting-point for a serious political debate. Moreover it is actually a hindrance to the efforts the party has since been making to restate its aims and principles.

The Social-Democratic government is facing great challenges. In addition to its traditional interests and obligations it has as its main tasks the replacement of capitalism on the Anglo-Saxon model by a European welfare state, and the provision of guidelines for the conduct of a deregulated global market. This is the mandate that the European electorate has given the social-democrat governments of Europe. Many Europeans put their hopes in the new Social-Democratic government in Germany. But the Schröder–Blair *Third Way* left an air of general disappointment.

In the media age, more than ever, we need a set of long-term policies. Those who cry for modernization must be made to define what they mean by the word. Words such as adaptability and flexibility are mere labels. A desire to improve one's social standing is laudable, and as many people as possible should be enabled to share in the benefits enjoyed by the more prosperous classes of society. But we must remember that Karl Marx's dictum, 'Being determines consciousness', is not a cast-iron principle. A person who has risen in the world is under no obligation to carry with him the intellectual baggage of the propertied classes. If we know where we have come from, we shall know where we have to go.

The guiding principles of social democracy have lost nothing of their attraction for people today. That much, at least, the CDU/CSU learned from their defeat. Now they are defending the social market economy against the 'modernizers' in the government camp. But the SPD has promised to combine the necessary processes of renewal with the principle of social justice and must resist the pressures of the neoliberal *Zeitgeist*.

Hombach and Mandelson, two 'modernizers', wrote: 'In the past the promotion of social justice was confused with the demand for equality of achievement. As a result the importance of individual effort and accountability was ignored and left unrewarded, while social democracy became associated with conformity and mediocrity instead of with creativity, diversity and excellence.' The question arises: Which past do the two authors have in mind in this catalogue of our opponents' conservative prejudices – the period of Willy Brandt's government? Or Helmut Schmidt's administration, perhaps?

Our disastrous results in the European elections, in the local elections in North Rhine-Westphalia and in the *Land* elections show that the electors, men and women alike, reject the new policies introduced by the Schröder government. If they persist in this course, the SPD will inevitably find themselves facing further catastrophic defeats. The time has come for the Social Democratic Party, the great popular party of the left, to redefine its course. At the same time we must not forget that feelings are not traded on the stock exchange. They belong to the heart. And the heart beats on the left.

Index